The Rules of Time

The Rules of Time

Time and Rhythm
in the
Twentieth-Century Novel

R. A. York

Madison • Teaneck
Fairleigh Dickinson University Press
London: Associated University Presses

Associated University Presses
440 Forsgate Drive
Cranbury, NJ 08512

Associated University Presses
16 Barter Street
London WC1A 2AH, England

Associated University Presses
P.O. Box 338, Port Credit
Mississauga, Ontario
Canada L5G 4L8

The paper used in this publication meets the requirements of the American National Standard for Permanence of Paper for Printed Library Materials Z39.48–1984.

Library of Congress Cataloging-in-Publication Data

York, R. A., 1941–.
    The rules of time : time and rhythm in the twentieth-century novel / R. A. York.
        p. cm.
    Includes bibliographical references and index.
    ISBN 0-8386-3803-1 (alk. paper)
    1. English fiction—20th century—History and criticism. 2. Time in literature. 3. Narration (Rhetoric). 4. Fiction—Technique. 5. Rhythm. I. Title.
PR888.T5Y67   1999
823'.9109384—dc21   98-25212
                                                                    CIP

PRINTED IN THE UNITED STATES OF AMERICA

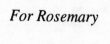

For Rosemary

Catching the very note and trick, the strange irregular rhythm of life, that is the attempt whose strenuous force keeps Fiction upon her feet.

—Henry James, *The Art of Fiction*

Contents

Introduction

Much recent criticism of fiction has been concerned with its ideological content, with its presentation of class, gender, race, and nation. It is certainly important to be aware of such things. It is particularly important to be aware of the assumptions that readers may unconsciously acquire from their reading of fiction—assumptions inherent in the style, point of view, and selection of scenes and characters—which they might wish to reject if they were fully conscious of them.

But such criticism is not the only kind possible. It illuminates some important aspects of novels, including the attitudes that the reader has to share with the author (at least provisionally, during the reading) in order to make the whole experience of reading readily acceptable and enjoyable; it articulates the common culture of reading that facilitates and is facilitated by literature. But it does not seem to me to elucidate what it is that ensures readers' absorption in the novel, their eagerness to read on, their delight in the characteristic tone and manner of the book, their sense of fulfillment at reaching the end. It does not elucidate what the novel has in common with other arts, such as music.

This book is going to investigate one dimension of novels that does, I believe, explain something of the aesthetic pleasure of fiction. Essentially, it will be concerned with the fact that readers are expecting something. This is certainly one thing they have in common with people listening to music. In listening to music, we are waiting at least for a return to the tonic chord, and in many cases also for the return of certain themes or cadences. In reading fiction, we are waiting for a resolution of whatever problems have arisen in the course of the work: a marriage, a victory, the solution of a crime, the discovery of a purpose in life—or for the definitive absence of these. What keeps us waiting is adventures, obstacles, conflicts, uncertainties . . . and various techniques of fiction, to

9

which I shall return. The satisfaction of the story is the overcoming of delays: if the detective arrives on the scene of the crime and at once arrests the man with a smoking gun, there is no story, no tension. We need to see in the situation depicted what the characters regard as a proper outcome, to recognize what there is that inhibits that outcome (the alibis, the locked room), and to appreciate what is being done to overcome the obstacles (the methodical questioning of witnesses, the moments of inspired insight). The text comprises a series of obstacles, a series of delays, and to this extent it is based on repetition: it repeats the sequence of (basic or secondary) problems and solutions. Repetition implies rhythm; we are conscious that each repeated unit occupies a certain time in telling and reading, which is longer or shorter than, or the same as, the previous units. And this process takes place at different rates: questioning witnesses is methodical, slow, repetitious; it offers only piecemeal and cautious advances towards a solution; the insight can be instantaneous. So, first of all, novels are likely to vary from each other in their pace: some present a world more filled with obstacles than others, some assume a more dogged perseverance as the way to overcome them. And second, any one novel is likely to contain some variation in pace: at some stages, progress will be rapid; at other times, the characters will be frustrated and the situation static.

All of this means that it is not enough to say that readers are kept waiting; there is a pattern to the way they are kept waiting, and I shall be claiming that a major factor in our appreciation of fiction and in our recognition of the distinctive qualities of individual novelists, or of periods of literature or of types of fiction, is just this element of pace. Pace may be rapid or slow, regular or irregular, constituted by external events or by psychological change, inherent in the story or imposed by the narrator's perspective, predictable or unpredictable. Readers may need to be patient, quick to adapt to change, sensitive in recognizing change, open-minded in deciding whether a change has occurred or not; they may need to cultivate such characteristics throughout the novel or to be prepared to deploy them as the text demands.

All this is ideological, even though I may seem to have disclaimed ideology. The way the text deploys the rhythm of events and of narration, the way it calls on the reader's patience or promptness, implies an attitude to the passage of time. (At the very least, reading fiction is an agreeable way of "passing time"; it ought to make us think about the way we want time to pass.) And attitudes to time are very much bound up with many of the qualities of mind we may admire in others and wish to develop in ourselves: there are qualities such as thoroughness, caution, decorum, solemnity, application, energy, determination, resoluteness, flexibility, and efficiency that entail a certain way of using our time. We may not necessarily see these virtues as ideological, because they are appreciated by people of a wide range of political, religious, and social attitudes; but, for one thing, a widely held ideology is still an ideology, and for another, it may well be that certain perspectives stress some of these qualities more than others.

Not only virtues are temporal; pleasure too depends on the pace of things. We are depressed either if we feel that things are happening too fast for us to cope with them or if we feel that they are happening too slowly to merit our attention; we are happy, relaxed, self-confident if we feel that the pace of events corresponds exactly to the speed with which we can respond to them. Our capacity for responding to stimuli—what in terms of information theory could be called our channel capacity—no doubt varies from person to person; it seems likely that it also varies from culture to culture. I shall be suggesting that novels set a model of a proper rate of processing information—and for the complexity of information that can be so processed—that at best gives us the sense of using to the full our mental power.

Overall, then, this book will hope to show that there is some congruence between the rate at which things happen in works, of fiction, the qualities of character that are implicitly praised in these works and the satisfaction we derive from them as we read. We now have to notice—reverting to a point hastily bypassed earlier—that the novelist has at his disposal a variety of techniques for controlling the rate at which things happen. We are first of all tempted to say that this can be simply a matter of the kind of happenings that are narrated (and therefore of the kind of happenings invented by the author), some of which do, in the nature of things, take longer than others. This is not entirely false. Certainly the total rhythm of the novel does depend on the number of obstacles the author creates to the resolution of the novel, or of each stage in the novel. So the hero may immediately rush to the villain's den to rescue the captive heroine, or he may carefully ascertain that she is indeed captive, reflect on his entitlement or obligation to rescue her, attempt to obtain assistance, consult his street map of the town, and the like. But this is only quite a small part of the truth, for the pace of narration depends not only on the events that are assumed to take place but also on the kind of attention the author thinks they merit. This is what is conveyed by the various novelistic techniques I refer to.

First, there is the issue of point of view, or focalization, as it is called by more precise theorists. It may be a surprise for me when a man with a gun bursts through the door; it is not a surprise for him. If the novel tells the story from my point of view, its rhythm will be brusque or rapid; if it tells it from the point of view of the gunman, its rhythm may be one of methodical preparation and predictable culmination.

Second, there is the factor that critics most frequently identify as relevant to pace, which is known by the key terms "scene" and "summary." The narrator may present an episode in detail, as if the reader were watching it onstage, so that conversations, for instance, are recounted verbatim; or substantial lengths of time may be summarized. The gunman may search for his gun in a cupboard, check its working, oil it, load it, reflecting on the deplorable increase in the cost of bullets, queue for a bus, and make his way step-by-step to my door, the reader closely attending to every move and hoping or fearing that at any moment he may be prevented from reaching me; or the narrator may simply tell us that he picked up his gun and went to his destination. The classic example of summary is the Flaubert novel in which several years are covered by the sentence, "He travelled." There are of course degrees in detail, so that the usual twofold distinction of scene and summary is obviously a simplification, though a valuable one. It may be useful to mention here a German term often used: the time spent by the narrator in telling the story is the *Erzählzeit* (telling time); the time covered is the *erzählte Zeit* (time told); the distinctive feature of the narrator's stance is the proportion of *Erzählzeit* to *erzählte Zeit*, a proportion that may approach equality in the case of scene, or that may approach zero in the case of Flaubert. Although it is obvious that this choice affects the pace of narration, it is not easy to say which way it affects it. On the one hand, summary gets a lot of time out of the way quickly and so may look like fast narration; on the other hand, a scene may show an event to contain a lot of information—a lot of points where something new happens, where some change takes place or seems to be about to take place—and so it too may look like fast narration, compared with the featureless periods that are summarized. Our feeling of speed appears to depend on how often we come across what we regard as an event in the text, what we see as a change, a novelty, a surprise. Since our view of this is not an objective matter, some people seeing tedious repetition where others see a scintillating deployment of nuances, there is bound to be some personal discretion in assessment of pace and rhythm, and this discretion will be used without apology in this book.

It may be worth commenting specifically in this context on the presentation of inner thought and of discussion. In general, it seems likely that readers regard action as inherently faster than reflection, for the obvious reason that it looks as if it is quickly bringing about a change in the situation. This is why thrillers are often praised as "fast moving." Introspection and debate are likely to look static, which is why "psychological novels" are not usually praised for being fast-moving but are expected to be slow, thoughtful, grave.

Third, there is the relation of narration and comment. Again there are specialized terms to note: linguists distinguish between *discours* and *récit*; *discours* is the presentation of reflections and judgments, which may refer to the present situation, to permanent values or to general expectations, and is normally associated with the present tenses (including the present perfect); *récit* is the telling of a story, of a series of events, and is normally associated with the past tenses. One way of characterizing the style of a text is to estimate the proportion of *discours* to *récit*; the higher the proportion, the more static the text and the slower the pace.

Finally, there is the possibility of nonchronological narration. The narration may employ flashback or, less frequently, anticipation (the word "flashforward," as far as I know, does not yet exist). The narration of the past or future may then be done either through scene or summary. The effect is complex. On the one hand, the main story is standing still during the inserted new timeframe of past or future, and therefore the reader has some sense of an arrest in the narrative; on the other hand, the intercalated episode has its own pace that will have its own effect on the reading process.

Overall then, the structure of the story is not unlike the structure of the sentence as presented by Sinclair (1972, 251–61). There is a basic logic: the subject calls for the predicate, the problem calls for the solution. Added to this basic logic are delaying factors: in the sentence, there are adjectives, adverbs, subordinate clauses, and the proportion of these to the main message and the order in which they appear influence the reader's perception of the sentence as advancing to a conclusion or as retarding it; in the story, there are shifts of point of view, alternations of scene and summary, passages of commentary, temporal dislocations. Given the length and complexity of most novels, the use and effect of these things can be extremely subtle. I hope that a reasonably detailed study will do something to characterize the value of some novels we enjoy because the interest of a sentence often does not come from its basic subject and predicate; it can come from the information—the excess information, one might sometimes be inclined to say—provided by delay. And I think that in novels too, it is often the delays, the frequency of delays and the kind of delays, that give real fascination and stature to the work.

The present study will be concerned with the twentieth-century English novel. The reason for this is partly that this period has produced many fine novelists (those studied here are a very limited selection), and I hope that readers will find that an increased awareness of their handling of time and narrative pace actually adds to their appreciation. More specifically, the handling of time and narrative pace does, I think, become fundamental in these writers because of a major shift in sensibility that is widespread in the period. I am tempted to label this shift "the death of the event." Nineteenth-century novelists such as Trollope, who is studied in the first chapter, construct their works on the basis of clearcut events; these events form climaxes in the novel, and the rhythm of the novel is made up of the contrast between the climaxes and the preparatory stages, in which characters consider what they can do or else take the first steps in doing it. The events are usually produced by the decisions of the characters; they are related to their motives and personality and they have an impact on the situation of other characters. Trollope, in other words, shows the interplay of different people as a series of public acts, and it is the pace of these acts that, in the first instance, determines the pace of the novel.

In the twentieth century, there is a turn to the development of sensibility, of private feeling and judgment, and away from public acts. A critic has aptly spoken of the modern novel as characterized by "quietism, purposelessness, inhibition or suspension of will, passive or static states of mind and feeling, and speculation free of connection with deeds" (Caserio 1979, xiii).

There is a turn away from events, in other words; and the changes in feeling and opinion that replace events may be much less easy to discriminate from each other than would be events; they are less easy to place in time and so less easy to recognize as forming a rhythmic sequence. One of Virginia Woolf's characters comments that "it's life that matters, nothing but life—the process of discovering, the everlasting and perpetual process, not the discovery itself at all" (ND, 132). A great many modern novels are marked by this love of "the everlasting and perpetual process" and by the corresponding indifference to the results of such processes. There are no final points in process, as thus conceived; which means, in strict logic, that there are no climaxes.

It is difficult to conceive of a novel in which there are no events and no climaxes at all. This would be a novel without a plot, which seems to be a contradiction in terms. What in fact happens is that in many respects modern novels do follow the pattern of Trollope and his like; they do tell stories about people who feel some lack and take steps, against some opposition, to overcome it. They therefore do create a rhythm in which the acts and decisions of characters play a large part. But this story-based conception of the novel has to compete in their works with what might be called a lyrical conception of the novel, one in which feeling, perception, atmosphere, self-awareness play a large part. These things, as far as the story is concerned, lead to delay; they hold the reader back from the solution to the mystery or the definitive success of the enterprise. This gives special significance to the four fictional techniques of control of point of view, of exploitation of scene and summary, of prominent commentary (or *discours*) and of nonchronological narration. The "lyrical" aspects of the novel may have a rhythm of their own (just as verse has not only a verbal rhythm but also a rhythm in the overall shape of the poem)—all the more since many of the authors very clearly sense that the quality of our feelings and judgments is bound up with our sense for the flow of time—and one of the tasks of the modern novelist is to relate the lyrical rhythm, the rhythm of emotional growth and of contemplation, to the story-rhythm. The novelists we shall be studying have different approaches. In some, the deviation from the traditional novel is modest, discreet, elusive, in others very clear; in some it involves an apparent suppression of the author, in others a particularly conspicuous manifestation of the author; in some there is a high coherence of the rhythm of events with the rhythm of feeling or of commentary, in others there are great discrepancies; in some the rhythm reinforces some recognizable assessment of the way of life depicted, in others it is a complicating factor that makes any such assessment more difficult. There is then great variety in the texts studied. What I shall be claiming is that they are all responses to an underlying concern: the concern with the values—partially compatible, partially conflicting—of continuity, growth, and novelty. I end by studying three recent popular novels; it will be apparent that to a great degree these novelists remain faithful to the Trollopian conception of the event as public climax and as expression of private character. But we cannot forget that the authors write in the context of a sophisticated literature that has more complex or varied forms of organization, and it will be of interest to see to what extent they show themselves aware of the sort of vision in which events are not primary.

The techniques of fiction writing that contribute to the establishment of pace and rhythm have been studied separately by many critics and theorists, often with much insight into the perspective they offer on the characters and themes of the novel; for an economical and lucid general account one should recommend Rimmon-Kenan (1983). But these features do not often seem to have been studied together to illuminate the sense of time that is implied in the works. Among the authors we shall be studying, several have made passing remarks on rhythm, while E. M. Forster devoted a chapter to "Rhythm" in his *Aspects of the Novel*; this, however—like E. K. Brown's *Rhythm in the Novel*, which is much influenced by Forster's work—is less about rhythm in the sense of temporal sequence and proportion than about certain patterns of symbolism. Critics have recognized the importance of time—and timelessness—in fiction, as for instance in Meyerhoff's wide-ranging study (1965) or in Church's thesis (1983) that the modern novel frequently seeks to arrest the flux of life, or in Orr's stress on the moment of epiphany in fiction, the moment outside time (1987). An important collection, with a rich bibliography, is Patrides (1976). The most substantial account of literary rhythm appears to be the two volumes edited by Delas and Terray, *Rythme et Ecriture* (1988–91), in which many essays discuss questions of the expression of the subject through rhythm, of the reader's expectation, and of rhythm as repeated alternation of event and preparation, all themes very pertinent to the perspective to be adopted here.

The present study will attempt to characterize the sense of passing time that is conveyed by each of the authors studied; it will partly refer to the explicit statements about time made by narrator or characters, partly to the inherent timing of the sort of events narrated, partly to the temporal perspective provided by the fictional techniques indicated in this introduction. The integration of these is not rigorous; it may be that future researchers will find a more systematic frame of study, or it may be that the reader's subjectivity is inescapable and that no fully rigorous analysis is possible. In either case, I hope that this book will demonstrate that the pleasure of fiction arises in part from the pace at which the characters perceive the flow of life and the pace at which readers handle the flow of information.

The Rules of Time

Anthony Trollope: *The Warden*

THE Warden (1854) is an ideal starting point for our study because its sense of rhythm may be totally imperceptible to many readers. The novel is short and simple; its pace seems regular, unhurried, and accomplished. If the novel appears to be one that has (on the whole) a classical surety of touch and reads like a typical Victorian novel, that is in part for the apparently negative reason that the reader hardly ever feels either rushed or held back. Time may be imperceptible because the lapse of time is indistinguishable from the characters' actions and decisions. In fact, the time scale of the work is very carefully and subtly orchestrated so as, on the one hand, to give some sense of the quality of the characters' experience and of their self-awareness and, on the other, to coordinate the reader's responses to the events depicted, to mark out what is good, what bad, what indifferent, what weighty, and what trivial.

One should, in fact, first of all quite simply note that references to time are extremely pervasive. Some of the meetings and avoidances late in the novel show something verging on an obsession with timetabling (and most obviously with the Bradshaw railway timetable), but the sense of living in a world of continuity and change is never far from the narrator or the characters. The first chapter is meticulous in its placing of events: the story takes place "a few years since" (1); the author recapitulates Mr. Harding's arrival in Barchester "early in life," carefully moves back a stage to point out that "a fine voice and a talent for music had decided the position in which he was to exercise his calling" (1), and notes that "for many years" he was a minor canon, at the age of forty acquired a living, and at the age of fifty became a prebendary. A new shift back recounts that he "had married early in life" (2). Soon the text shifts to 1434, carefully explaining the change, and recounts the history of Hiram's Hospital, which is to be the subject of contention throughout the work, leading up to Mr. Harding's behavior as warden of the hospital. In other words, it leads back to the present of the story, and this is further reinforced by a shift to the present-tense "Mr. Harding is a small man, now verging on sixty years" (9), ending with an illustration of his character from the past (his having spent money on the publication of a book of church music). The second chapter then continues with the present tense, but it immediately refers back and then immediately hints at change: "Mr. Harding has been now precentor of Barchester for ten years; and, alas, the murmurs concerning the proceeds of Hiram's estate are again becoming audible" (11). These last words are a near repetition of a phrase in chapter 1 (6) and mark out the chapter opening as the launching of the real story; in other words, they articulate very forcefully the shift from a gradual, coherent development to a time of polemics and suddenness.

Three points arise. First of all, the text requires close attention to time on the part of its readers; second, it conveys a strong sense that the explanation of institutions and characters is to be found in the past; and third, it gives every appearance of regarding continuity as normal and desirable. So, the sentence about Mr. Harding's career being "decided" by his talents may seem characteristic: it is in the order of things that a long-lasting activity should arise—without choice—from a given potential. There is in *The Warden* a strong love of the given, a lyrical conservatism apparent in, for instance, the author's attitude to Archdeacon Grantly, the apostle of changelessness:

> Who could be hard upon a dean while wandering round the sweet close of Hereford, and owning that in that precinct, tone and colour, design and form, solemn tower and storied window, are all in unison and all perfect! ... The tone of our archdeacon's mind must not astonish us; it has been the growth of centuries of church ascendancy; and though some fungi now disfigure the tree, though there be much dead wood, for how much good fruit have not we to be thankful? (64)

There is irony here, obviously enough; but as well as the irony there is a sense of naturalness and order, offered at the least as nostalgia.

This is, in fact, an instance of a frequently manifest aspect of the book and one that tends to alleviate change. In Trollope (and in some other nineteenth-century novelists), the proposition of *discours* to *récit*, of commentary to narration, is high. In other words, we see not just what happens to Mr. Harding and his fellows, we see what Trollope—or a fictitious narrator not unlike Trollope—thinks it all means, and therefore what kind of person this narrator is.

He is reflective, a connoisseur of characters and expressions, humorous; he has a strong sense of the social relevance of what he narrates. He is relaxed and good-humored, if capable of indignation and pathos. He is patient. All this means delay for any reader whose chief concern is to find out what happens next; much of the art of *The Warden* is precisely to make these reflections and comments interesting—diverting or grave enough to educate the reader away from wanting more story. A single example will be sufficient. When Harding tells the bishop that John Bold, the radical who has instigated the campaign against his tenancy of the hospital, is attached to his own daughter and may become his son-in-law, the bishop does nothing. This doing nothing calls forth quite a lot of commentary:

> The bishop did not whistle; we believe that they lose the power of doing so on being consecrated; and that in these days one might as easily meet a corrupt judge as a whistling bishop; but he looked as if he would have done so, but for his apron. (46)

The pomposity of the bishop's office meets with the mock pomposity of the narrator's role—and with the sharp point of the note on corrupt judges; the reader is turned away for a while from his or her complex expectations about Harding and his family to admiration for the wit and worldliness of the narrator. In doing so, it looks as if the narrator is pointing to a need for change (for really incorruptible judges), but perhaps more deeply he is pointing to what is claimed to be a permanent fact: the inescapable fallibility of human beings.

This suggests that this is a book in praise of inertia. But the recognition of change is emphatic. It is, in fact, a book about the destruction of the past. Mr. Harding's regret, at the end of the book, pronounced simply and pathetically to the "bedesmen," the beneficiaries of the hospital, is essentially that "our ordinary quiet mode of living should be disturbed" (298). There is irony again, and harsher irony, for the disturbance arises from the bedesmen, who have shown themselves to be dissatisfied with their ordinary quiet mode of living. But one way the text is to be read is as the account of Harding's martyrdom by disturbance

Hence the novel's anxious sense of beginnings, of what is novel, of what disturbs: so, in the second chapter, to which we have referred, "such

matters [as abuse of ecclesiastical office] have begun to be talked of in
various parts of England. . . . Men are beginning to say that these things
must be looked into" (11). Mr. Harding is "becoming uneasy" (13); later
he tells the bedesmen, "I want no changes—at least no changes that shall
make you worse off than you now are, as long as you and I live together"
(75). He will decide that the publicity arising from their complaint
prevents them from living together; he abandons his occupation of the
hospital. And this is a decline: their situation really is to change for the
worse; the last page of the story proper (before the brief conclusion of
chapter 21) recounts the fate of Bunce, the most conservative and faithful
of them: "Poor old Bunce felt that his days of comfort were gone. The
hospital had to him been a happy home, but could be so no longer" (303).
Continuity is comfort; change is irrevocable deprivation. Hence the
characters' timidity at change. A striking and finely dramatized instance
is the first intrusion of John Bold into the tranquil atmosphere of the
hospital, where the warden is playing the cello to his (not very apprecia-
tive) wards, to break the news that he intends to challenge the system
they live by. The scene leaves Harding anxious, plunged into the "first
moments of much misery" (39). Elsewhere too there is a frequent sense
of foreboding, a sense that novelty means misery; Bunce, for instance,
later has "deep grief seated in his heart, for he perceived that evil days
were coming" (104).

But change does not just evoke lamentation; Mr. Harding can come to
accept it, if not to welcome it; with great authenticity of character, he
faces, at the end of chapter 6, Bold's criticism of his status and love for
his daughter (95) and is able, "with flowing eyes and a full heart," to
reconcile his concern for her future happiness with his concern for his
own future impoverishment. And in his final great gesture of renunciation, he recognizes the rightness of change. He says to the Advocate
General, Sir Abraham Haphazard, who has been retained to defend the
status quo: "I cannot boast of my conscience, when it required the
violence of a public newspaper to awaken it; but, now that it is awake, I
must obey it" (259). The awakened conscience is a severe, "violent," but
imperative novelty.

Harding then changes. This is a vital feature of his character, and in
general the characterization of the novel is lucidly structured in terms of
determination, changeability, and a characteristic pace of speech and
conduct. Harding clings to the past, is indecisive and slow—but he

makes the fundamental change of renouncing his charge. Bold is eager for reform, impetuous, hasty, and obstinate—and he too changes, renounces his attack. Archdeacon Grantly, the chief defender of clerical privilege, is against change and doesn't change. Tom Towers, the London journalist who backs Bold's campaign, is for change and doesn't change. The sense of pace and fixity that informs the basic conception of the characters and their function in the plot is also apparent in the detail of personality and the patterning of particular scenes; so, when Harding discusses with the archdeacon their response to Bold's enterprise (chapter 9), the archdeacon is "impatient," dismisses any "splitting of hairs," theatrically demonstrates surprise, "continu[es] to pour forth his convictions," and speaks "in a somewhat peremptory manner," while the warden has several moments of silence until finally "it burst forth from him" and he declares his misery "with a somewhat jerky eloquence." The culmination of the scene is that the archdeacon accuses Harding of cowardice, a term that reduces him again to silence and preys on his feelings ever after. They are an active character and a passive character; Harding is passive, even inert—usually—in his behavior as in his speech, as against the prompt, efficient, persistent speech and action of his son-in-law; and it is Harding who verges on saintliness.

The point is important: saintliness tends to exclude purposiveness and planning. Harding's conception of the future rarely extends beyond his apprehension of public shame; so the discussion with the archdeacon ends with the warden "resolved to bear it all—ignominy, suspense, disgrace, self-doubt, and heart-burning"—and to accept Dr. Grantly's guidance. The central character of the novel, then, does not take the actions that drive along the plot and that create the various events that constitute its rhythm. But he does put an end to the plot. By deciding to abandon his claim to the wardenship, he makes the whole debate irrelevant and cancels out the tension of the story.

The Warden is the story of two decisions, and the brilliance of the story—its economy, its elegance, its sense of conflict and order, and the sense of personal growth and discovery that it communicates—depends on the relationship of the two.

Bold announces his campaign by visiting the warden in the hospital; Harding responds by consulting the bishop. In a pair of basically comic scenes, the bedesmen conspire to sign a petition against their warden and the archdeacon attempts to dissuade them from their conspiracy. The newspaper *The Jupiter* denounces the hospital system, and the church team decide to retain Sir Abraham Haphazard. Then comes the first crucial decision; persuaded by his beloved Eleanor Harding, Bold agrees to end his campaign. The story, it seems, is over; the threat to normality is over. This is rather surprising, since it happens in chapter 11, out of twenty-one chapters. And, in fact, things carry on. Bold has withdrawn, but when he goes to visit the archdeacon on his own territory (a visit recalling his visit to Harding), the archdeacon doesn't withdraw but violently announces the continuation of hostilities. Bold attempts to persuade his abettor, Tom Towers of *The Jupiter*, to withdraw, but Towers, like Grantly, is uncompromising and refuses. Now comes the major decision of the book: Harding does withdraw from the controversy and sacrifices his position. To complete the symmetry brought about by this transformation, he is now sure and even obstinate. The moral point is this: the novel seems at first to be about power and possession. Some characters—Bold, Grantly, Towers—think in political terms. This political strife is ended by love; if one wishes to be harsh, one can say that Bold is blackmailed by his beloved to abandon his political principle. But Harding, in the second half of the novel, doesn't see the situation as a political one. He sees it as one of self-judgment, one of spirituality or of comfort. His renunciation is, on the political level, unmotivated (since the legal process against him has been abandoned), and the more touching or noble for that; he renounces because he discovers in conversation with Sir Abraham Haphazard that the political world is not one of principle or repute but one in which success alone counts. "How could a successful man be in the wrong?" Tom Towers incredulously wonders (221); the novel as a whole demonstrates precisely that success is likely to be in the wrong and that the desire for power and effectiveness that goes with it—and that generates the action of the novel—is likely to be an aspect of its wrongness. Harding's decision—much delayed—is, in a sense, a conversion of the text, which turns from a preoccupation with who is going to win to a concern for how purity and rest are possible.

The symmetry of all this is a vital characteristic of the work and very strongly marked. So, Herbert acutely characterizes Trollope in terms of his combining comic patterning with "realistic fluidity or amorphousness" (116). Certain pairs of chapters are clearly patterned. Chapter 4 shows the wicked (i.e., demanding) bedesman Handy persuading his fellows to rebel against Harding, only to be denounced in the climax of the chapter by the virtuous Bunce; chapter 5 shows the pompous (i.e., prosperous) churchman Grantly seeking to persuade the bedesmen to abandon their rebellion, only to be deplored privately in the thoughts of the virtuous Harding. Chapter 6 recounts a party at the warden's house and ends with a frank discussion between Harding and Eleanor about their future and especially about Harding's esteem for Bold, while chapter 10 recounts Harding's solitary worrying and ends with a discussion between Harding and Eleanor in which Harding repeats his esteem for Bold. Chapter 10 also echoes chapter 9: in chapter 9, a prolonged debate ends with Harding submitting to Grantly; in chapter 10, a prolonged, intimate conversation ends with Harding seeking independence of Grantly. Chapter 6, moreover, anticipates chapter 9: in the former, Harding welcomes a theoretically hostile possible son-in-law, and in the latter he suffers abuse from a theoretically sympathetic actual son-in-law. Chapters 12 and 13 give a new pairing: in 12, John Bold, frustrated by Grantly's insensitive abuse, nevertheless finally goes to London to see Towers; in 13, Harding, frustrated at *The Jupiter*'s insensitive abuse, goes to London to see Sir Abraham. Two things need to be said about all this: one is that the rhythm of the novel in general is set up by a series of repetitions and that what is repeated is either unsuccessful persuasion or unsuccessful appeals; the second is that in all this, the actions appear almost to be the product of these virtually predictable processes of action and reaction. There are hints that the whole enterprise resembles a game. The archdeacon, with intense sarcasm, refers to Bold's campaign as a "little game of backgammon" (176); at the end of the same chapter (182), Bold finds himself checkmated. The game has changed, admittedly, but the idea of a turn-taking game is one that seems to inform the whole structure of the text, and to add to its tension, its orderliness, its comprehensibility. Perhaps it also adds to the distance between character and reader and makes the action a more remote spectacle.

This comprehensibility depends on a number of very important rhythmic features. First of all, there is a general tendency for the chapters to be self-contained units with clearly marked beginnings and ends. Life, in this novel, carries on through distinct stages, within each of which the issues at stake are lucid and coherent. The chapter is defined chiefly (apart from the typographical display of chapter headings and blank space at the end) by continuity of characters, each chapter normally relating an episode involving a set group of characters and limited by some pattern of social activity. Thus, chapter 4 shows the bedesmen and ends with the irruption of their leader, Bunce, while chapter 5, seen from the point of view of the gentry, shows the archdeacon's visit to the hospital, at which he harangues the bedesmen; the reader can easily identify and name the central activity of each chapter. (The coherence of the chapter is further enhanced by vocabulary, the word "petition" pervading both of these.) Some chapters are more complex. So, chapter 3, the first in the story proper, contains two related episodes, each too short to make a chapter of anything like normal length: Bold's visit to Harding and Harding's visit to the bishop, both shaped by the normal rhythm of a conversation, in the first case properly restrained and businesslike, in the second more confused and sporadic. The point presumably is to set up a story without excessive concentration on these introductory scenes and to give a sense of the immediate complementary of attack (by Bold) and defense (from the bishop).

The integrity of the chapters is strengthened by a very clear emphasis on openings and closures. One common marker of the beginning is to relate the chapter explicitly by time to the previous one; chapters thus start, "Bold at once repaired to the hospital" (3), "On the following morning" (9), "When Eleanor laid her head on her pillow that night" (11). Or there might be a specific reminder of the previous chapter's closing phrases: chapter 5 ends with Harding in a state of much anxiety and uncertainty, and chapter 6 begins "after much painful doubting"; chapter 6 ends with Eleanor snubbing John Bold, and chapter 7 begins, "Although Eleanor Harding rode off from John Bold on a high horse." There may be conspicuous antithesis, as between the end of chapter 10, where Harding assures his daughter that she need make no sacrifice for him, and the beginning of chapter 11, which is called "Iphigenia" and starts with Eleanor "in her warm-hearted enthusiasm"—with impractical sentimentality, the author may hint—deciding that self-sacrifice is the means to adopt. There is continuity but also distinctness; a new start is to be made, a new move played, even if this means gratuitous contradiction.

Chapter endings are if anything even more clear-cut; the signs of finality are emphatic. Two ends with Harding taking his departure; 4 with the comment that "there is no help for spilt milk" (in other words, that the chapter is written and cannot be changed); 5 with the archdeacon, having compelled the bishop, his father, to a decisive act, returning home; 6 with Eleanor firmly walking away from Bold after threatening to think the worse of him, and so on. Something has been done, in these chapters. Something small, perhaps—there has to be enough left to do to encourage us to read on—but the reader senses life to be progressive and irreversible.

Finality does not necessarily mean climax. The novel is sparing in climaxes. Some chapters (1, 8, 16, 18, 21) contain no major climaxes; these—with the exception of 16, to which we shall return—are chapters of exposition or chapters that confirm some state of affairs that has been attained. Some (3, 7, 14) present a major event followed by a more or less lengthy reaction (one may think of reaction shots in the cinema). Some (9, 10, 13, 19, 20) present a fairly intense discussion or commentary on some given state of affairs, with a comparatively brief introduction and conclusion, and serve as amplification, that is, as rhetorical emphasis of the gravity of the present instant. Some (2, 5, 6, 15) present an early shock, followed by some relaxation of tension, and then by a second high point; these depict the ongoing activity of struggle and effort.

Two chapter endings call for special comment: the fine if somewhat sentimental pathos of the farewell of Harding and Bunce at the end of chapter 20, with Bunce reflecting in a spirit of sacrificial finality, "I have now to forgive those who have injured me—and to die" (303); and the pause at the end of chapter 17, after Harding has made his decision to abandon his post: feeling a "glow of comfort," "he stood still a moment to collect his thoughts, and reflect on what he had done, and was about to do" (260). Immediately, he is about the comparatively trivial business of facing up to the indignant archdeacon, and this expectation marks the very end of the chapter in cliff-hanging mode. But this pause also marks the stillness of a real change, the moment between decision and implementation, the end of indecision and pain. Time, that is, is not just progressive; it brings fulfillment and calm—if it brings self-knowledge and with it the capacity to act in a way faithful to one's real past.

The most dramatic chapters are those that build up to a single great climax: the denunciation of the bedesmen by Bunce in 4, Bold's conversion in 11, the denunciation of Bold by Grantly in 12, Harding's conversion in 17. These are sudden and major changes or moments of judgment; they merit high concentration and high emphasis; they are touchstones for the integrity of moral life and rightly stand, in some senses, by themselves. But they are also integrated into the continuing ebb and flow of feelings and relationships, and that is what the shifting patterns of climax and lull in the novel demonstrate.

Quite conspicuously set against these excitements are lulls, some of them displaying an almost outrageous retreat from action. Chapter 6 ends touchingly with the conversation of Harding and Eleanor. The reader is left in some tension, wondering how the relationship of Harding and Bold and that of Eleanor and Bold will develop, and in particular what will become of Bold's campaign. Chapter 7 begins with two pages of reflection on the psychological state of the lovers, intelligent and digni- fied in phrasing but far from surprising in content (Eleanor is proud but loving, Bold is crestfallen); then comes a quotation from the *Jupiter*'s editorial on the hospital case. This is an important step in the story, since it contributes greatly to Harding's awareness of public disapproval, but the ironic tone of the author and the prosy style of the newspaper mean that it is hardly exciting in itself. The narrator then leaves it to the imagi- nation of the reader to guess the effect of this on Harding—a formulation that implies that it is readily predictable—quotes the reactions of the bishop, archdeacon, radicals, and bedesmen to the article, commenting that no decision was made by the church party except the decision not to respond to the newspaper, and finally explains why Sir Abraham has been prevented from forwarding the legal cause by parliamentary business, again described in terms of heavy humor and at some length. Not much has happened in this chapter. We are being kept waiting. And the next chapter is not very different, consisting basically of a lengthy (and, to modern readers, tedious) satire on various church personalities as personified in the Grantly family. It is the next chapter that brings us something really new, the violent criticism by Grantly of Harding's timo- rousness. The effect is shocking, and the more shocking because of the general ebbing of energy that seems to have been going on before this moment. Our attention has been fixed on the small-scale and unsurpris- ing; we have become accustomed to humor and inertia. But we suddenly find that there are extremes of conduct too, that life is not all mildly amusing or mildly pathetic, that transformations are possible.

The finest example of the lull in the book is chapter 16, "A Long Day in London." The chapter has rightly been noted by critics for maintaining the interest and sympathy of the reader over some twenty pages during which nothing substantial happens. It is regarded, for instance, by W. Wall as the most absorbing in the novel (22). Harding has come to

London to meet Sir Abraham Haphazard; he naively fails to realize how difficult it is to see the Attorney General and is unprepared to wait for a whole day to contact him. He cannot spend the day in his hotel for fear that Archdeacon Grantly will follow him to London (as indeed he does), find him at the hotel, and upbraid him (as he does, too late). So, out of inexperience and timidity, this elderly innocent has to spend a day away from home. There is much emphasis on the length of time and on the stratagems to which he is driven, simply to fill in time. Harding seeks a place where he can find comfort; first, he "takes sanctuary" in Westminster Abbey, where he is critical of the service and somewhat embarrassed not to be attending purely for reasons of faith, and where he spends much time meditating on his future impoverishment and its impact on his daughter. "Confused and ashamed," he goes out into the alien brightness of the open air and has a meal at what is implied to be a distinctly unsuitable restaurant, certainly one where he is felt by the habitués to be much out of place, until finally he finds an incongruous rest in a "cigar-divan" where he drinks coffee, reads a magazine, falls asleep, and dreams of Barchester until, refreshed, he arrives at Sir Abraham's chambers in perfect time to keep his appointment. The day has been an ordeal, in which the preoccupations of Barchester have been added to the anxiety of London, and through this ordeal, unconsciously, a certain confidence has come, which enables Harding, in the next chapter, to judge the unreflective pragmatism of Sir Abraham and to respond to it with his own conscious commitment to principle—to innocence, in a more solemn sense. A chapter of rest anticipates the chapter of greatest decisiveness in the work; the lull is a gathering of strength, in which the reader is shown Harding's weakness before coming to discover his strength.

In the structure of the novel, then, on the large scale, action alternates, in a measured way, with hesitation. The same is true of the detail of the text, and the pace of Trollope's prose seems generally leisurely because his characters like to "dilate upon every feeling" (149), to "think long and deeply" (39), and because the narrator seeks to present decision only in the context of reflection and therefore of indecision. The effect of this technique is that the major events of the novel are much anticipated and much recapitulated: Harding's renunciation of his post as warden, the climax of the whole book, is anticipated from the moment of Bold's first charge, to which Harding already reacts with "the first shade of doubt" (39); soon he is slowly pacing under the lime trees (those images of the unchanging growth of conservative England) as he debates at length within himself until "he became all but fixed in his resolve that some great step must be taken to relieve him from the risk of so terrible a fate" (79)—a great step, in which Harding is all but fixed; the formulation of hesitation, of indecision, is acute. His reluctance to accept the advice of Sir Abraham when it appears to favor the status quo (127) again displays his tenuous grasp of power and anticipates his final, open confrontation with the lawyer, and "as he paced up and down the room he resolved in his misery and enthusiasm that he could with pleasure, if it were allowed, give up his place, abandon his pleasant home, leave the hospital" (130). The resolution is getting near; it seems almost to have been made, but for that question of "being allowed." Chapter 10, "Tribulation," is dominated by Harding's inactivity as he walks and sits in his garden; sits, hardly moving a limb, for two hours, in his drawing room; and finally contemplates with a "gleam of joy" the "escape" of abandoning the hospital and living alone with his daughter in a cottage (thoughts to which he returns more anxiously during his "long day" in London). Thought anticipates action, at great length; the novel largely comprises repetition of this baffled thought, with minor shifts of emphasis and attitude, until suddenly the decision emerges. In conversation with Sir Abraham, "Mr. Harding declared vehemently that he could not wait, and Sir Abraham began seriously to doubt his sanity" (256). He has waited a long time—the reader has waited with him—but at last the moment has come.

And what is to follow is not really more events. It is the solemn confirmation of the event that has now occurred: letters, conversations, narratives, asserting that Harding really has, permanently, resigned. The novel, one can say, is designed essentially to give weight to two dignified utterances: Harding's declaration to Sir Abraham that "I would sooner that [Eleanor] and I should both beg, than that she should live in comfort on money which is truly the property of the poor" (258) and the formal letter to the bishop in which he reasseverates his decision: "It has seemed to me that this right [to his income] is not well made out, and I hesitate to incur the risk of taking an income to which my legal claim appears doubtful" (277). The warden is honest; he knows his decision is the result of weakness, of lack of conviction, of his not being of the right caliber; he is careful not to assert that Bold was right in principle; the text does not claim that his choice is a rational one. But the reader admires him for at last deciding for himself, allowing his doubts to outweigh the archdeacon's pressure. The fascination of the book, that is, is in the point at which indecision tilts over into obstinate self-denial; and the rhythm of the work is such as to give this moment value as an authentic self-discovery.

Self-discovery tends to override the short-term rhythm of the chapters. We have seen that chapters tend to be self-contained, moving from an initial problem to a clear conclusion. The case is clearest with such basically comic or satirical scenes as that of the bedesmen's conspiracy in chapter 4; the question set by the chapter is, "How many of them will sign?" and the answer is given—and has to be given—within the chapter, as each of them does fall into temptation—except the noble Bunce, who provides a conclusion by denouncing the rest. Much the same is true of the other scenes of persuasion; a striking and dramatic case is chapter 11, where John Bold allows himself to be persuaded within a few pages by Eleanor's "vehemence" to give up his campaign and the glory he expects from it. But Harding differs from most of the other characters in the persistence of his thoughts: he worries and remembers. In the "conference" with the archdeacon, the reproaches of *The Jupiter* are still "fresh in his memory" (129), although they have taken place two chapters—and some appreciable length of time—previously; he recalls his own previous experiences, such as the financial difficulties brought about by publication of his book and his reading of cases such as the Saint Cross one, which parallel his own position (138). "All manner of past delights" (144) are present to him as he ponders on his impending loss, and he visualizes very precisely—both in emotional tone and in financial calculation—what his future prospects may be. When Sir Abraham advises him to "sleep on" his decision, he responds forcefully—and these are his last words in the crucial chapter: "I have done more than sleep upon it. . . . I have laid awake upon it, and that night after night. I found I could not sleep upon it; and now I hope to do so" (260). "Night after night": the continuing quality of his life is at stake. For him, time has a consistency. There is a similar moment of self-awareness in John Bold; when he is rebuffed by Dr. Grantly, the narrator comments—apparently summarizing the character's own thoughts—"That was certainly the bitterest moment in John Bold's life; not even the remembrance of his successful love could comfort him" (181). Deep feeling is feeling that is significant in the development of a life, and that is what the structuring of the novel as a whole seems to bear out.

The Warden as a whole, then, demonstrates a certain pace of life and thought; a cautious, grave pace, in which change is rare. It shows the vulnerability of that pace to vehemence, to suddenness and violence, under the pressure of conflict, and it shows the restoration of the norm, if on a more melancholy note. And it persuades the reader that this sort of alternation of pace is the appropriate one. It is appropriate because it allows clear exposition and aptly weighty or intense formulation to both parts of the sequence of events, to intrusion and transcendence, and because it affords us an image of wisdom and reflectiveness in the personality of the narrator. This seems to imply a system of contrasts between thought and action and between dullness and haste. Essentially, the book opposes the deep, reflective, hesitant, developmental manner of Harding to the prompt, active, energetic, resolute manner of Grantly; it recognizes that the deep can closely resemble the dull and that the active can closely resemble the hasty. It recommends, to all appearances, compromise rather than fixity, and peace rather than polemics; but it shows that fixity and polemics provide the challenge that brings novelty into the world and that converts self-preservation into self-development. It is therefore very deeply concerned with time, with the way individuals change or continue. Trollope shows that such themes can be handled with special aptness through the genre of the novel; what I want to suggest is that the novel is an apt form because it allows certain patterns of rhythmic construction.

The novel can use rhythm mimetically, that is, it can imitate the familiar experiences of waiting, planning, reflecting, remembering, preparing, deciding, acting, and so on. It can also use rhythm rhetorically, that is, it can use the reader's sense of suspense, tension, contemplation, completeness, or redundancy to affect his or her response to the events of the story (and so to the characters and themes). If there is a primary rhythmic motif in *The Warden*, it is that of indecision; the central vision of the work is of Harding's failure to decide on change while he is under attack, and of his decision to change when the attack has ceased, at which time this indecisiveness, this mismatch of his inner life and of external pressures, gives way to a calm, grave celebration of his weakness and decisiveness. The coincidence of mimesis and rhetoric makes for sympathy, and this sympathy is part of the process of characterization in the novel; we feel Harding to be a personality worthy of consideration because we wait with him and because we accept with him his final decision.

To sum up: *The Warden* depends on decisions and on empathy; it is purposive and rhetorical. Broadly speaking, the purposes drive forward the action, creating events that may beget other events. Empathy (or, more precisely, the narrator's display of empathy) may lead to reflection, discussion, description, and analysis; it reduces the frequency of events and slows the pace. The continuing interest of the novel depends on a delicate balance of writing that pushes on the story and writing that makes it seem more significant and so more deserving of our respect. Most nineteenth-century fiction no doubt shows these qualities, though a good deal of analysis would be needed to find out exactly how they operate in different works. But there seems to be a considerable change in approaches to these matters in the twentieth-century novel because there seems to be in the twentieth century an important change in attitudes to events and to personality. The rest of this study will consider some modern novelists in order to describe these changes.

D. H. Lawrence: *The Rainbow*

UNLIKE *The Warden, The Rainbow* is not concerned with decisions. Very near the end of the book, Ursula, the dominant character in its latter half, does have to make a choice; the effect is to bring home strangely to the reader the extraordinary rarity of choices up to this point. And it proves to be a somewhat muffled choice anyway. Having failed her university exams due to her overwhelming preoccupation with her lover, Anton Skrebensky, during her last term, she has to choose between marriage and spinsterhood as a schoolmistress (439). She can choose who she is to be; the implication is extraordinary, within twenty pages of the end of a novel in which choices have been few. And a few pages later, she perceives her relation with Skrebensky to be over. "Have you done with me?" he asks, and she replies "It isn't me. . . . You have done with me—we have done with each other" (446). "It isn't me": the choice of personality has been dropped; the possibility of decision has lapsed, replaced by the recognition of a state of affairs. The movement is typical of the novel. It is a work in which things happen to people, and they recognize it. It is because the changes in Lawrence's characters can be recognized only retrospectively that one may speak of an unconscious in his psychology; consciousness comes after the event.

This is the more important because the text appears to reflect only the feelings and states of mind of the characters; the author does not speak as a distinct personality, and the rhythm of the book appears to be the rhythm of the characters' emotions. It thus purports to be more exclusively mimetic than such works as *The Warden*. This is only an appearance, since it is the author who chooses which character's emotions to depict at any moment, and there are some very skillfully handled shifts in focus. The control of pace in Lawrence has been praised by critics such as T. Slade (1969, 53, 57); they are conscious of his sense of the pulsation of life (Worthern 1971, 66), of the ebb and flow of feeling, (Vivas 1961, 203), of the intermittence of vision (Hough 1968, 45); of his alternation of agitation and stillness (Bersani, 179). Leavis stresses the sense of development, personal and generational, in *The Rainbow* (148). It is Tony Pinkney who emphasizes the crucial point that there is a complexity of rhythm brought about by the "decentring" of the event in much of *The Rainbow* and its submerging into the broader rhythms of natural and human life. A typical case occurs with Will Brangwen and his daughter Ursula (207). The father angrily reprimands the child for treading on seeds in the garden. The scene starts, very briefly, with her sudden emotion: she is violently startled as her father shouts at her; his words are quoted, at greater length. The next paragraph cites the shock of both father and child, and the following one cites her retreat from feeling; this provokes hasty anger in the man, and he briefly speaks. The next paragraphs analyze at greater leisure her resentment and go on to recount her overall psychological development over some years, ending with the comment that her connection with her father was strong but tense. This page, then, recounts a moment, an unexpected and uncontrolled moment, no doubt typical of such strains; and while the overall concern of the passage is with the growth of the child, the rapid references to the feelings of the man serve to offer an outside view of the occasion of her feelings and to strengthen the tense disproportion between moment and state. There is a rhetoric in the book; it is a rhetoric that relates intensity to continuity, and that attunes the reader to growth in sensibility rather than to any judgment of the characters who possess it. Lawrence criticized Thomas Mann because "Death in Venice" did not have "the rhythm of a living thing" (P, 1:308–13); the concept defies precise definition but may relate to this acute sense of the characters' intense and continuous life.

There is an overall structure to the time sense of the book; it lies in the discrepancy between two forms of time. On the one hand there is the time of will, of progress, change, discontent; on the other, there is the time of inertia or of circularity (and the ambiguity here is important), the time of passivity, routine, the seasons. In Lawrence's own terms, it shows a will to motion and a will to inertia (P, 1:447) (the theme is acutely analyzed by Kermode in his *Lawrence*). The story is mostly one of people who want change but often have little sense of what change they want or how to obtain it; typical is Fred Brangwen: "He wanted change, deep, vital change of living. And he did not know how to get it" (226). It seems that Lawrence is displaying in his work, for one thing, the recurrent natural patterning of the seasons and generations with the associated psychological developments (cf. Stevenson 1992, 143–46), but also, perhaps more importantly, a generalized historical aspiration to greater freedom and self-awareness—the tendency "out of the nothing-ness and the undifferentiated mass, to make something of [oneself]" (263). Specifically, there is the move, as Mudrick puts it (16) from family productivity to individual aspiration. Since the self-awareness is precisely being aspired to rather than achieved, it is manifest in the bulk of the novel as an ill-grasped discontent. It therefore excludes any clear formulation of a goal or of any stages in movement towards attainment. The novel starts with a powerful picture of the cyclical, earthy pattern of farming life, develops through such characters as Tom Brangwen, with his fascination with the other, the foreign, and ends with Ursula, the detached intellectual who strikingly denies her past. The villagers who have grown up with her object to her changing: having known her since she was born, they regard any change as mere pretense. But she insists she has profoundly changed, through her education, her employment as a teacher, and her contacts with people from outside: "What was true of her ten years ago was not true of her now" (318).

And yet this desire for change is oddly combined with a sense of inevitability, of fate. Tom insists early in the novel that a person's nature cannot be changed (17), and if he and the other characters do in fact undergo some transformation, it is often with a sense of the inevitable, as when he first meets his future wife: "It was coming, he knew, his fate. The world was submitting to its transformation. He made no move: it would come, it would come" (32). Will Brangwen finds his job as a handcraft instructor to be a "supernatural fate" (387). Ursula has an inevitable attraction for Skrebensky (274); later, she feels equally out of control: "He was waiting for her to decide on him. It had been decided in her long ago, when he kissed her first" (411).

The book is much concerned with transformations, with transfigura-tions, and these are often emphatically presented. Characters find "a baptism to another life" (90). Marriage is like a natural change of state, "like a chestnut falling out of a burr" (135). Ursula, as she first comes to know Skrebensky, finds her whole world being transformed and feels, in biblical terms, that "now a new state should come to pass" (277); soon after, "she felt she was a new being" (294). People may suddenly discover themselves and each other through a recognition of the new or the alien; so Tom, in the course of an intense conversation with his wife, finds her frighteningly "transfigured" (89) and, in recognizing this, discovers for the first time the force of his own desire: their sudden intimate discovery of each other is in his eyes "the transfiguration, the glorification, the admission" (90–91).

But transformations are precarious. The pattern of events in *The Rainbow* is summarized in a symbolic detail. During a seaside holiday with her family, Ursula observes a wave bursting against a rock "enveloping all in a great white beauty"; but the rock emerges, as black as before, unchanged, unfree, unaesthetic (402).

Most specifically, this anticipates the drama of the return of Skrebensky, which occupies most of this chapter. Ursula's "unnoticed" sexuality, aroused by her first meeting with him some years ago, is to burst out into absorbing passion. But it does not set her free; it yields to frustration, incomprehension, and betrayal; it leaves the black hardness of the everyday. And this is characteristic of the lives of many of the characters, through the generations, who strive towards fulfillment, towards beauty and freedom, but find themselves forced to adapt to the ordinary.

For this reason, many of the chapters, especially in the later part of the book, trace processes of adjustment, of lapsing from intensity: chapter 7 is about the intense differences of Will Brangwen and his wife, Anna, chiefly focused on his interest in church architecture and craft, and ends modestly enough with his building a woodwork shed and recognizing his limitations, the unintelligible element within him (195); chapter 8 is about the childhood of Ursula, as well as about tension between her parents, and ends with her unconsciousness of her father's secret self as he works in his shed (222); chapter 9 is about the death of Tom Brangwen (narrated with superb intensity) and ends with the tranquil conversations of his widow with her granddaughter Ursula. Chapter 10 reverses the usual pattern, but chapter 11 reverts to the norm: 11 is about her first love for Skrebensky and ends after his departure with Ursula's soul, "cold, apathetic, unchanging" (309), while 12 is about her lesbian attachment to a schoolteacher and ends with her disillusion, as the teacher marries her uncle Tom. The more the characters seek individual fulfillment, the more they are likely to end in stagnation.

But the chapters may also be seen as accounts of repeated discoveries of potential, recognitions of the difference and complementarity of people, movements that terminate a phase of life; each is a determination of willed individuality. So, chapter 9 starts with the death of Tom Brangwen in a flood that sweeps away the form of the cultivated earth, his death depriving him of individual character and making of him an absolute, an abstraction (233), a strange, alien, intriguing object, and proceeds with the children's disturbing experience of the funeral before concentrating on Ursula's relationship with her widowed grandmother, a relationship that ensures a calm continuity of the generations but also gives a context for Ursula's childish anxiety about love and about the vastness of human experience. Chapter 10, revealingly called—like a later chapter!—"The Widening Circle," begins with the frictions between the Brangwen children and the more "common" children of the village, and proceeds to Ursula's excitement in going to secondary school, where she can escape from the restraints of her home village, and then her isolating herself from her own family. The chapter ends with her encounter with Christianity, concluding with what we take to be her reflections (though the text is so immersed in them that she is no longer named) on the acceptance of the body within Christianity, in which the crucified flesh is to be "a strong gladness and hope to them [the crowds in the street], as the first flower blossoming out of the earth's humus"—an image of birth as transcendence of the natural, as creation of the new. The child expecting love within the context of history, the adolescent expecting sacrificial sensuality in the context of redemption: these are the climaxes that arise alike from strangeness and the sense of limits.

And if there is repetition in this way, there is progress too; the reader may perceive each new beginning as starting at a point of selfhood broadly comparable to the terminating point of the previous chapter, and each ending is therefore a higher development than the previous one: so chapter 11 will end with Ursula's being brought by the sensual intensity of first love to a point of excess, her body even becoming sensitive to the point where clothes become uncomfortable: the aspiration to a more abundant physical and emotional life has the price of an ever more acute discomfort at contact with the outer world.

Such development tends to be manifest in the form of narrative summary. Summary, of course, appears in a great many novels; one is almost inclined to say in all, but some do adopt a form verging on the dramatic, in which only perceptible events and speeches are presented to the reader (the Jamesian tradition of the dialogic novel tends very strongly in this direction). Summary is normally, no doubt, perceived by readers as slowing the action. Lawrence was conscious of the ordinariness of much of life, and of the gradualness of change, and chose to reduce both to summary, allowing moments of change to stand out conspicuously. Chapter 7, "The Cathedral," recounts the first year of the marriage of Will Brangwen and Anna Lensky and their discovery that they find more of themselves as they cope with the conflict between them caused by their different interests and aspirations (the conception that the major attraction of marriage is quarreling is typically Lawrentian). The conflict is most powerfully conveyed in the account of a visit to Lincoln Cathedral, where Will is carried away by the mystic, timeless, womblike atmosphere, while Anna, mistrusting and ironic, is eager to maintain her own separate identity. The passage ends with a vigorously ill-tempered argument in which Anna interprets a wooden carving in the cathedral as a malicious portrait of a woman, while Will—more pious and himself a woodcarver—insists that it depicts a monk. The acuteness with which the dialogue is captured, the balance of taunting and sullen defensiveness applied to an apparently objective and factual issue, is persuasive and memorable. And then Lawrence starts to deepen his analysis by focusing—in summary form—on Will's response to this teasing, on his frustration, anger, disillusion, his fear of losing the certitudes that have supported him (190).There is a move forward here: Will's feelings have developed, become vulnerable to skepticism, to the Mephistophelean spirit of the everyday; he stands back from his wife's aggression. And as he stands back, so does the author, who can judge at a certain distance these "vital illusions"; Will is being seen, at least for the moment, as typical of a certain psychological stance, the search for self-engendered elevation. And the narrative goes on to still more rapid summary: "She had some new reverence for that which he wanted, he felt that his cathedrals would never again be to him as they had been." By now the crisis is over and the reader is waiting for the next thing to happen; in fact, there is more summary of gradual change in the two characters, culminating in another, briefer quarrel towards the end of the chapter, some four pages later. The couple have settled into a modus vivendi; they are learning to be different and to combine love with resentment. The domination of summary essentially symbolizes a retreat from open dialogue—which means open conflict—into introspection and imperceptible change.

The summary, unlike the scene, is, then, primarily devoted to the sense of the ordinary, of inertia, of stagnation, of the state in which time simply passes, a state of unfulfillment and preparation (as also in much of chapter 10, for example, on Ursula's adolescence). There is much stress in the book, in these passages of summary, on the gradual and repetitious. A short passage that gives the taste of the book in this respect is the one between Tom's first meeting with Lydia (given in direct dialogue) and the point where he goes to ask her to marry him (38–40). He feels a loss of vitality at the end of their conversation and thereafter is dazed, unsure, expectant; twice she visits him, and once he drives her and her daughter in his cart; he is angered by her separateness and gradually comes to show his fury; she responds with renewed openness. The process of the two getting to know each other continues, still slowly, gradually, with repeated intermissions; and so, "one evening in March," a culmination comes: he orders Tilly to bring a clean shirt, one of the linen shirts he has inherited from his father, and the next scene starts with beautiful, concrete precision. The waiting has been empty but important; it has been marked by the gradual, the incidental, the repeated—and by the insistence of a vocabulary that unites the couple in their "new birth." In one sense, nothing much has happened over these two pages; but from this suspension of activity, an act has at last emerged.

Within such sections of summary, there is very strong cohesion. This is sometimes a matter of the inherent coherence of subject matter, as with the account of Anna's growth towards the beginning of chapter 4, "The Girlhood of Anna Brangwen" (94–95). The sequence of paragraphs itself spells out clearly a logical analysis of the subject matter; after a brief piece of dialogue with her father, we are told that "the Marsh life had indeed a certain freedom and largeness," and the next paragraph starts, "So Anna was only easy at home"; by a straightforward antithesis, the next paragraph starts, "At school, or in the world, she was usually at fault," and goes on to her dislike for the people she meets outside the family, a dislike restricted at the beginning of the following paragraph: "Still she kept an ideal: a free, proud lady absolved from petty ties." The next paragraph then starts a shift to her father's viewpoint, starting with his response to this "ideal": "Her father was delighted." It is easy to admire in Lawrence above all his intense sensuousness; but there is much also that is meticulously intellectual and analytical.

The feature can be found again in much more detailed psychological analysis, as in the lengthy treatment of Anna's first pregnancy and the strain this puts between her and her husband. A passage of summary covers some four pages (166–70) leading up to the striking and disturbing scenes where she dances naked before her mirror, wondering at her pregnant figure, and then where she is observed doing this by her husband, who is alienated and angered by the sight. The summary passage before these scenes is used as preparation, as lull and explanation. The passage is essentially one that in classical rhetoric is called "amplification"; it reinforces the sense of her joy and of his disquiet by the antithesis between them and by the reformulation of what is essentially the same information, which allows, however, for many surprising and convincing refinements. So, the depiction of Anna starts with her "walking glorified," treating the sounds of nature and of town as her Magnificat, and goes on to her happiness "in showers of sunshine," her love for Will, her finding an image of her flowery happiness in a painting, her response to flowers, love, the warmth of summer, and the fullness of autumn, the light, the clouds, the moon; this alternates with Will's silent struggle to accept her separateness, his sense of abandonment, his compelled "reverence of her conception," his gentleness as a black shadow, his "strange, dark tension," his forcefulness and dissatisfaction and the like. The writing is highly consistent, the vocabulary repetitious, the imagery consistently sensual and unified by the sense of season, light, and weather, the relation of the characters delimited by antithesis and conflict. And this allows development—the development from summer to autumn and therefore close to the moment of birth, and the development in the balance of love and resentment, inclining gradually to cruelty and shame, so that the dancing gains a sense as a new escape, an escape from man to God. The reader's waiting, the exposure to repetition, analysis, and increasing complexity of feeling, leads at last to the moment of completeness, when a change has to take place.

Feelings, in fact, alternate. People go from delight in each other to fury; "the recurrence of love and conflict" (155) that marks the relationship of Will and Anna is characteristic and makes for much of the form of the novel, which to this extent is not purposive; people adjust from day to day to their own—barely predictable—feelings, without, usually, setting themselves any clear goals; this means that the novel is in principle interminable, and the interest of the work lies in the balance between the development of the characters towards a vaguely apprehended fulfillment

of freedom and articulacy, on the one hand, and the fluctuating intensity
of their momentary sensations, on the other. Not only is the whole novel
incapable of absolute termination for this reason; particular scenes and
episodes seem to be unpredictable and arbitrary in their ending, leading
to great irregularities in length. The novel, that is, reproduces the common subjective viewpoint in which we do not know in advance what we
shall consider to be the end of an episode in our life. In chapter 2, "They
Live at the Marsh," for instance, (and almost any chapter would provide
similar examples) we have: five pages recounting Lydia's past, her first
husband, her exile from Poland, her mourning at her husband's death;
leading straight on to a page on her reactions to Tom Brangwen and then
to two pages on their feelings at their wedding, ending with a brief
conversation between them as they prepare for bed at the end of the
wedding day; three pages on their life together, including some lengthy
bits of talk by her that he perceives as puzzling, leading to an analysis of
his growing feelings of estrangement from her, an analysis lasting some
three pages; then an extremely concrete and lively dialogue between him
and her daughter Anna, and a series of concrete scenes and concentration
seen from Anna's viewpoint; just over a page on Brangwen's depression
in winter and the end of Lydia's pregnancy, and finally the remarkable
section on Brangwen's handling of Anna during Lydia's confinement,
which occupies some seven pages. This one night has occupied approxi-
mately a fifth of the whole chapter, which as a whole covers the best part
of a year; the author's attention, it appears, has suddenly been focused on
the conflict and dependency of father and stepdaughter and on the
movement of resistance and appeasement, which in some ways parallels
the relationships of male and female seen, sometimes more abstractly or
analytically, throughout the chapter; the suddenness relates obviously to
the normal high drama of childbirth, with its danger and pain and the
impending change in family relationships; but there seems to be also a
strange enlivening of the author not unlike that which sometimes affects
his characters.

Since Lawrence works in states of mind, in blocks of time, his timing
is often imprecise. It is true that he keeps careful track of characters' ages
(with occasional minor inaccuracies, noted in Anne Fernihough's Penguin edition). But the text may distract the reader's attention from strict
chronology. At one point in the chapter on the marriage of Tom Brangwen and Lydia Lensky, it is announced that she is pregnant (61). The

dating of this is not clear. On the next page, there is a reference to her state during pregnancy, and soon after that it is November (62); after this, there is a reference to Tom's feelings "towards the end of her pregnancy." There is then a lengthy flashback to the early days of the marriage and the relationship of Tom and Anna, including much precise dialogue and several concrete scenes, and the text then returns to the summer and the "later months" of Lydia's pregnancy, beginning in autumn. The birth takes place in January (71); the reader may well have lost track of the actual passage of time, thanks to the overlap of the flashback with the basic narrative. The birth is in fact announced with the words "one afternoon"; and this casual dating of "one evening," "one day," even "one springtime" is common in the novel, giving a curious sense of the accidental. Similarly, the birth of Lydia's later children in chapter 4 and of Anna's many children in the later part of the novel is not at all clearly dated, and it seems that families grow in some haphazard and imperceptible way. A particularly characteristic and frequent device that tends to obscure chronology is the scene that can be read as depicting either a single occasion or a repeated event (Genette, in *Narrative Discourses*, notes similar structures in Proust). A typical case is one where the child Anna is playing with Tom, where Lawrence reports that Tom "would" call out on hearing his son crying and that Anna "would shout in delight" in response (80); but these signs of recurrence disappear in the next line, where Tom simply "shouted" a song. And the rest of the scene, with Anna singing, forgetting the words, and being interrupted by the servant Tilly, appears to be so specific that it can only be an account of a single occurrence. The individual event, presented with great precision and concreteness, with a strong sense of the rhythms of excited speech, of the interplay of parent and child and the more distant response of the servant, is presented as typical.

In *The Rainbow,* the sense of immediacy is strong. (Sagar stresses the vividness of Lawrence's writing [1966, 72].) Vividness is not a term much used now; it may seem archaically uncritical. But Lawrence *is* vivid. A single example, and amongst the most impressive sections of the novel, is Anna's behavior while her mother is giving birth (71–76). Uncomprehending of what is happening, but conscious of some loss of attention, the child repeatedly calls for her mother, refuses to be undressed by her father or Tilly so that she can be put to bed, sobs convulsively, but is transformed into "a new being" when she is taken out into the rain to see the cows being fed, at which she becomes calm and affectionate, takes an interest in the cows' eating and sleeping, and at last falls asleep herself. The passage gives an extraordinary sense of being an unedited, "real-time" depiction of obstinacy and yielding, the child repeating the phrase "I want my mother" eight times in the course of the passage and each time being met by soothing reassurances from her father and the servant, despite Tom's growing frustration and anger. The text strongly conveys her stiffness, her refusal to "move her limbs to his desire," and the sexual undertones are quite insistent, recalling all the other points in the novel on the distinctness of the sexes. Contact with other people is a struggle, and the rhythm of persistence convincingly captures this insight.

Against this may be set the very fine and detailed sense of time that arises in solitude, notably in the episode of Tom's death (226–31). He returns late at night from a pub in heavy rain; he is drunk enough to be vague about what is happening around him and to feel an unfocused bonhomie, chatting at length to his horse and to himself, disciplining himself to concentrate on the road, finding himself struggling to stay awake but nevertheless falling asleep, completing in an automatic way the routines of depositing his property in the house and of putting away the horse, patiently and in good humor leading it to its place and reassuring it, disconcerted and then astonished as he suddenly finds the depth and strength of the water, and then rapidly shifting from enjoyment of this strange world to fear, uncertainty, dismay, and helplessness, until he is instantly knocked down by the water and struggles ineffectively until he strikes his head; and then the narrative grows more distant, more fragmented, as his wife and son bit by bit realize that he has come home, that the embankment has broken, and that Tom cannot be found, ending with Mrs. Brangwen, certain of her husband's death and waiting almost tranquilly for a boat to rescue her from the water. The point of view acutely follows Tom's vague attempts to cope with the threat of the water and the very different, rational, and businesslike attempts of the others to locate him, his yielding to a destructive nature and their attempts to survive it, and especially the shift from self-satisfaction to consternation, the discovery of the limits of the human when face-to-face with an overwhelming otherness.

These qualities are found in other of Lawrence's works: the effect is to produce an alternation between, on the one hand, intensely visualized scenes and, on the other, pages recounting the inertia or gradual growth of the characters. Readers easily recall the scenes of intense experience: in *Sons and Lovers,* there are Mrs. Morel amongst the lilies, Paul collecting his father's wages from the mine office, his flirting with the village girls, his first night in Clara's house, his waiting for his mother's death, and many more; as the text proceeds, these come to form islands of real experience in the reader's memory, standing out above passages of description (as of the village in the opening pages), explanation (the account of Paul's brother William's career and departure for London, which however culminates in the finely evoked brief scene in which miners carry him in in his coffin), or abstract psychology (as in much of the treatment of the relationship between Paul and Miriam). What matters here is less a measurable lapse of time; it is rather a sense of incommensurability, for reader and character alike. Times that totally absorb the attention through the fascination of the new and the challenging, times that allow change and self-discovery, times that therefore move in their own rhythm, alternate with the slow, sometimes almost stagnant motion of routine work, of waiting, of the gradual acquisition of artistic and professional skills, with, that is, a kind of time in which change is imperceptible. What matters, in other words, is not the duration of time but the kind of time, the kind of rhythm, the presence or absence of an acute attunement to impending change.

There is a well-known statement in a letter by Lawrence: his characters, unlike the fixed characters of traditional fiction, "fall into the form of some other rhythmic form." The principle of alternation, of pulsation which they share with external nature, overrides their humanistic individualism. This has an important formal result, expressed by Worthern in his remark that Lawrence's "idea of a novel was not of an artistic entity, but of an occasion for continual exploration and recreation" (1979, 70). It might be more precise to say that Lawrence has modified our idea of what an entity is like; since his works do not, characteristically, recount an approach to some preset goal, they are not delimited by a clear conclusiveness; the artistic entity is the process of self-definition. The patterning of the story depends in part on symbolism, as critics have often pointed out. In other words, certain scenes are connected with the preceding and following parts of the story not so much because they contribute to the progress or problems of the characters but because they seem to sum up some pattern of events or relationships. They therefore constitute pauses in the onward movement of history and invite the reader to see time as the repetition of an essence, while also giving a very sensuous and specific presentation of a single occasion. Lawrence's writing is rhythmic in that it offers regular repetitions, circlings back to a set purpose; he speaks of the "curious spiral rhythm" of Verga (P, 249), and a modern critic has stressed Lawrence's own "incremental repetitions" (Stewart 1986, 171). Cohesion is given by such things as the heavy rain Tom Brangwen meets as he feeds his cattle while his wife is in labor (75), which anticipates the heavy rain that is to drown him much later; Anna's vision of dawn and sunset as a rainbow spanning the day in hope and promise (187), which anticipates Ursula's vision of the rainbow at the end of the whole book, or the overwhelming imagery of darkness that pervades much of the novel and especially impends over the whole of the last chapter. But if such scenes imply repetition of an essence, they can also show the sudden revelation of an essence, as in the very fine account of Anna and Will harvesting sheaves of corn together (113), making manifest a tension between desire and delay, or in Ursula's vision of the horses shortly before the end of the whole work, a scene in which, as Niven puts it, symbol and rhythm counterpoint theme (79). In the final, very brief chapter, prominently entitled "The Rainbow," Ursula is recovering from her separation from her lover, Skrebensky. This is the stage of loss and disruption; the encounter with otherness comes as she walks in the countryside near her home and suddenly sees a pack of galloping horses, from which she has to take refuge, and that seem to her to incarnate a menacing vitality. This encounter with force is an ordeal from which she emerges into illness. As she recovers from illness, she comes to see afresh her home environment, with its harshness, ugliness, bleakness. And then, less than a page from the end, she sees the rainbow: precisely described as it comes into form and color, it all at once becomes an image of people's potential for renovation, as it powerfully dominates space, rising from the undignified new houses to the vault of the sky (458). A meaning has been achieved; what was anticipated in Ursula's former anxieties and speculations is here attained, for a moment. The novel stops without resolving practical problems. Ursula is deserted, insecure, unemployed. For a moment she can love the world she lives in; but the suddenness of the vision and the suddenness of its ending leave the reader aware that the novel cannot finally impose an order on the multiplicity and change of life. Every novel, according to André Gide, should end with the words, "Could be continued": such rapidity, almost arbitrariness, of conclusion is one way of signaling that this novel could have been continued (as indeed, in a way, it will be continued in *Women in Love*).This suddenness is in part an avoidance of real finality; such endings are not the natural or inevitable conclusions of the stories, and they allow for continuation and change. The vision of intense animality is in part an escape from repetition, even from a benign repetition: freedom means freedom from sameness, freedom even from consistent personality, and this is manifest in brusqueness and difference.

The alternation of scene and summary has been particularly significant in the shaping of Ursula's development into a full individual, independent, willful, and self-conscious, as she detaches herself, more completely than any previous member of her family has succeeded in doing, from the natural order of farming life, subject to the seasons, the inescapable tasks of the land, and the geographical limits of a small rural community, and her steps towards selfhood are presented with increasing thoroughness as she matures. So, for instance, her schooldays, in the chapter "The Widening Circle," are told through a strangely intense and rapid alternation of general summary and acutely chosen detail, as here:

Up here, in the Grammar School, she fancied the air was finer, beyond the factory smoke. She wanted to learn Latin and Greek and French and mathematics. She trembled like a postulant when she wrote the Greek alphabet for the first time. (250)

The "trembling postulant" gives a sudden access to her intimacy; but in a later chapter, such as the second one of the same title, that intimacy is much more steadily maintained. She trembles again when given a present as she leaves a teaching job: "She was tremulous with pride and joy. She loved the two books. They were tokens to her, representing the fruit and trophies of her two years which, thank God, were over" (393). All of this appears to be quite close to her own thoughts: even the last sentence, because of the sensitively grasped paradox and the exclamatory "thank God," does not quite read like a summary of a lasting state of mind but rather like the record of an immediate response; and the chapter as a whole remains close to this style of depiction.

Moynahan (1963, 52) appears to regret the "staggeringly disproportionate ratio of descriptive passages to dramatic scenes" in *The Rainbow*. The disproportion differs when one realizes that the descriptions are re-

productions of a gradual, tentative, restrained learning process. The pace
of the novel slows, as Niven notes, from generation to generation (1978,
62); this is because each generation has more to learn. So, for instance,
Ursula's experiences as a schoolteacher start with a very detailed account
of her first day at school, of which her first impression is the sight of a
fellow teacher rubbing a paper on a jelly tray (an early form of duplica-
tion), focusing on the detail of the small, repeated movements of his
hands (344); time passes—as it does in new experiences—in tiny
moments. Gradually a routine establishes itself, and the style changes to
summarizing narrative, sometimes rather distant, in which the signs of
time passing are fairly emphatic: "The first week passed in a blind confusion. . . . Soon Ursula came to dread him [the headmaster]. . . . Then she
began to get on. . . . From the first moment she set hard against him. . . .
So she taught on" (350–51). But this is broken by one of the most dread-
fully direct scenes in the novel (and indeed in fiction), the one in which
she beats a disobedient pupil and so at last attains command over her
class (368–70). "Something went click in Ursula's soul": she has suddenly acquired the brutality required for school teaching (for teaching a
class of fifty in a poor industrial area); she has suddenly become strange
to herself. And she finally recognizes this as a stage in life, a difficult
move on the path to liberation (377). She is conscious of her own
strength and cruelty, qualities that go here with sudden intense activity
and that are an important part of what Lawrence conceives as an authentic contact with the livingness of the outside world; they will be further
apparent in the passionate horses of the last chapter, and here they appear
as a moment of energy that both contrasts with the dull alienation of
school life and encapsulates the harshness it contains.

Two particular dimensions go to reconcile progress and retrogression:
on the one hand there is the strong sense of past and future, in their
relation to the present; on the other there are the moments of stillness and
timelessness. First, one can recall the constant temporal density of the
characters' lives. They are always aware of having a past and a future;
they have recollections and apprehensions. This sense of other times may
even transcend their own lives; a moving episode has the young Ursula,
after her grandfather's death, acquiring peace and security from her
grandmother's tales of her Polish youth that place the individuals in a
broader context, "within the great past" (242); the adult Ursula will retain
a passion for the past (342), recalling the farm and her drowned grandfa-

ther as she waits for a tram to her urban and modern employment as a teacher; as she approaches the end of her university career (before the return of Skrebensky), she seeks to understand her own identity in terms of her past: "Already it was a history" (405). People live in time, and the novel makes that temporality palpable. And it formulates the impoverishment that is brought about by the discontinuity of time, through the industrialist Tom Brangwen Junior: for him, "each moment was like a separate little island, isolated from time, and blank, unconditioned by time" (320).

But if people are conditioned by time, they may also escape from time. The escape is manifest in the "timeless stillness" (76) into which Tom Brangwen falls during his wife's labor, in the "poised, unflawed stillness that was beyond time" that Will and Anna feel on their honeymoon (135), in Ursula's final ordeal as, agitated by the sight of the horses, she sits by a desolate road and finds herself liberated from time and change; she is "like a stone, unconscious, unchanging, unchangeable, whilst everything else rolled by in transience" (454). The novel cannot ultimately assert changelessness, and Ursula's final aspiration, to which the vision of the rainbow responds, is "to create a new knowledge of Eternity in the flux of Time" (456). And perhaps the whole form of the novel is an attempt to at least adumbrate such a knowledge; to present the vastness and uncertainty of flux but also to point towards the moments of impersonal, unwilled experience that might go beyond that flux.

Virginia Woolf: *Mrs. Dalloway*

*M*RS. *Dalloway* was originally to be called *The Hours*. It recounts the events of a single day in June 1923. The chronology of the day is strictly followed, and it is emphasized by frequent references to the striking of clocks, which enables the reader to time almost any event fairly precisely (to within a quarter of an hour in some cases); there is no summary, and all the events are presented in conversation or in the consciousness of a character. The major exception to this endeavor to directly reproduce a day as seen by various people at different times is that there are flash-backs; often information about the past of the characters is given by their own memories, plausibly aroused by sights, sensations, meetings; but information is provided about one character in what appears to be autho-rial intervention. This is then very obviously a book about time, about the impact of time on the sensibility of the present, and an attempt to find a new way of depicting the flow of time in a novel. The conception is new in that the novel is neither quite based on purposes nor on empathy: purposive acts are secondary to perception and memory, and empathy is qualified by ironic fascination.

For Woolf, the sense of purposive action has declined to the point at which it is barely possible to conceive of the events in the novel (if indeed they are events) as stages towards the attainment of a goal, and so as to some extent climactic. Woolf had even expressed in her diary (23 November 1926) the theory "that the actual event practically does not exist—nor time either" and asserted in a critical essay that "nothing happens to us as it did to our ancestors; events are seldom important" (CR, 24). For her, it is process that matters rather than result; and so events need to be considered lyrically; their effect in the reader depends on comparison between them, on a recognition that this section is more or less detailed, wide-ranging, change-producing than that section, and that this difference is a crucial function of the nature of experience or of the author's handling of it. Their effect, in other terms, is essentially a rhythmic one. *Mrs. Dalloway* to a considerable extent shows purpose replaced by pattern as a governing factor in the shape of the novel. And yet the order of the novel is not that of a timeless abstraction. The quality of life it displays does depend on two things: on characters' fixity or lability of purpose, and on the coincidence of purposes. Thus, Clarissa is fixed throughout on organizing her party and knows what it means to Miss Kilman, to Peter Walsh, to Lady Bruton, to Ellie Henderson; but she has intermissions in her purposiveness, so that the rhythm of the novel is a rhythm of ebb and flow. Into her day come the acts of other people—Peter's return, her husband's absence, the news of Septimus's death—so that the rhythm of the novel is a rhythm of events. The time of the novel is two-dimensional; it corresponds to the model offered by Jaques (1982) in which clock time advances regularly but is intersected by the transverse time of memory and anticipation.

The work is extremely concentrated; although it may seem at times to aim at depicting the whole life of London on the given day (rather as Joyce, earlier, had sought to give an image of the life of Dublin on a single day), and although for this reason it includes quite large numbers of people who have some contact with the central characters in the streets of the city or observe the same things as them, the basic concern of the work is with a small number of characters: Clarissa Dalloway; her husband, Richard, a prominent politician; her daughter; two of her old friends, Sally Seton and Peter Walsh; Miss Kilman, a friend of her daughter much resented by Clarissa; and, in one of the strangest and most risky aspects of the work, Septimus Smith, a young man suffering from mental disturbance as a result of his war experiences; his wife, Lucrezia; and the doctors who are treating him. The risky aspect is that Septimus has virtually no contact with the Dalloway group of characters and that the reader may therefore think that the novel really forms two quite separate stories arbitrarily stuck together. Septimus commits suicide in the course of the day, and one set of events in the book is therefore the sequence of happenings that lead up to this. Externally there are his passing through the streets and parks of London with his wife on his way to a consultation with a psychiatrist, his return home, and his death as he hears his own doctor about to intrude into his home. More importantly there are the internal events: his shifts of mood from hallucination and depression to calm affection and then very suddenly his choice of death. The book is, however, more centrally focused on Clarissa; she too has strong and unpredictable fluctuations of mood: from joyous appreciation of the fine day, to depression because she thinks her husband has chosen to lunch without her, to various tones of memory. Externally the chief events of her day are those involved in preparing for a party she is to give in the evening: ordering flowers, repairing her dress, talking with Peter Walsh, newly returned from India, and inviting him to the party, talking briefly to her daughter and Miss Kilman and inviting Miss Kilman, and the like. The two series of events coincide only because one of the guests at the party is Sir William Bradshaw, Septimus's psychiatrist, whose wife mentions his death to Clarissa. The party gives a sense of unity to the day. It brings together in the flesh various people who have been separated up to then—including especially Sally Seton, whom Clarissa and Peter have both remembered from their youth with much enthusiasm but who arrives at the party unexpected and uninvited; it brings together symbolically Clarissa's love of life, manifest in her sociability, and her awareness of death, manifest as she hears of the suicide with horror and a certain respect; and it brings together also her public, formal, social self with her sense of solitude and individual uniqueness (as seen in the alternation of her social chatter with her momentary vision of the old lady next door through her windows).

This means that what counts as an event in the development of the work is extremely varied, and some of these events might seem to some readers trivial. The novel includes an attack on the idea of proportion; it contains itself a major disproportion between the anguish and death of Septimus, on the one hand, and the small annoyances of Clarissa on the other. The events that most strike us in the life of Septimus are his threat of suicide, his attempt to persuade his wife to suicide, his horrifying vision of a dog turning into a person, the brief interlude of calm, affection, and relaxation, and the sudden death that immediately succeeds this. In the life of Clarissa and her circle there are far more happenings, but they are far less intense, and in another sort of novel might well have been mere details of circumstance. So there are such things as: inviting to the party in turn Peter, Lady Bruton, Ellie, and Miss Kilman; Peter's arrival at Clarissa's home, his sudden bursting into tears as he recounts the complications of his love life, his aimless following of a young woman in the streets, his falling asleep in Regent's Park, his sudden

decision to actually go to the party; the numerous memories of Sally
Seton and her unexpected appearance at the party. The tone is particularly clear in the very last words of the novel, which one might expect to
convey the greatest climax of the book. In fact, they do not convey a
climax as such at all but only readiness for one. Peter has arrived at the
party, has had a few words with Clarissa, of a fairly formal kind, and has
had a lengthy and intimate conversation with Sally, while Clarissa is
occupied with her other guests or with her private musings. The last lines
show sudden feverishness as Sally goes on to speak to Clarissa's husband
and daughter, while Peter remains, suddenly feeling terror and ecstasy,
"extraordinary excitement" of which the occasion is hardly apparent, and
instantly identifies the cause:

It is Clarissa, he said.

For there she was.

And so the novel ends. The terror, ecstasy, and excitement are not the
effect of some Dionysian tragedy but of the opportunity to speak to an
old friend he has last seen a few minutes ago. This needs to be seen in the
context of the whole work; earlier, Peter has been recalling his acquaintance with Sally and Clarissa in their youth and seeking to define the
importance of Clarissa to him: despite much apparent ordinariness in
conversation and manner, she had the gift, "that woman's gift," of being
at the center of things, of being a personality who cannot be overlooked:
for all her unexceptional qualities, "there she was, however; there she
was" (83). The end of the book confirms the middle of it; Peter's anticipation confirms his memory. The text is centered on a personality
(Clarissa has reflected on the social pressure to form herself into a center,
a radiancy [40]); and this centeredness is enough to marginalize the death
of the stranger, to allow Clarissa's social round to weigh against Septimus's destructive passions.

This disproportion is visible in the rhetoric of the writing, too. The
handling of Septimus's visions and fears is constantly intense; the technique is usually to plunge the reader directly into his consciousness and
to dramatize this consciousness by suddenness, by discontinuities and
surprises; so, for instance, the first appearance of Septimus and Lucrezia
ends with Lucrezia desperately trying to interest him in the everyday
spectacle of some boys preparing to play cricket; his inattention forces

her to persist, repeating the word "look" five times (on three occasions this is described as her imploring him, on the other two as her repeating the word); her persistence symbolizes her normality. Septimus's derangement is apparent in the sudden shifts from his rapid vision of Evans (a character as yet unidentified but apparently connected in some way with the dead) to his gravely visionary transposition of Lucrezia's "look," which he takes to be the voice of the unseen, greeting him as a savior of mankind (27).

The sections on the other characters on the contrary tend to mute their climaxes. So, the memory of Sally has been one of the major preoccupations both of Peter and of Clarissa throughout the day; little is known of her present state, and she appears to be an almost mythical figure of youthful vivacity. But she does come to the party. And she is barely recognized:

> "Clarissa!" That voice! It was Sally Seton! Sally Seton! after all these years! She loomed through a mist. For she hadn't looked like *that*, Sally Seton, when Clarissa grasped the hot-water can. (188)

The final reference, incongruous as it may seem, is in fact a passionate one; Clarissa has remembered herself at Bourton, in her bedroom, presumably about to wash, saying aloud, "She is beneath this roof!" (37), her quasi-lesbian delight in Sally's presence then being transferred, so intense and coherent is her feeling, to her memory of the hot water. The act of metonymy, the association of passion with hot water, is in the past. It is here revived in memory; Sally's actual presence produces at first hackneyed expressions of surprise and, if anything, dismay, "after all these years"; only after a moment does Clarissa "kindle all over with pleasure at the thought of the past" (188); the conclusion is almost lost. Other parts of the novel are perhaps even less climactic; so Clarissa's first interview with Peter, after five years absence in India, starts with her unable to remember his name and ends when it is interrupted by the entry of her daughter. Clarissa, it is true, announces Elisabeth "emotionally, histrionically, perhaps" (52); Elisabeth says, "How d'y do," Big Ben strikes, and Peter leaves; the following section ends unglamorously with Peter falling asleep on a park bench. "There are tides in the body," Richard Dalloway reflects later on (124), and the remark sounds like a justification for Woolf's whole process of depicting lives through waves of feeling and perception. Critics have commented on the pulsational or wavelike movement of Woolf's novels (Di Battista 1980, 26; Gordon 1986, 193), on her feeling for "the innermost rhythm of life" (Vogler 1970, 38), on the alternation of outgoing emotion and withdrawal into the self (Kiely 1990, 141; Bennett 1964, 63) or of immixtion in process and the feared interruption of the process (Bloom 1990, 71). On this occasion the tides refer very simply to Richard's having lost interest in the not very interesting lunch party with Lady Bruton (who herself has fallen asleep on the previous page), and his yawning, in a state of torpidity, as he follows an acquaintance, Hugh Whitmore, on some shopping. This is a world, often, of low animation; the undertaking of the novel is to show that within this restraint there is the memory of passion, the continuing intensity of some feelings, notably Clarissa's hatred for Miss Kilman that animates her at her party ("That was satisfying; that was real" [191]), and the growth of a sort of unity.

This unity is in large measure the work of the narrator. What concerns Clarissa is spatial discontinuity. Noting the old lady in the neighboring house, she reflects on their separateness: "The supreme mystery . . . was simply this; here was one room; there another. Did religion solve that, or love?" (140). And the author appears to imply that art solves it, the art of the novelist that can penetrate the minds of several characters and so eliminate the boundaries between them. The process is shown almost ostentatiously in a number of passages of *simultanéisme*, in the term used of contemporary French writers such as Apollinaire, that is, of writing that presents—in the sequence of the text—perceptions that take place simultaneously in the world of the novel. An early example is the car that is heard as Clarissa is shopping for flowers in the opening pages of the novel. Clarissa does not see it, but the shopkeeper comments on the noise of its backfiring and goes to look at it; the observations of passersby are recorded; one of them comments in an unidentifiable but no doubt humorous accent that this is "the Proime Minister's kyar"; he is heard by Septimus Smith (his first appearance in the novel), and Clarissa leaves her shop, reflecting that "it is probably the Queen." This brief slipping from mind to mind through the mediation of a public event is then followed at much greater length by an account of an advertising airplane that attracts the attention of a great many people, many of whom never appear again, or perhaps only once, discreetly, as a kind of game or witticism on the author's part. This means that what is happening in the novel is not so much an event in the imagined world but a change in the narrator's attention, and that the narrator's attention is not confined by relevance or an everyday sense of interest. The effects presumably intended are, first, a sense of general contemplativeness, distinct from the specific purposes of the characters and from the chains of cause and effect that we normally expect in practical life; second, and more specifically, a sense of the way the spectacle of modern life—the city and high technology—unites disparate people in an aesthetic curiosity not unlike that of the author; third, a view of this aesthetic contemplation as being that of a symbol of freedom, as the plane soars above the care-laden and socially restricted people on the ground; and fourth, a recognition that amongst these disparate people are Clarissa, the prosperous, emotionally rich, socially active woman, and her rhetorical counterpart in the pattern of the novel, the excluded and emotionally impoverished war veteran Septimus.

The novel has become static; it very blatantly insists on what has been called spatial form (Frank 1945; Smitten and Daghistany 1981) rather than the sequence of happenings. The writing of such passages has to maintain the curiosity of the reader sufficiently to imply that a total meaning will emerge in the temporary absence of plot; it also creates a sense of emptiness, of waiting, which delays the beginning of the story proper (the return of Peter Walsh) and to this extent again mutes the intensity of change. Later such *simultanéisme* will have a sharp ironic edge. Septimus in Regent's Park has a vision of his dead army friend Evans approaching him in a gray suit, and he is moved to prophetic lamentation for the deaths of the war. The man in the gray suit happens to be the respectably clad Peter Walsh, who, himself preoccupied with his somewhat confused love life, sees Septimus and Lucrezia only as a pair of quarreling lovers (77). Later, Peter will be passed by the ambulance bearing Septimus's body and reflect on the efficient and humane work of the ambulance as "one of the triumphs of civilisation" (165). Coincidence brings together these alien people, but it merely emphasizes their alienness; it disunites.

In addition to such changes of focus, the rhythm of the novel is affected by very brusque and marked changes of emotional tone. This does not exclude a great subtlety of tone in many parts of the text. Clarissa's inner monologue as she sets out to buy flowers at the beginning of the book, for instance, is interesting and persuasive because it expresses a number of constant elements in her emotional life through the brief allusions of a busy and well-bred person: she notes the shop-keepers "fidgeting in their windows" and has to remind herself (in parentheses) to "not buy things rashly for Elizabeth"; she notes the silence and the "slow-swimming happy ducks" of the park, and with some irony recognizes her old friend "the admirable Hugh." We do not yet know who Elizabeth is, but we learn that she comes readily to Clarissa's mind, as an object of generosity, as a temptation; the external world runs alongside a stream of recollections and desires, adding—at this stage—its tranquil enjoyment to produce an even but spontaneous and unpredictable readiness for varying kinds of happiness.

Clarissa is not free from intrusions; if she regards the visits of Peter Walsh—despite his emotional excess and his disorganized private life, despite his shedding tears before her—as a part of the continuity of her social existence (a renewal of an old acquaintance), she nevertheless knows that some things are alien to her: the brief worrying views of the neighbor, her daughter's deplorable interest in the baleful Miss Kilman, the obligations that make social life a chore, her husband's political responsibilities. Life, however prosperous and orderly, is precarious; it poses the challenge of preserving one's own purposes, one's own memories, one's own sense of being a separate and integral person, amidst the fluster of small duties. One of Woolf's crucial concerns, as Brown shows, is the "chasm in the self, [the] disruptive moment of unmaking which remakes all self-experience" (1989, 119). And the strange, almost ungainly rhythm of the novel, veering from lyrical memory to lively dialogue, from fantastic description to petty curiosity, from bleak introspection to unforeseen catastrophe, is an image of that precariousness of the tonality of life.

If Woolf is capable of subtlety in the emotional events she presents, she is capable of extremity as well. The most obvious cases arise, again, with Septimus. Septimus's first appearance is in the context of the mysterious car, and he is given some special emphasis, first by a more precise description than is accorded most of the passersby in this section (which of course slows the pace of narration), including a reference to his apprehensive look, and then by an odd, unattributed expression of concern: "The world has raised its whip; where will it descend?" (15); then gradually the text modulates, through impersonal description, to give us Septimus's thoughts—which are very different from general, good-humored curiosity: "This gradual drawing together of everything to one center before his eyes, as if some horror had come to the surface and was about to burst into flames, terrified him" (16). The novel will end with a happy "drawing together" at the center of Clarissa's party; here, suddenly and prematurely, the drawing together is one of horror or terror. Septimus will often later be the focus of such disturbing visions, as shortly after, with his vision of the birds singing to him in Greek; his mental disturbance is an extreme form of the incompatibility of subjective and objective worlds, which is manifest in many ways in the book. The movement to horror is a movement into the private, and such movements into the secrecy of the self are common throughout the novel. An instance is the way Septimus's anxieties alternate with his wife Lucrezia's more rational worries and with her view of him, mediated by the external record of her speaking to him and preparing to walk away (24); this, through the transition of a brief conversation, gives way to a stranger's view of the "queerness" of both Septimus and Lucrezia—and then to her exclaiming at the independent horror of her own situation isolated in London.

But change can take place equally within a single character (to such an extent that the idea of consistency of character or of personality seems under threat). A case is Clarissa's "sudden spasm" as she sees herself in the mirror, bringing to an end her sliding memories of her fascination with Sally Seton and of Peter Walsh's intrusion; the moment is echoed after the return of her husband by her sudden sense of desperate unhappiness, of which she then has to seek the cause. Clarissa is a sudden person; her life oscillates between concern for others and anxiety at herself, and if there is a move towards harmony and social grace, the move is awkward and devious. Another striking example, again marked by suddenness and discontinuity, is the moment when Clarissa is politely informed by a maid that her husband is lunching out (32). This is a shock—which she carefully distinguishes from "vulgar jealousy"— which forces her to think about time and space, about the erosion of time, and about the "exquisite suspense" of her entering her drawing room. There is a remarkable stylistic change, the hesitation producing a complex, hesitant, but controlled syntax and a strange marine lyricism as her entry into the room is compared to a diver plunging into the waves, which do not break but "only gently split their surface, roll and conceal and encrust as they just turn over the weeds with pearl" (33). This is a special moment; not a pleasant one, but one that is acutely distinct and in

which self-awareness is intensified by change. The change seems disproportionate; entering a drawing room is not really, one might feel, much
like the sea-change that is hinted at here. One thing *Mrs. Dalloway*
implies is that such a sense of proportion would be crude and literal;
Clarissa is interesting in part because of her lack of fixity, because of her
literary imagination. And this leads to a certain indefiniteness of the
character. Is it Clarissa or Virginia Woolf who spends so long over this
hesitation? Who is responsible for the comparisons, for the contemplation of the vanishing "colours, salts, tones of existence"? The text articulates and ornaments the sense of imminent change and the sense of loss
through time; the rhetoric communicates itself clearly to the reader; but
who is speaking?

Special moments are one of the chief concerns of the book; the point is
made quite early—and this time through the sensibility of Clarissa—and
developed through the texture of the whole work. Critics have noted the
crucial status in it of the moment, the "moment of revelation," the
"moments of vision" (Hungerford in Bloom 1990, 29, Beja 1990, 36).
Returning home from her shopping trip, Clarissa feels the satisfaction of
her familiar home, feels "blessed and purified"; and says to herself that
"moments like this are buds on the tree of life, flowers of darkness . . .
(as if some novelty rose had blossomed for her eyes only)," and reflects
that one must pay those who benefit one—servants, dogs and canaries,
her husband—"from this secret deposit of exquisite moments" (32).
Simply put, this seems to mean that such moments give strength to carry
out the social obligation of good companionship. But the imagery is rich
and complex; memory, it seems, turns a private aesthetic vision—
through accumulation, deposit—into money, the stuff of public communication and of the moral life. The novel thus becomes a meditation on
how far riches of private experience can be transposed into external
goodness. It is perhaps ironic that this moment is immediately succeeded
by the "exquisite suspense" of her apparent exclusion from her husband's
lunch, by a moment of personal anxiety that drives Clarissa briefly away
from society. And she will go on from this to meditate on the nature of
such moments, including the moments of failure. The reference here to
her failing her husband at Constantinople is one that will recur; the
consistency of the character lies largely in the recurrence of memories,
focused precisely around such moments. And she sets such moments of
failure with men, and also the routine unchanging solitariness of some

aspects of her life, against her moments of intimacy with women, her moments of illumination: "a match burning in a crocus; an inner meaning almost expressed" (35). Enlightenment is brief and partial, but this approach to the meaning (to borrow a phrase used in a different context by T. S. Eliot) is what gives life some fortitude.

And certainly the texture of the work is to a considerable extent made up of these special moments: most notably for Clarissa—and bearing out the quasi-lesbian implications of the passage just cited—there is the memory of kissing Sally Seton (38) (interrupted as are many of the positive moments of the book; Clarissa's memories of Peter Walsh's interruptions of sensitive scenes form one of the leitmotivs of the text). Special moments mean memory, and the temporal quality of the book is very much made up of the constant presence of memory, especially, of course, the memories shared by Clarissa, Peter, and Sally of their youth at Bourton—what the author in her diary called the "caves behind the characters" that link up finally (30 August 1923), but also the memories of war they share with Septimus and Lucrezia and with Miss Kilman, a victim of war in that she has been persecuted because of her German family origins. *Mrs. Dalloway* is a book about aftermaths, about what is left for Britain after a war that has brought deprivation and trial (a recurrent image is that of the stoical Lady Bexborough opening a bazaar as she hears of the death of her son) and what is left for middle-aged people after the intense emotions of youth.

As well as moments of enlightenment for the characters, *Mrs. Dalloway* contains moments of enlightenment for readers. Memory may link up in ways that suddenly become perspicuous for the reader. So, Clarissa, meeting the pompous official Hugh Whitbread in her walk to the shops, recalls that Peter Walsh "had never to this day forgiven her for liking him" (6). This memory is confirmed when we see Peter himself, who recalls in detail his grounds for objecting to Hugh, with his priggish obsequiousness, and especially Sally's indignation at his kissing her (80); at the end of the novel, Clarissa remembers Sally accusing Hugh ("of all people") of kissing her to punish her for her belief in votes for women (199), and Sally confirms it to Peter (208). With Peter's appearance we understand why he is so hostile to Hugh; with Clarissa's recollections we realize that forgiveness is possible. Clarissa is perhaps too indulgent, Peter perhaps biased by his admiration for Sally, and perhaps too crudely, too romantically opposed to the merely social; a single occur-

rence becomes multivalent and reveals or constitutes the character of
several individuals; likes and dislikes are part of the fabric of time and of
the interplay of ideologies. And the reader recognizes these things, one
by one as the novel proceeds, each little enlightenment contributing its
item to the kaleidoscope of a society.

There is then a balance of repetition and development. In some
respects continuity may have the upper hand, to quite a surprising extent.
So with the musician Breitkopf, remembered from Bourton. He is
remembered by Clarissa, singing Brahms "without any voice," as part of
the background to the vibrant figure of Sally (38); by Peter as a
(deserving) victim of Clarissa's youthful laughter as he sings "without
any voice" (169); by Sally, "singing Brahms without any voice," as part
of what she shares with Peter (199). The repeated phrase transcends the
difference of character and perspective; there is a persistent sameness in
the book, as in many of Woolf's novels, a sort of unchangingness, most
strongly apparent in the lyricism of atmosphere, the images of flowers
and moonlight in which so much of the text is bathed. If the Breitkopf
example is mildly humorous, there is also something elusive about it; the
reader may not find it easy to recall exactly where or by whom the key
phrase was last used, and there is to this extent a dissolution of sequence
and of personality. In general, the book is one that does not orient itself
towards a conclusion, to an achievement or a defeat; it is a book about
readiness for feeling, about openness to "life." "What's the sense of your
parties?" the asocial Peter might ask Clarissa (133) (he has, in fact, asked
himself, "Why does she give these parties?" [52–53] but without thinking
out an answer); her reply would be, "They're an offering," an offering,
apparently, to "this thing she called life" (133). She admits the vagueness
of this; but vagueness seems to be inescapable (the book, in other words,
is vague), and she goes on to attempt a definition in terms of an acceptance of the sequence of time, of one day following another, of the
chances of meetings and experiences, which seem—astonishingly to the
reader—to exclude death (134). Clarissa thus justifies the form of *Mrs.
Dalloway*, with its routine sequence, its suddenness of incident, its
aesthetic moments; and she defends it as a bulwark against death. The
novel as a whole, however, through the figure of Septimus and through
the memories of war, accepts death as part of a general yes-saying. "Fear
no more," Clarissa frequently says to herself: on hearing of her husband's
lunch appointment (32), as she sits peacefully sewing before Peter's

incursion, feeling contentment build up and break like a wave renewing itself, as "the whole world seems to be saying 'that is all' more and more ponderously" (43), as she reflects in darkness at her party on Septimus's death (204). Shakespeare's poem is about the tranquillity of death as an escape from the excess of life. It plays a complex part in the structure of the novel. Clarissa, as Peter fairly crudely intimates, has a "horror of death" (167); she "fears time itself" (32) because of the transience of life; her talismanic recourse to Shakespeare's line seems to be at once an attempt to exorcise this horror—and so, by implication, a reminder of it—a withdrawal from the tensions of life, an attainment of rest, and an acceptance of the inevitability of death evoked in the unquoted last lines, "Golden lads and girls all must, As chimney sweepers, come to dust." And, of course, such tranquil acceptance is questionable. The one death we see in the novel, that of Septimus, is not accepted but chosen, not a peaceful escape from turmoil but an expression of turmoil destroying a rare moment of peace. Septimus, as Graham puts it (in Patrides 1976, 190), "casts off his temporal selfhood"; looked at positively, his death is an assertion of the mystical unity that he perceives in his heightened state of sensibility. But it is also an act of panic; and Clarissa accepts time, accepts the norms of social life and sanity, and rejects death.

Leaving Clarissa, Peter Walsh experiences a moment of timelessness, of repose. But this moment is not a transcendent liberation: "Effort ceases. Time flaps on the mast. There we stop; there we stand. Rigid, the skeleton of habit alone upholds the human frame. Where there is nothing, Peter Walsh said to himself; feeling hollowed out, utterly empty within" (54). Timelessness is lack of feeling and submission to habit. Much of the novel is about habitual ways of life; but these for most people are given meaning by the aura of feelings they bring with them. Septimus is the limiting case of a deprivation of life caused by inability to feel, by his inability to comprehend the horror of war and the price he pays in delayed horrors.

But if Septimus is the extreme, lack of feeling is always a risk for Clarissa too; cold, in Peter's eyes, lacking in warmth in her own, even her past threatens to escape her: reflecting on her memories of Sally, she finds that "she could not even get an echo of her old emotion" (37). Slowly, partially, the feeling returns as she muses on her memories; but it gradually merges into a reflection on herself, on her achievements, on the immediate moments of light and beauty, of "this June morning on which was the pressure of all the other mornings," and finally on the practical business of repairing her dress. Memories merge with actualities; and in the merging, the sense of the moment is asserted and then lost.

Feeling can take the form of obsession and so of repetition. Once again, Septimus with his everpresent concern with the war is the extreme example; but Clarissa shows herself chained to certain smaller concerns. Hearing of her husband's lunch engagement, she thinks with frustration of his host, "Millicent Bruton, whose lunch parties were said to be extraordinarily amusing" (32). A few pages later, she is starting to recover from the shock and reflects on the self-discipline she is capable of, "never showing a sign of all the other sides of her—faults, jealousies, vanities, suspicions, like this of Lady Bruton not asking her to lunch" (40). After a slightly longer interval, and in the midst of her conversation with Peter, when she might well have been preoccupied with pity or annoyance at his undue emotional expression, she silently, privately, but very bitterly reverts to the memory of her husband lunching with Lady Bruton: "He has left me, I am alone forever, she thought" (51). From self-discipline to neurotic exaggeration seems not to be very far. For some time the novel turns away from Clarissa; when it returns to her, she is preoccupied with the difficulties of her relationship with her husband: "She had failed him, once at Constantinople; and Lady Bruton, whose lunch parties were said to be extraordinarily amusing, had not asked her" (129). The moment is another brief and delicate one, another suspense at the breaking of a wave, for Richard comes in, holding flowers for her—but failing to tell her, as he had decided to do at Lady Bruton's quite boring lunch party, that he loves her. She asks whether Lady Bruton has asked after her, and husband and wife sit for a while in affectionate companionship. Richard has invited Lady Bruton to the party and, sure enough, very near the end of the novel, she appears at it, is told that Richard has enjoyed his lunch party, and asks after Clarissa's health (196). Emotion rises and fades; the trivial impinges on the profound; life reverts to discipline and exterior decorum. Society gives a structure to the individual, prey to excess and imagination. The novel shows this disciplining of the individual tragically and satirically in its treatment of Septimus, whose life never reverts to normality but is made a victim of the doctor's cult of Proportion, which is the same as the Conversion by which European power is imposed on other nations (109). Conversion is control; Clarissa outwardly has self-control and survives; Septimus is subject to control by others and suddenly dies.

The inner life is one whose movements are sudden and secret, Peter Walsh reflects, hidden as in deep seas, manifesting themselves only in bright glimpses. And having said this, he hastily turns his attention to Richard Dalloway and his views on politics (176). Peter, pondering on his decision to go to the party, after all, is in no hurry; his style is repetitious, complex, uneven, epithet-laden; if this is a discovery, a recognition of "the truth about our soul," it is also a speculation, a way of filling in time, of going "on and on"; and so it is typical of the idle, displaced, ineffective half-intellectual. But for all his limitations, Peter here formulates one of the structural principles of the book and refines on Clarissa's sense that "life" is made up of routine and exquisiteness; in Peter's sense, the inner life is made of persistence, of repetition or obsession, of memory and history; the public life is made of routines, of rituals, of common spectacle, of coincidence; and the quality of our experience is made of uneven shifts between the two. This is therefore a work of monotony and surprises, and these qualities articulate a complex and shifting sense of the priorities in life. In the final scene, social order will coincide, briefly, with personal fulfillment; but more radically *Mrs. Dalloway* challenges the reader to decide whether life is undifferentiated flow or whether there are peaks, moments of public propriety or private intensity, which give a shape to our lives.

E. M. Forster: *A Passage to India*

IN many respects, *A Passage to India* appears to be a work of the highest rationality. It is a work of clear exposition, cohesive events, coherent characters, mature judgment. It depicts a stable, objective world through the eyes of sensible people. So, in the opening chapters we see Dr. Aziz receiving a summons from his superior, Dr. Callendar; we see him setting off by bicycle; we see the bicycle puncturing and Aziz arriving late. A few chapters later, we see Callendar losing his temper because of Aziz's unpunctuality and Aziz's attempts to excuse himself. In another early episode, we see Aziz's refusal to attend the bridge party arranged, without great sincerity, by the collector to allow Indians and Europeans to meet, an explanation by flashback of his refusal, an account of what he does instead (he plays polo with a British officer he meets by chance), and then his dispute with another Indian about his absence from the party. Events make sense; they illustrate the normal motives and social structures: obedience, rivalry, self-esteem. Specifically, they illustrate the national stereotypes of colonialism: British arrogance, Indian poverty, and inefficiency. Events fit neatly together, one thing happening at the same time as another and the two coming together at a precise point.

The neat fitting together of events can contribute to the elegant comedy of much of the book. So, Aziz visiting Fielding, the British schoolteacher who is sympathetic to Indians, for a tea party (chapter 7) finds him complaining at losing his collar stud. With somewhat absurd helpfulness, Aziz gives him his own. No more is said about this for some time; but Ronny, the fiancé of Adela Quested, a newly arrived English-woman who is attending the party, arrives and is annoyed to find her hobnobbing with Indians; to express his annoyance, he comments on the typical Indian sloppiness shown by Aziz's failure to wear a collar stud. On a larger level, it seems a curious coincidence, curious enough to somewhat detract from the potential gravity of the final chapters: that three of the major figures of Chandrapore, where the earlier parts of the novel are set, should all end up in the native state of Mau, where the novel concludes. In fact, it is quite logical: Godbole, as he makes clear quite early on, has been offered a major post in the educational system there, befitting his academic status and his profoundly Hindu mentality. Aziz, disillusioned of British rule by the ordeal of the false accusation against him, chooses to live in an Indian state and not surprisingly is able to find employment in the one where his old acquaintance Godbole is influential. Fielding is on an official tour of inspection of education in the Indian states. Everything is motivated; the writing is craftsmanlike, which means that it gives a picture of events as both plausible and significant.

This leads to a very clear sense of climax within some chapters. Fielding's tea party is a nice example: starting with a general account of Fielding's character and background, the chapter goes on to Aziz's arrival, early of course. A charming and perceptive account of Aziz and Fielding's conversation as they get to know each other, slightly awkwardly but with much good will, leads to the arrival of Mrs. Moore and Miss Quested, conversation gradually enlivening as Aziz recalls his previous friendly encounter with Mrs. Moore and starts to feel himself the star of the occasion. The pace slows slightly with the inhibiting effect of Godbole's arrival and then comes to a first climax—an ironic, playful, teasing one—with Aziz's invitation to the ladies to accompany him to the Marabar caves. This arises as near accident; Aziz does not want to invite them to his home, since he is ashamed of its condition, and instead invites them on this large-scale and expensive expedition to a place of which no one seems to know the attractions. So, a state of relaxation and good humor, of mutual curiosity, has been attained: "Into this Ronny dropped" (69). This line occupies a paragraph by itself; Forster seems almost to be parodying the clear articulation of the chapter, in which interracial harmony, involving the more liberal and flexible characters of the novel, is very brusquely disrupted by the voice of authoritarian colonialism. Ronny immediately hurries his charges away to see a polo match (a quintessentially British activity), paying little attention to the Indians and resentful when Aziz interprets for him; there are lengthy good-byes; the chapter is concluded. Except that it isn't quite. There is something hanging over, which is now settled. Adela politely refers to Godbole's singing, and Godbole, after all the good-byes, sings, in a disturbingly inconclusive manner. The chapter as a whole builds up to climax, to conflict, to avoidance of the alien, coinciding with the normal end of a social occasion; it ends in anticlimax and confusion.

A still more effective demonstration of logic and emphasis appears in the trial scene (chapter 24 of part 2). The scene starts with the heat of the season and goes on to Adela preparing to give evidence and the Europeans discussing the prospects of the trial. The trial begins amidst trivial bickering about seating and then goes through the due formalities of the prosecutor's speech and the calling of the first witness. All this is somewhat delayed by heckling and by disputes about secondary issues such as the exact status of the caves or, somewhat more crucially, the question of the absence of Mrs. Moore, a potential witness: details that plausibly demonstrate the tension between the races, the displacement of activity into the secondary that the Europeans think of as typically Indian but of which they themselves are equally guilty, and the threat that legal process will be subordinated to political power; details also that keep the reader waiting for the essential business of the trial and verdict, as Forster makes plain, commenting almost too explicitly that "the crisis was still to come." Adela gives her evidence in a thoughtful, careful, slightly hesitant manner, recounted at first in a long paragraph of summary and then moving into direct dialogue, until we reach the crucial question as to whether the prisoner had followed her into the cave where the assault is alleged to have taken place. A moment's delay as one of the Britons comments, "Now we've got 'im"; but they haven't got him, for after a few more exchanges of question and answer, Adela withdraws her charges. In a grand climax, the magistrate dismisses Aziz "without one stain on his character," Aziz faints, and the court collapses into uproar. There is an anticlimax again; the punkah-wallah, briefly mentioned at the beginning of the trial, continues to operate the punkah, "unaware that anything unusual had occurred"; perhaps these things don't really matter all that much after all. But apart from this final note, the construction of the chapter is exemplary; background, preliminaries, orderly development of a schema, delay, climax. A major change, a gesture of undoubted integrity in an atmosphere of muddle, bewilderment, and bias, is given its full weight.

As well as clarity of sequence, there is in the novel a complex patterning, the contrast between Miss Quested and Fielding in the first section giving way to the conflict of Miss Quested and Aziz in the second and the tension between Fielding and Aziz in the third, each part ending with a partial overcoming of separation and distance. Within each of these sections, there is further development. Part 1 parallels the development of Miss Quested's engagement to Ronny, interrupted by her first contact with Indian people (including Aziz), with the development of Fielding's friendship with Aziz. The second part opposes a first movement, in which Miss Quested and British India are in the ascendant and expel Fielding, to a second movement, in which Aziz and native India discredit Britain and welcome Fielding. In the third part, the variation is between the totally native India of Godbole's religious ceremony and the final approximate harmony of Aziz and Fielding. The overall shape of the story is clear: it moves from a state of British domination, in which natives seek acceptance, to a native state in which the Briton Fielding has only limited acceptance. Symbolically, this is a move from a highly differentiated and codified social order to a world of confusion and randomness. It parallels a shift from expectation and promise to disappointment and waiting, as Colmer puts it (1979, 119). The hypothesis that is being played out here, in ironic, contemplative, spectacular modes, is that order means division but that order is quite good and division quite bad. The first part identifies the characters who are capable of change; the second shows first Miss Quested's unconscious succumbing to the disorderliness of India and then an elucidation of this disorderliness, manifest through Aziz's bitter sense of racial division and injustice; the third part celebrates disorder as a divine transcendence of division and finally demonstrates that some degree of division is inevitable.

Maturing is a structural principle within the novel, as in the whole tradition of the European novel; we see it most strongly precisely in Adela's recantation, which is the culmination of her gradual facing up to her own uncertainty; under constant pressure from her associates to take the straightforward strategy of denouncing Aziz, she nevertheless hesitates. Aziz is arrested in chapter 16. By chapter 22, Adela is asking if she has made a mistake and asserting that Aziz should be released if he is innocent (192–93); as the trial proceeds in chapter 24, and as she actually sees Aziz again, she first of all asks herself again, "Can I possibly have made a mistake?" (210), then, as she rises to give evidence, reflects on her will to tell the whole truth and her painful rehearsals of the effort to do so. At first, she is elated by the ease with which she finds she can answer, as she again visualizes the events of the day in question; when the crucial question comes, she finds she cannot visualize Aziz following her into the cave and says, with due decorum and restraint, "I'm afraid I have made a mistake" (218). She has always been characterized by her sincerity; "If one isn't absolutely honest," she asks Mrs. Moore at one early stage of the novel, "what is the use of existing?" (89). She finds the difficulties of absolute honesty; she overcomes them gradually. She learns, and the novel shows that learning happens through gradual self-discipline and sudden self-awareness.

There certainly are strong climaxes in the novel; there are also chapters that appear to build up to some meaningful conclusion only to deny the reader the satisfaction of a clear change. The first few chapters, for instance, end with the description of the Marabar Hills, Aziz talking to Mrs. Moore, a wasp, the reaction of some missionaries (not otherwise mentioned) to the announcement of the "bridge party," tension between Mrs. Moore and Ronny, and Aziz playing polo with a chance-met subaltern. The missionaries seem to be merely a bit of light satire. Others of these climaxes do have some importance later in the work, from the point of view of plot or of theme. The wasp will gain importance symbolically (as Brown points out), notably in the final part of the novel where God-bole, at a moment of religious intensity, recalls Mrs. Moore amidst "a throng of soliciting images" including the image of the wasp on a stone (277); the text asserts that his equal feeling for the wasp and the woman is what makes him godlike. Mrs. Moore's interest in the Indian Aziz and her discomfort with her son contribute to her mythical status as a protector of the Indian people against injustice and, more practically, contribute to the arrangements for the crucial visit to the Marabar caves. Aziz's game of polo will be recalled, with unconscious irony, by the subaltern during the agitation about Miss Quested's charges against him (the subaltern contrasting the decent, polo-playing Indian with the evil Aziz) and will be echoed near the end of the novel by his riding with Fielding. A network of potentially significant incidents is being constructed; but at first sight they look trivial, and at times even less interesting than the events to which they succeed, such as the planning of the bridge party, the encounter with Fielding, and Aziz's quarrel with his superior. The characteristic event in these opening sections appears to be a fading away of interest, under the pressure of the oppressive ordinariness of colonial society; the reader may feel some frustration and may expect the newcomers in India, Mrs. Moore and Miss Quested, to feel similarly.

And there are aspects of the work that very clearly amount to an assertion of the irrationality, the incoherence, and the unintelligibility of the world depicted. Characters, first of all, do not always behave with Fielding's thoughtful deliberation. Things happen suddenly in Forster, as Page points out in discussing the murder in *A Room with a View* (1987, 38). Mrs. Moore, to take a sympathetic example, acts on impulse. She tells Aziz, at first meeting him, "I don't think I understand people very well. I only know whether I like or dislike them" (17), and Aziz replies, "Then you are an Oriental." To be Oriental is to be without calculation; this is why the spontaneous Mrs. Moore can seem to bridge the two cultures. Meeting an Indian family at the bridge party, she "had an impulse" (37) and invites them to visit her, an invitation that of course goes wrong. Even the more organized Miss Quested—for whom planning "had been a passion . . . from girlhood" (128), but whose frankness and sincerity sometimes lead her to an "outburst" (40) that disconcerts her companions—almost lets her engagement to Ronny slip accidentally. Asked at the tea party if she will stay in India, she replies that she couldn't do so: "She made the remark without thinking what it meant" (66)—which is, of course, that she will not be marrying Ronny—and only belatedly thinks she should have said it to him first. Then, at the polo match to which he takes her after the tea party, she makes "the undigested remark" (75) that they should reconsider their engagement; in fact, "the 'thorough talk' so dear to her principles and temperament had been postponed to too late"; she feels the ordeal of decision "slipping away like a dream" (76). Things are happening to her; control has gone, and timing has gone with it. A few pages later, after the car accident involving the Nawab Bahadur, Ronny looks at her and she shyly recants her breaking of the engagement—"and they became engaged to be married in consequence" (85). In consequence: there is some trace of logic round here. "The accident was over": the car accident, but perhaps also the accident of the disrupted relationship. The engagement will later be canceled, and Ronny will realize that it was itself accidental.

And yet, in a sense accidents are never over. Life in India is quite accidental. The Marabar caves episode will be another accident that proves that the engagement itself is accidental, that it doesn't respond to the lasting characters of the two people but only to the awkwardness of circumstances and is best forgotten. The action in *A Passage to India* stems from the difference between those characters who (for part of their career, at least) believe in progress, in gradual personal growth through learning something of other people (Miss Quested, Mrs. Moore, Fielding), and those who, through political or social conservatism, religious fatalism or anticolonial distrust, think that no real change is likely and view all activities as small-scale gestures—perhaps ultimately futile—within an established code of social contacts; hence the discrepancy between Miss Quested's wish to learn something of India and Aziz's haphazard picnic. The novel is made up of accidents and the cancellation of accidents. So, Aziz's invitation to the Marabar caves is accidental, and many accidents surround the visit itself: Fielding and Godbole arrive late, delayed by a level crossing; Aziz and his relative Mohammed Latif almost miss the train as it starts early; the Englishwomen's servant Antony has, in fact, been bribed to stay away—as is charged at the trial—but with no malicious intent, and it is accidental that this should provide plausible evidence against Aziz. These things make possible Adela's isolation at the caves and her hallucination of attack; they arise from mere incompetence.

In general, the Indian sense of time is free of the mechanical reliability expected in Europe. Unpunctuality is rife; the Bhattacharyas' acceptance of the Englishwomen's invitation and their failure to actually attend is characteristic of a life free from planning. Life in India has no sense, especially of conclusiveness. "That was the climax, as far as India admits of one," the narrator comments of Godbole's Hindu ceremony in the final part; the conception that a civilization might have no sense of climax is one that seriously threatens the novel as a genre. The outstanding example of Indian inconclusiveness is Godbole's song, which appears as an anticlimax in its chapter and is itself inherently anticlimactic. It comes suddenly and ends apparently in midtune. He explains that the song itself is about an unfulfilled desire, being an invitation to a god, which the god does not accept: "I say to Him, Come, come, come, come, come, come. He neglects to come" (72). The effect is a memorable one. As with some of the previous examples we have noted, the text will return to this moment and give it added point. In the final section of the book, Godbole meditates in the course of a ceremony in which his choir has sung to God with what may be equal ineffectiveness. This meditation culminates in the reflection that he has to place himself in the position of Mrs. Moore and pray on her behalf to God to "Come, come, come, come" (281). And on almost the last page the atheist Fielding asks the Muslim Aziz after Godbole and gets an apathetic answer:

"Does the old fellow still say 'Come, come'?"

"Oh, presumably." (310)

As we read, what strikes us is the pointlessness of things, the alienness and unintelligibility of people from a different culture, and the fact that this pointlessness is precisely what Godbole seems to wish to convey (if "wish" is not too strong a word). Anticlimax becomes spectacular. This is part of the Indian experience, and it is part of the irony that the novel inculcates, a radical irony that questions any sense of purpose or expectation, any differentiation of life into the significant and the trivial, and therefore any climax or rhythm. And yet one crucial note qualifies this: Miss Quested at one point (228) blames on Godbole's song the state of "living at half pressure" that led to her hallucination of being attacked by Aziz; undifferentiation and shapelessness lead to the high tension of accusation and trial. The ambivalence of the work emerges clearly from M. Orange's comment on the scene (in Das and Beer 1979, 156–57): "Expectancy has been celebrated . . . the moment itself (rather than the structure of potential realization and futurity built upon it) when prolonged, absorbs eternity. Significance resides in waiting." Orange's interpretation eloquently states an important aspect of the novel. It is indeed an important aspect of many novels, and many modern novelists might accept that "significance resides in waiting." But there are other kinds of significance: the significance of Fielding's refusal to stand up to show respect for Ronny, of Adela's recantation, of the awkward rediscovery of friendship between Fielding and Aziz. What Forster shows is that significance resides in what we attend to wholeheartedly.

This means that much of the handling of time and narrative in the book is confusing or disproportionate. To take one important issue, the central event of the book is never narrated. At the end of chapter 15 of part 2, Adela enters a cave, thinking partly of the boredom of sightseeing, partly of marriage. Chapter 16 switches back to Aziz (from whose viewpoint the beginning of this last paragraph in chapter 15 is seen), who is in "his cave." He intends to rejoin her and is told by the guide that she has gone into "a cave"; Aziz and the guide pointlessly call for her, and Aziz glimpses her field glasses, dropped on the hill. After some conversation with Fielding, who has now arrived, and Mrs. Moore, including well-meaning queries about Adela's whereabouts, he is told by a servant that she is being driven back to Chandrapore. And so it seems the incident has come to a vague and confusing end. It hasn't; this is the beginning of Aziz's ordeal of accusations. We can deduce from the account so far that Aziz is innocent of any assault on Adela; but what we don't know—and never are to know—is what happens to make her accuse Aziz. We can recall what has happened to Mrs. Moore in another cave, a few pages earlier, though in very different circumstances: accompanied by a large crowd of servants—another of these Indian muddles or accidents—she has been struck by panic: "For an instant she went mad, hitting and gasping like a fanatic," and she has been terrified by the echo, which is "entirely devoid of distinction," "monotonous," "utterly dull," because it is a negation of meaning. The cave typifies Indian irrationality, and it disturbs Mrs. Moore for this reason. Does Miss Quested, though alone, have some similar sense of the limits of intelligibility? We have to wait until the trial scene for her to recapture her memories of the incident, and then she fails to do so; she simply cannot recall the prisoner Aziz entering the cave (rationally enough, since we have every reason to think that he did not enter it). But the vision she has at the trial, a vision above "the insipidity of the world" (219), is presented only as a vision of caves and of herself both inside and outside one of them. A mystery, a puzzle, remains at the heart of the work. The cave is rather dismissed by Page as a "narrator's trick" (1987, 108–9); whether it is a trick or not depends on our willingness to believe that there are experiences we do not comprehend—experiences, we might say, that we do not fully have. This is a moment in a sense outside time, and certainly outside the narrative that has concerned itself at the crucial point only with Aziz's vague and somewhat embarrassed time-filling. One of the characteristic qualities of *A Passage to India* is its mixture of discreet social comedy with an adumbration of the metaphysical; what happens here is that the comedy actually replaces the metaphysical, which therefore long remains as a subject of curiosity and expectation for the reader, until the reader finally admits that there is no revelation, or a revelation of nothing.

The chief voice of indistinction (a paradoxical status in itself) is that of Godbole. In a conversation with Fielding soon after the arrest of Aziz, Godbole, bereft of any sense of proportion or relevance, spends a good deal of time asking him for suggestions for the name of the school he intends to open in Mau (a school that we later learn, at the time of Field-ing's inspection, to have declined to the role of granary). At the proposal that it should be called either the "Mr. Fielding High School" or, as a second best, the "King Emperor George the Fifth," Fielding interrupts to ask the crucial question as to Aziz's guilt. But for Godbole this is not the crucial question: he unhelpfully declares that everyone and everything is responsible for the attack on Adela: "When evil occurs, it expresses the whole of the universe. Similarly when good occurs" (169). Fielding is, not surprisingly, irritated by this and seeks to assert that good and evil are different; Godbole obfuscates the issue and asks him if at Marabar he has seen any interesting antiquities. This is funny, but it is funny because of a refusal to discriminate, which we may also find disturbing or tempting. The chapter—bitty, fragmented, inconclusive—seems to be holding up the story, delaying any businesslike progression to evidence and trial (to the classic courtroom drama beloved of authors such as Trollope); and if we find any delight in Godbole's fascination with the trivial it is in part because we are accepting his perspective (or lack of perspective). After the trial, Fielding attempts to dissuade Aziz from his resentment of Miss Quested, criticizing him because his emotions are disproportionate to their occasion, and Aziz responds that the question of proportion does not arise in emotion, which cannot be weighed out like potatoes (241–42). The Western feeling for life, it is implied, is quantitative: scientific, mechanical, commercial; Aziz asserts the alternative, that of intuitive spontaneity, at the cost, here, of an unpleasant, arrogant unforgivingness. There is much plausibility in the refusal to quantify, but it risks allowing a world of chance and unpredictability.

The Hindu religion, as Forster depicts it, favors this sense of the sud-den and unpredictable: the ceremony at the end of the book culminates in a burst of noisy expression that occurs punctually at midnight, little as punctuality may be observed in most aspects of Indian life (277). And it transforms the world; the shouting, noise, throwing of colored powders, amount to a redemption of the world: "All sorrow was annihilated, not only for Indians, but for foreigners, birds, caves, railways, and the stars; all became joy, all laughter; there had never been disease nor doubt, misunderstanding, cruelty, fear" (278). The moment is all-embracing and retrospective; time and separateness disappear; the idea of the "before" vanishes. But we who have been reading on from page to page and recall what has happened before, between Indians and foreigners, in caves and elsewhere, who recall much doubt, misunderstanding, cruelty, and fear, can hardly accept this as other than a brief fiction. And indeed the narrator will endorse our skepticism within a few lines: Can such experiences really be remembered and expressed? Are they really events at all if they cannot be integrated into the normal sequence of everyday life? "The adept . . . may think, if he chooses, that he has been with God, but, as soon as he thinks it, it becomes history, and falls under the rules of time" (278). What happened in the cave has somehow not become part of history (as the changing relationships between colonist and colonized that arose from it clearly have); it has somehow not fallen under the rules of time. The novel his left a gap in its sequence, and the gap is the possibility of timelessness.

The narrator or author is the crucial voice here, and much of *A Passage to India* is characterized by the intercession between event and reader of the personality of the author. (In technical terms, there is a high proportion of *discours* to *récit*.) A great proportion of the text is taken up with essayistic writing, generally showing the good-natured irony we tend to think normal of E. M. Forster from his other works. The effect is of distance and delay. A striking example occurs in the midst of the narrative of the Marabar outing. The party has arrived at the caves, by elephant, and Aziz is eager to maintain a good impression while feeling somewhat lost in a Hindu culture that is almost as strange to him as to his English visitors. There is a brief conversation in which Miss Quested makes an effort to be polite and Mrs. Moore doesn't, and Aziz explains that a meal is about to be served, to keep them nourished until breakfast. The conversation ends with Aziz solemnly—too solemnly—taking responsibility for any deficiencies in hospitality, and the text then records his feelings of satisfaction at the success of his hospitality up to now (134). So far, the text, then, is recording the developing relations of the characters; it is sensitively tracing the awkwardness of contracts across cultures; it is showing an attractive respect for the positive aspects of the characters on both sides: Aziz's pride and concern, Miss Quested's wish to play her part. All this is an image of development, of growing warmth, which has a clear rhetorical function in that it will make the sudden cataclysm all the more extraordinary and shocking; and this development will resume at the end of the next paragraph when Aziz starts to remind the older woman of their first meeting in the mosque, at the beginning of the novel. But this paragraph itself is oddly detached and static. It begins with a reflection on Aziz's sense of hospitality and possession, which it presents as not individual to him but characteristic of Asian civilization; it then goes on for a hundred words or so analyzing Aziz's nonpossessive relation to Mrs. Moore and Fielding, ending, before the return to dialogue, with the words, "Their images remained somewhere in his soul up to his dying day, permanent additions." This last sentence is particularly hard: the events of the novel are recent at the time of publication (they occur in the epoch of Post-Impressionism). Aziz is a young man. When did he die? Even apart from this perhaps overliteral curiosity, the sense of an intrusion is strong; the narrator judges, distinguishes, summarizes, foretells. The story is standing still; the narrator is seeing the events as no more than illustrations of the kind of person Aziz is.

It seems that something quite complicated is happening. The narrator is displaying a Western confidence in analysis and assessment. But he invites the reader to see this intellectual distance as alien to the main movement of the text, to see the process of communion as primary. There is then a dual perspective, within and without the scene, which anticipates the complicated perspectives of Adela's moment in the cave. But the first-time reader has no reason to know what is being anticipated and may react against the gratuitous pomposity of the narrator; we may want to "trust the tale and not the teller" and not quite know how far we dare do so.

The narrator's attitude is largely one of ironic detachment; it is through the acts and reflections of the characters that we grasp the issues of significance and love that make sense of life. The narrator seems almost hostile to such gravity of commitment, and his strategy is rather to delay the crucial acts of choice and self-discovery. He delays them by such near digressions as that, in an early chapter, in which he describes, over several lines, Aziz's energy in walking and the fatiguing effect of walking at all in India, where the soil is "hostile," either resistant or too soft (12–13). The passage may seem to be rather prosaic geography, barely up to the level of a competent travel book, but there is more to it than that. For one thing, it contributes—in a way that could just about be called symbolic—to a sense of the difficulty of effort in India and of the variety and unpredictability of life there; for another, it marks the time taken by Aziz to get from an unsatisfying contact with a European, Dr. Callendar, to a pleasing contact with another European, Mrs. Moore. This time—together with some time spent in reflection in the mosque—adds to the psychological plausibility of the following scene, since it allows Aziz to recover his self-confidence and self-assertiveness; and it acts as an articulation for the reader, who is able to see the two episodes as distinct and contrasting, and so to be aware both of the contrast in character of the two Europeans (Mrs. Moore is the person who believes that Europeans have a duty to "be pleasant" to Indians) and of the variation within Aziz's conduct. In other words, the pace ensures clarity and ready intelligibility, qualities not strongly marked in India as Forster presents it but provided by his manner of narration.

The issue recurs with special force in the case of conspicuous symbolism, of what may be seen as imposed meaning. When, for instance, in the opening chapter of part 2, the scene-setting description of the Marabar caves, we read that the rocks "rise abruptly, insanely, without the proportion that is kept by the wildest hills elsewhere, they bear no relation to anything dreamt or seen" (116–17), we recognize at once the metaphor and the hyperbole. We recognize, at least in broad terms, what point the narrator wishes to establish; we may start to recall references to insanity or disproportion in the rest of the work, or examples of abruptness of various kinds. But how do we assess this? Are we to see this as a struggle by the author to apply a pathetic fallacy that inclines to the self-contradictory (since it asserts that the hills are not pathetic)? Are we to see it simply as an exordium, a rhetorical punctuation mark? There is the balance, complexity, and allusiveness of the sentences, the progressive curiosity implied in the paragraph organization, the echoing of vocabulary and metaphor, the play of negatives, the shifts from scientific precision and explicitness ("the caves are readily described") to incompleteness ("Their reputation—for they have one—does not depend on human speech"—on what then?); all these things suggest a form of writing that spins, very explicitly, around a hollow, a lack of inherent sense. The point comes to a crux in the last lines, concerned with a hollow boulder, which sways readily in the wind and "hence" is known as the Kawa Dol (118). This name will recur and become part of the scenery of the book, often with some sense of menace or fragility. But the pretense of explaining it here is scandalous. To that large proportion of English-speaking readers who have no knowledge of Indian languages, the term *Kawa Dol* can only be explained by a translation, which is conspicuously not provided. Meaning is denied, but paradoxically a relation of meaning is asserted, as the hollowness within the boulder corresponds to the hollowness of the sentence.

This uncertainty might be approached through Forster's own concept of rhythm as interrelatedness, which Stone (1966, 341) tellingly uses in his account of *A Passage* as he speaks of the rhythm not of a mobile but of Indian sculpture as the deployment of repetitions, parallels, echoes. This is not what *rhythm* means in our present study, but it does point to the constant sense of readiness to find analogies and symmetries that is required of Forster's readers.

When at the bridge party Fielding invites Miss Quested to his tea party and explicitly does not invite her fiancé Ronny, she suddenly has a vision of her married life. It is a vision of exclusion. She will continue to see the colors of India, the crowds and the bathers, but not the force behind them: "She would see India always as a frieze, never as a spirit" (41). The novel clearly criticizes her detached intellectualism, while it respects her recognition and judgment of it. In doing so, it implies a difficulty in coming to terms with India. It certainly seems to declare that India has to be understood as change, in time, and not as stable, spatially distinct essences. But what precisely the spirit is, what kind of change or potential for change it implies, is far from clear. In fact, Forster more than once stresses the indefinability of life in India. The point arises in connection with the restoration of Adela's engagement. Immediately after the breaking off, during the drive with Nawab Bahadur, Ronny and Adela see an unidentified green bird and react in a European spirit of rational classification: "They would have liked to identify it, it would somehow have solaced their hearts" (78). When, a few pages later, the engagement is resumed, there is some regret at this rationality: "Unlike the green bird or the hairy animal [which has caused the motor accident], she was labelled now" (85). Miss Quested's liberalism leads her to deprecate labels, but the refusal of definitions seems more fundamentally non-European and perhaps relates to an unlimited flux that is the "spirit" of India. The Europeans return to their normality, Miss Quested playing Patience with Mrs. Moore and discussing with her "the day generally, whose rough desiccated surface acquired as it receded a definite outline, as India itself might, could it be viewed from the moon" (90–91). Time is comprehensible at a distance; "rough" and "desiccated," the events as they are lived through form an uneven continuum; only the distance of narration, of recollection, turns them from a surface to a shape, introduces the delimitation of figure and ground. Very near the end of the book, the day at Mau resists such articulation. "Looking back at the great blur of the last twenty-four hours, no man could say where was the emotional center of it, any more than he could locate the heart of a cloud" (306).

The novel itself seems to have an emotional center; it is about Adela's recantation. Around this center cluster the components of a story, the stages of a development and of an explanation: the setting of Chandrapore and of British rule in India, the arrival of the English ladies and their attempts to discover India, the circumstances of the "crime," the arrest, the subsequent tension, the trial, the aftermath; all this is rhetorically emphasized and elucidated by a skillful handling of pauses, delays, alternations of detailed depiction and general summary. In all these ways, it follows the norms of clarity, decorum, and respect for moral development and social order that can generally be expected from a major work in the tradition of Western liberal humanism, the Trollopian norms of rationality and rhetoric. It has the lunar distance that eliminates hazard. But much of the novel has no such distance. Throughout there is the sense of the indistinguishability of moments, of the continuous play of chance and caprice, of the priority of life over meaning. Signs of the non-European; anticipations of the postrational.

Katherine Mansfield: Stories

KATHERINE Mansfield's story "The Stranger" is about impatience. It concerns John Hammond, a middle-aged man whose wife, Janey, has been away from home (which is presumably in New Zealand) for ten months visiting their daughter in Europe, and it recounts the short time from his waiting for her boat to dock at the harbor to their arrival at a hotel and their first private contact. During this time, John talks with other people waiting for the boat, meets his wife, and observes her farewells to her fellow travelers. They take a short cab drive, settle in at the hotel as her luggage is delivered, and finally have a brief conversation. The story is some 5,000 words long and perhaps narrates some one hour of experience; in other words, a slow reading would take nearly as long as the events recounted. Here is a first paradox; the story is about impatience, but the style of narration is rather leisurely. This might be read, in principle, in one of two ways: either the narration is a demonstration of thorough, sound, systematic storytelling with proper attention to pace and decorum—in which case the implication might be that the haste of the central character is inappropriate—or the narrator is deliberately teasing the readers by withholding the climax that they, like Mr. Hammond, can quite legitimately expect. The reunion of married people after a long break is surely an occasion for eagerness, to say the least; if Mrs. Hammond had returned to find her husband calm and resigned to the delay in her arrival, she might naturally have been upset by his indifference. The situation, we shall see, is actually quite subtle.

The first point to note is the quite heavy emphasis on Hammond's impatience. The opening words of the story are: "It seemed to the little crowd on the wharf that she was never going to move again." The exaggeration is a normal conversational one and certainly not surprising when we learn that the crowd has been waiting for two hours. Still, it may shock a little, especially given the sudden plunge of the reader into the situation, with that initially obscure "she" and "again" (Who is she? When did she last move?). The feeling of a possibly excessive pressure is reinforced by the very heavy stress on the rapidity or brusqueness of Hammond's manner: he has a "quick, eager glance," his eyes "searched anxiously, quickly, the motionless liner," he obsessively consults his watch, he paces quickly up and down—all this within a couple of pages, and persistently counterpointed with the obstinate slowness of everything else: the "old chaps lounging against the gangways" (who, Hammond manages to persuade himself, are not simply idlers but "fine, solid old chaps," "solid" no doubt meaning "slow"), the dusk, which "at least might have the decency to keep off for a bit" but which "came slowly, spreading like a slow stain over the water," the Captain "hanging about in the stream."

This is getting comic, as Hammond's irritability struggles desperately and repeatedly with his sense of respectability and his good nature; it is a comedy born of repetition and disproportion. In other words, it is a comedy depending essentially on a sense of time, on the difference between the pace that is natural to the central character and the pace that is imposed upon him by circumstances and on his inability to cope moderately with this difference. The comedy continues discreetly, throughout the story: rushing onto the liner, the first of the waiting crowd and immediately behind the harbor master, he is greeted by his wife saying coolly, "Well, darling! Have you been waiting long?" She then insists on saying good-bye to all sorts of people ("It was plain as a pikestaff," Hammond consoles himself, "that she was by far the most popular woman on board"), tips the stewardess, and at the very last moment insists on going off to see the ship's doctor, though denying that she has been ill ("That was rather queer of Janey, wasn't it?"). Arriving at the hotel, they seem to be coming closer to the culminating moment of intimacy. Hammond hastily avoids his acquaintances in the public rooms in his longing to be alone with his wife, only to be interrupted ("Would you believe it!") by a porter with the luggage, and at this moment Janey starts showing a quite uncalled-for interest in letters from their children, their father heartlessly insisting that "later on will do." All this is approaching farce, suggesting the Feydeau series of contretemps and obstacles, even though in Feydeau it is not usually marital love that is thus impeded. And this comic perspective throws an important light on the sense of the story: Hammond's impatience is not just natural and respectable; it is also essentially a manifestation of power and possessiveness. Decent, responsible, outgoing, and efficient as he may be, he is also a butt for amusement because of his failure to apprehend what other people are like, his failure to see that other people have other priorities: "They knew, every man-jack of them, that Mrs. Hammond was on that boat, and he was so tremendously excited that it never entered his head not to believe that this marvellous fact meant something to them too." At this point, Hammond's excitement may be quite endearing; so, perhaps, is his first vision of her "between two great clumsy idiots." But we gradually realize that his affection is always of a patronizing and restricted kind, so that his reflection, "How little she looked to have come all that long way and back by herself!" is in fact a way of subordinating her, of denying her independence and responsibility, and is quite consistent with his rejoicing that she is "not a day changed. Just as he'd always known her" and his satisfaction at seeing her luggage labeled with her married name as "Mrs. John Hammond." In short, Hammond is, at bottom, the pompous and self-regarding buffoon who is the mainstay of many comedies—though presented with Katherine Mansfield's usual restraint and discretion.

The rhythm of the story up to now has been a largely comic one; it comprises a number of brief and partially successful attempts by Hammond to gain control of Janey. But the climax of the story changes the pattern as well as the tone of the whole. As Hammond at last embraces her, he feels weariness, his thoughts turn self-pityingly to his own excitements during the day rather than to her ten months away: "There we were, hanging about. What kept you so long?" And the answer, given slowly, hesitantly, thoughtfully, is that she has been held back by death; she has nursed a young man who has died in her arms of some heart trouble, and the delay was caused by medical formalities.

This news retrospectively makes a new kind of sense out of the story; the delay is no longer a simple annoyance, one of many, but is rationally intelligible (the two hours' waiting, we should remember, follows on the departure of "the doctor's launch," Janey has been eager to see the doctor, and even though he is usually unobservant about clothes, Hammond has noted that she is wearing black). The story is a cohesive one, and what gives it its cohesion is the ultimate challenge to the self-assertive pride that typifies Hammond: death and the demands death makes on those who have contact with it. Janey's preoccupation with death arouses immediate jealousy in her husband, of a quite clearly sexual kind: he is particularly aware that the young man has died in her arms and that this physical contact comes obviously by her own will, whereas he implies that her behavior towards him has been generally passive and cool. And this concern of hers for another person has, in his eyes, made a radical difference between them; in a final sentence that elegantly inverts the first, he reflects that "they would never be alone together again." The phrase, moreover, echoes a thoughtless but revealing hyperbolic expression Hammond used at the beginning of their conversation: "I feel I'll never have you to myself again." At the end, that vague discontent has become a profound anxiety. And no doubt he is right, at least in the sense he gives to the words: no doubt he will never again be the only object in her thoughts. The story has attained a new level of decisiveness; from trivial delay it has slipped to significant change, as Hammond has passed from complacent ignorance of other people to a sudden confrontation with death and with the variety of people's attachments.

How is this discovery handled by the processes of narration? Mansfield apparently totally suppresses the personality of the narrator, which gives the impression that the text is nothing but a record of the consciousness of the characters, or of a single character, in this case Hammond. Undoubtedly she achieves an extraordinary success, equaled by very few other authors, in this elimination of narratorial comment or interpretation, leaving an impression of impersonality, objectivity, even inscrutability, in which the reader has to decide for himself or herself on the value and significance of the events portrayed. But this absence of the narrator can only be apparent; the narrator actually survives in the occasional references to things Hammond doesn't see (such as his wife's expression of concern when he queries her health), in the occasional explanations that seem not to be in Hammond's consciousness ("The blow was so sudden that Hammond thought he would faint"), in certain patterns of imagery that the reader finds difficult to associate with his unsophisticated and immediate frame of mind (the grip of the chair he feels as he is shocked by Janey's news of the death [362] recalls the grip of anxiety as he waits [357]), in certain visions that appear to be that of the author rather than that of the character ("the great blind bed, with his coat flung across it like some headless man saying his prayers" [363]). Above all, the act of narration appears in patterns of pace and rhythm.

Someone other than Hammond has decided what to narrate in detail, what to summarize, what to omit.

Given the general orientation of the text to the consciousness of the central character, it is inevitable that detailed, apparently unedited narrative should predominate. But this itself has a particular effect. Since readers are accustomed to narratives that (like any other form of communication) are governed by the principle of relevance and do not contain material that does not advance the point of the story, they will be conscious of the various factors of slowness: repetition, recounting of trivia, searching for exact formulations. So, we have, for instance, dialogue that repeats information given as unspoken thought:

> There wasn't a pair of glasses between the whole lot of them.
>
> "Curious thing, Mr. Scott, that none of us thought of glasses." (350)

We have dialogue that is completely uninformative, as far as the relationship of the Hammonds is concerned:

> "All well?"
>
> "All well."
>
> "How's mother?"
>
> "Much better."
>
> "Hullo, Jean!"
>
> "Hillo, Aun' Emily!" (354)

We have an attempt to analyze the impressions given by a rather unsatisfactory kiss:

> It seemed to him there was a tiny pause—but long enough for him to suffer torture—before her lips touched his, firmly, lightly—kissing them as she always kissed him, as though the kiss—how could he describe it?—confirmed what they were saying, signed the contract. (361)

All this comes from Hammond's consciousness, and it makes his consciousness seem somewhat strange to us. The first example is, of course, an instance of his making conversation while waiting; the activity is normal enough, even if it does drive people into remarks as pointless as this, but the narrative technique underlines the pointlessness and lets us see it as a reflection of Hammond's wish to dominate, to be the center of attention. The chain of greetings is perhaps a little too analytically treated; according to the narrator, the voices "flew to greet each other," but this hardly reads like flying—it looks like a rather obsessive interest in the circumstances of waiting, as opposed to the purpose of it. And the puzzled analysis of the much awaited kiss is very strange: Hammond seeks to describe his sensations to himself, becomes a spectacle for himself; the heightened self-awareness brought about by delay seems to have excluded the intended climax. In short, the chosen method of moment-by-moment narration is one that is essentially alien to the central character's apparent concern for rapid assertion of will and possession; it shows how far life is a matter of dependency and distance, of waiting for other people and of seeking to discover oneself.

The technique of immediate and exhaustive depiction is, in any case, not quite fully maintained. In the earlier parts, at least, of the story, there is some display of economy. There is, for instance, the turning of the ship to come in:

> At last! She was slowly, slowly turning round. A bell sounded far over the water and a great spout of steam gushed into the air. The gulls rose; they fluttered away like bits of white paper. And whether that deep throbbing was her engines or his heart Mr. Hammond couldn't say.

This is certainly not rapid narration, but it is a condensation, insofar as it takes much less time to read these fifty words than it does to watch a ship turning. The word "slowly" does much of the work here; that and the throbbing put the emphasis on the recognition of change, on the effect rather than the process, and so imply that moments are being selected by the narrator in view of their importance. The point is even clearer in the one obvious omission that appears in the text: a row of dots covers the time from Hammond's sending for someone to collect the luggage from the ship to the couple's arrival on the wharf. The time cannot be estimated exactly; they have to wait for someone to ensure that the luggage will in fact be collected, walk to the gangway and down it (possibly amidst the general impediments of other disembarking passengers), and find their direction on the wharf. This is no doubt a matter of some minutes. That these minutes are not narrated is a sort of courtesy to the reader, since they can easily be reconstituted, as we have just seen. But there is more to it than that. First, the gap appears to promise a sudden shift in the narrator's attitude; the waiting, we might feel, is over, and we shall now come to the real business of marital communion. This is partly true; we are indeed approaching a sort of climax. But it is not the sort of climax we might be expecting, and we are not approaching as fast as we might think; the narrator is almost teasing us by taking us, fairly slowly, to what may seem to be an anticlimax, to an imperfect and understated contact between the couple. And that teasing is part of the point of the story; we have to learn not to share Hammond's impatience and to reprove ourselves—with humor, no doubt, but not without gravity—if we have been seduced by his eagerness, if we have shared his irritation with waiting crowds and the stewardess needing to be tipped. And second, the omission is not just a courtesy, not just a passing-over of redundant material; it also conceals a difficult transition. Just before this point, Mr. Hammond has been anxious: "And again, as always, he had the feeling he was holding something that never was quite his—his." "As always": the narrator is intruding here, generalizing beyond the moment. And the generalization is one that might apply to quite a lot of Mansfield's characters, including many less dynamic than the present one: it concerns the sense of separation from the desired object. This focuses forcefully what is perhaps the central theme of the story. Hammond reacts with brutal energy: "For God's sake let's get off to the hotel so that we can be by ourselves!," and, momentarily, the narrator appears to share his brusqueness, suddenly—magically, so to speak—placing him on dry land and in a more positive frame of mind: "She took his arm. He had her on his arm again. . . . No more going without his tea or pouring out his own. She was back." The stability achieved here is not going to last, of course, but the brief feint of satisfaction, of delay overcome, of a problem solved, at least writes into the story—obvious as the irony may be—a not quite unsympathetic sense of the desired orderliness of life.

This is the rhythm of what Hammond wants, not of what he has to put up with. The effect is a double one: the moment strengthens such element of sympathy for him as has existed throughout the story so far and so prevents it from becoming too facile a satire on male possessiveness; but it also prepares for his final defeat by making the revelation of Janey's separate concerns come as a surprise, as a sudden blow disproportionate to her mildness of speech and gentleness of manner; it stresses the un-predictability of other people, it shows that their difference from us is incalculable.

It goes, in short, towards allowing the story to be read as an account of a revelation, of a moment in which the familiar is seen afresh (freshness here implying suddenness), and it allows the reader to experience both the unenlightened feeling of a wish for conclusiveness and comfort and also the moment of enlightenment, the discovery of otherness. Certain aspects of narrative proportion in the story as a whole arise from this same structure. The period of waiting accounts for some ten pages and contains various subdivisions (waiting for the boat, boarding, moving to the hotel, receiving the luggage); the final, revealing talk occupies some two and a half pages and is essentially a continuous whole. It appears to be essential that an enlightenment be set against a norm, and it appears that the character of a norm is to be protracted and repetitious; it is there-fore essential that the part of the story enacting the norm be fairly long and the part enacting the revelation—by contrast—be fairly brief. But it would also seem to be essential that the account of the moment of enlightenment not be too brief, though the reason is not quite as clear-cut. The reason for length in the presentation of the norm is one of mimesis; life is long-drawn-out and repetitious, and the story should imitate these characteristics. It is not clear that the length of the climax is governed by considerations of imitation. On the one hand, it might be argued that an important discovery (such as that of the profound difference between oneself and one's spouse) is bound to arouse many rapid thoughts and that these ought to be depicted by the writer of fiction; on the other, it might be argued that an important discovery about the nature of human life should not be rushed, that on grounds of dignity and respect for the bases of human life a decorous slowness should be observed. If either of these arguments is correct, there has been a change of attitude to the whole business of storytelling; the bulk of the story is governed by a wish to depict the actual, the climax by a wish to do justice to it. (This is especially clear if we take the second view, that of dignity and profun-dity; even if we take the first, we are considering how much psychologi-cal activity *ought* to be presented). There is a shift from the actual to the normative; rhythm in this way enacts the significance of the story.

Many of Katherine Mansfield's stories follow a similar pattern of expectation and reversal. Fullbrook (1986) sees such reversals, very pertinently, as "moments of truly existential wonder and terror" and rightly stresses their discontinuity with the normal course of (male-dominated) life (32). An earlier critic (Hormasji 1967) notes that Mansfield's subject matter "is the prosaic and the ordinary, the life of the everyday." But he is too simple in saying that "the events which happen in the lives of her characters are not memorable or of any major import" (85). This is true enough, as far as public import is concerned. For the characters themselves, the events are revelations that may utterly disrupt the ordinariness of their lives. The very fine story "The Garden-Party," for instance, again produces an encounter with death as its climax but sets this in a somewhat more complex context: the central character, Laura, wishes to cancel her family's garden party when she hears that a neighboring workman has died, but she is overruled by the rest of the family. At the end of the day, she is sent to deliver a parcel of leftover food to the house of the dead man and is moved at seeing the body, which she finds both impressively serene and somewhat embarrassing. The pattern of contrasts between context and climax is complex: life against death, bustle against repose, middle-class decorum and complacency against working-class unrestraint, enjoyment against gravity, dissipation of emotion against concentration. And the structure is somewhat more complex than in "The Stranger" because of the many moments of fine visual observation that make small climaxes in the preparatory part of the story (but that eventually have to be reinterpreted as mere incidents of hedonistic life) and still more because of the moments of tension in the preparatory section as first Laura and then—less radically—her father worry about the propriety of life continuing in the presence of death. The preparatory section is thus not a case of simple waiting but rather of the uncertainties of adolescent impulsiveness or adolescent decency and so acquires an interest in itself and not simply as preparation for a conclusion.

But other Mansfield stories give a more worrying problem to anyone seeking to find patterns in fiction. These are stories in which, one is rather tempted to say, nothing happens; stories in which there seems to be no climax, which might as well, as it seems, have finished a page earlier or gone on a page longer; stories that are nevertheless not demonstrations of literary incompetence but impressive stories that a sensitive reader can read with full absorption and a sense of an enriched life. If this sort of description is accurate, it would seem that, for some fiction at least, climaxes don't matter and that rhythm doesn't therefore matter; all that matters is the delicacy, subtlety, convincingness, humor, or pathos of the writing; it is the quality of the reading experience that matters rather than its shape. And undoubtedly there is much truth in this, and it is a truth that applies to many writers of the period we are considering (as well as to previous writers, such as Chekhov, obviously one of Katherine Mansfield's major influences). Many modern writers do not obviously seek climax; one might even say that their works are a struggle to produce fiction without climaxes, or at the very least to mute such climaxes as may be inevitable.

An example of such writing is "The Voyage." This recounts a night boat journey (between the two islands of New Zealand?) in which Fenella, a young girl whose mother has just died, is taken from her father's home by her grandmother to stay with her and her grandfather. Grandmother and granddaughter get on the boat, say farewell to the father, consider buying sandwiches but find them too expensive, go to bed, are visited by the stewardess, arrive on shore. and go to the grandparents' house, where they find the grandfather in bed. During all this time, Fenella has been given charge of her grandmother's swan-necked umbrella, which she has carefully preserved and which she hooks onto the grandfather's bed-rail as they arrive. And that is the story. A hasty reader could certainly say that "nothing has happened," or at least nothing major; the important event in Fenella's life is the death of her mother, and the important change—a fairly normal, even routine one in the circumstances—is that she goes to live with new people. But the death takes place before the story, and the life with the grandparents takes place after it; it seems perverse to focus on a transition, which in itself contains no events beyond the banal: grandmother's prayers, her loosening of her stays, Fenella's not eating a banana.

But there is an event, an event so miraculous as to be almost imperceptible. It is one that depends in large part again on the degree of sympathy or intimacy with the central character that the story allows. The narration essentially follows Fenella's observations, but (unlike the treatment of John Hammond) it does not reproduce her consciousness continuously, and it says little about her response to the things she sees. But the response is not totally absent: she is awkward at the beginning, clutching her hat to keep it on and giving "an undignified little skip" to keep up with her hurrying elders; she seems to be pecked by the umbrella "as if it too wanted her to hurry"; she sees that her father looks tired and sad; she finds the farewell of grandmother and father "awful" and turns away; she asks anxiously how long she is to stay and gets no answer—except a present of a shilling that persuades her that she is going away forever; she notes that her grandmother is praying and later is afraid that she is going to do it again; she overhears the stewardess sentimentally commenting on her as a "poor motherless mite." And as they reach land, the text for once reproduces her thought very explicitly: "Oh, it had all been so sad lately. Was it going to change?" And as they reach the new home, it does change: there is a white cat "folded up like a camel," and a white-bearded grandfather, and it is the grandfather's good humor that ends the story: "And he ruffled his white tuft and looked at Fenella so merrily she almost thought he winked at her." So, there is here, as in "The Stranger," a discovery: whereas Hammond in the midst of his excessive pride and security finds death, Fenella in the midst of her anxiety finds life and welcome. The distinctive thing about "The Voyage" is not that there is no climax; it is that the climax is an event that can be seen as climactic only in the given context—it might elsewhere be dull or trivial. And the story does much to mask the climax, which is not surprising, since a meeting with a grandfather is a predictable result of a journey to the home of grandparents, and indeed he has been briefly mentioned (and it is certainly not surprising that a grandfather should smile and have a white beard); it is not conclusive, since we have no guarantee that this welcome is going to continue; it is very brief (a half page out of ten), and the indication of both sides of the contrast, Fenella's anxiety and the grandfather's good humor, is extremely understated and might be overlooked on a cursory reading (the pathos of Fenella's voyage being appreciably undercut by the narrator's humor and by her own sensitivity and curiosity in observation). This, one might say, is a kind of minimalist narration, in which the procedures of expectation and contrasting fulfillment are deployed as discreetly as possible; but they are deployed nevertheless and make for much of the satisfaction the story gives us.

"The Voyage" is the story of a kind of grace, of the gift of happiness as a compensation for hardship, and of the ordeal of an ill-prepared waiting for such grace. It is a story because it implies that the sequence of events in time makes sense and affects the quality of our experience, that waiting affects the way we receive the thing we have waited for. It presents, subtly and imaginatively, an attunement to the future. The short story tends to be a study of waiting, expectation, and apprehension. Our study shows the same to be true of many novels; Katherine Mansfield brings these things to the forefront of the reader's attention. Her work is fascinating, it demands the reader's most delicate sympathy because experiences of the sort depicted might not seem to the uninvolved observer to constitute an event at all because it does not constitute an obvious anecdote with an obvious finality. The correspondence of expectancy and culmination is tenuous; it depends, for one thing, on the author's control of atmosphere through image, recurrent phrasing, point of view, and pace, and for another on the reader's sense of the incompleteness of some kinds of experience and the fullness of others, the conclusiveness of death and love. Two structures are superimposed: a structure of fictional culmination and a structure of discovering ultimate values, and they work together to create a sense of the elusive satisfactoriness of life.

Elizabeth Bowen: *The Heat of the Day*

BOWEN'S *The Heat of the Day*, a novel of over three hundred pages, is focused on four short periods: the first Sunday in September 1942, when Harrison, an agent of the British security services, warns Stella Rodney that her lover Robert Kelway is a German spy and threatens to denounce him unless she enters a sexual relationship with himself; a day "some weeks later," a Saturday in early October, when Stella and Robert visit his family home in the countryside and when Stella has a further lengthy discussion with Harrison; Stella's visit—in "late autumn"—to Mount Morris, an estate in the Republic of Ireland that has been inherited by her son Roderick (who is in the army) from her husband's cousin Francis, and the day of her return, when she warns Robert of Harrison's charge, despite Harrison's instructions not to tell him (the episode specifically timed because the news of the victory at El Alamein on 3 November is received while Stella is in Ireland); and then Roderick's visit to Cousin Francis's widow and, on the same evening, the meeting in which Harrison reveals that he knows Robert has been informed and threatens to "foreclose" immediately on his bargain with Stella but does not do so, and the night of the following day, when Robert and Stella openly discuss his guilt and Robert falls to his death while seeking to escape pursuers as he leaves her flat (this episode also specifically timed because it coincides with the Allied landings in North Africa on 8 November). These few episodes therefore cover about two months; much of this is spent in waiting, and the culminating events take only a few days.

The novel is therefore an extremely condensed one; it deals with a short period, in which a shocking discovery is made and its impact rapidly worked out. A brief coda shows the gradual eclipse of this period in memory. Even within this period, it leaves substantial lengths of time unaccounted for and presents only the crucial points of threat, intensification, crisis, and dénouement. It is not difficult to see this as essentially a dramatic structure, presenting the turning points of a set of relationships directly through the words and actions of the characters. Drama, of course, has little option but to present events in "real time" (though some twentieth-century plays have used a narrator to obscure this feature) and therefore has to select the events that unmistakably reveal changes in the characters and their relationships. Novelists do have an option, and those modern novelists (following the example of Henry James above all) who have imitated the immediacy of drama have been voluntarily disciplining themselves, reducing the potential of the author's intervention and imposing a quite distinctive rhythm of narration. Time in such novels appears as blocks of intensity, with nothing (or little) in between. Bennett and Royle (1995, 82–103) see this dramatic quality of narrative as a fundamental challenge to stable perspective, objective knowledge, and especially to rectilinear time. While this may be less new and less disturbing than they claim, or than their elusive manner of writing may imply, it certainly does seem to be true that what Bowen offers her readers is not an impersonal series of events but a series of events and relationships as seen, variously, by characters at given moments.

This discontinuous view of emotional life is intensified by the author's liking for starting the chapter in midscene or in midconversation. So, chapter 1 starts "That Sunday," as if the reader already knew which Sunday is concerned, and the action starts with Harrison already attending a concert while he considers his impending visit to Stella. Chapter 2 starts with, "Stella Rodney stood at the window of her flat," and shows her awaiting Harrison's visit; she has not previously been named and we do not at first know what she is waiting for. Chapter 3 starts with a slightly different approach but one that equally implies a fresh start; chapter 2 has ended with Roderick phoning his mother, and chapter 3 starts, "Roderick never came to the flat without giving warning." Similarly, chapters may be cut off very economically in midaction: chapter 1 ends with Harrison tearing himself impolitely away from Louie, who has attempted to make his acquaintance: "He stood in a sort of aftermath of suspicion, not yet sure she might not have picked his pocket, then walked the other way." Chapter 2 ends with Stella informing Harrison that Roderick is on his way, but it does not recount Harrison's departure or the end of their conversation. Chapter 3 ends with Stella holding a brief telephone conversation with, presumably, Robert, in which she mentions Roderick's arrival;

the last sentence is "forty-eight hours," which must be her answer to a question about the length of Roderick's leave. Again, the reader has the sense that the conversation could not have ended like that and that there must be at least some unreported final formalities. Much of the characters' doings are being relegated to the secondary and omitted.

One qualification needs to be made to this account so far that will be developed later. It is a point implicit in our description of the four stages of the action. The second component of the plot is that of "intensification"; the term implies an admission that this component does not radically change the situation and that it adds to the complexity of characterization and to the tension of mystery and indecision without adding anything essential to the plot. Similarly, we shall see that the "minor character Louie," who receives quite a lot of attention and indeed is the last figure to appear in the text, relates quite tangentially to Stella and Harrison. The concentration of the book is therefore not absolute; the text does include some things that might be regarded as secondary. Because of the work's generally elliptic nature, these gain an odd emphasis; there is a sense of things not quite meriting their place in the work, of the author's perhaps having some cryptic grounds for nevertheless being fascinated with the ordinary.

It may have been noticed that many of the phrases already quoted from the book refer to time. Lee (1981, 182–83) notes the extraordinary stress on time, on watches, clocks, and the like (though she seems to regard it as a rather strained attempt to create an ominous mood). The fact that a chapter ends with the words "forty-eight hours," for instance, is no chance. It relates to a characteristic feature of wartime life. People were much concerned about the leave-periods of their family and friends in the army, and the figure mentioned is easily recognized as one of the standard lengths of permit. And whether because of the conditions of war or through some more permanent interest of the author, the concern with precise definition of periods and moments of time is extraordinarily acute in the novel. "How many moments *are* there," Robert's young niece asks him (253); it sees almost that the novel as a whole is directed to the nature of the moment and of the way moments belong to continuous time.

In writing about fiction, Bowen insists on the need for actual, even development in the onward movement of the novel but recognizes the need for what she considers merely "*apparent* variations in speed" (CI, 250). She considers such variations as essentially rhetorical, designed either for emphasis or for attunement to the reader's varying responses. Elsewhere, she attributes the way the author can "open and shut time like a fan" to the nature of the story, which "demands (because of its proportions) some particular sort of timing of its own" (Aft, 139). We have seen that *The Heat of the Day* begins with reference to a day of the week. In fact, it soon goes on to time of day, season, and, symbolically, the sequence of life and death: "That Sunday, from six o'clock in the evening, it was a Viennese orchestra that played. The season was late for an outdoor concert; already leaves were drifting on to the grass stage— here and there one turned over, crepitating as though in the act of dying, and during the music some more fell." Before long we come to a neat reference back to earlier the same day, "The Sunday had been brilliant," and then an identification of it as the first Sunday in September. Harrison leaves the concert as eight strikes (19), and at the beginning of the next chapter, "it was some minutes since [Stella] had heard eight strike" (20); at the end of her conversation with Harrison, he remarks, "I'd no idea, do you know, that it was getting so late" (39), a banal remark and typical of his gracelessness but also made somewhat sinister by the novel's apparent obsession with the clock and by what is presumably Stella's response, "It might have been midnight" (39). In fact, when Roderick arrives, having had a meal after his phone call, it is, very plausibly, a quarter to ten (43).

Time can be measured by cigarette ash. Harrison, in the opening interview with Stella, having lit a cigarette, soon finds the ash accumulating and has to search for an ashtray to knock it off (25) (and continues to fidget with ashtrays afterwards). Roderick, arriving after his departure, is intrigued, Sherlock Holmes-style, by the full ashtray on the mantelpiece: "Why should anyone *stand* to smoke for so long?" (49). Time and tension go together to produce a tiny clue, acutely picked up. The seasons are also clearly indicated, despite the short period of time directly involved: the "day of October size" (169), "the narrowing of autumn"; and the feared "obliteration of everything by winter" (139), later the snowdrops (307). Stella keeps clear track of time, referring explicitly to the two months of the events (181, 275) and conscious of them as a special time, a time of crisis. Robert too focuses on the two months (190), and he can identify with almost surprising accuracy reference to particular dates: he recalls immediately the night Stella returned from Ireland and even "that night we were looking at my tie" (262)—which, without his realizing it, was the day of Harrison's first visit.

Conversely, the novel sets the events of this crisis against quite a full background of earlier events through flashback or incidental reference. First, this moment of 1942 is set in the context of the war; this happens on the strategic level with the reference to the "war turning" at El Alamein (171), which contrasts with the references back to Dunkirk and the fall of France in 1940; and it happens on the personal level with the account of Stella and Robert's meeting soon after Dunkirk (at which he has been wounded; his limp remains as a permanent reminder of his past and may play a part in his death). This account of their meeting contains a very explicit statement of one aspect of the time-sense of the novel: "They were the creatures of history. The relation of people to each other is subject to the relation of each to time, to what is happening" (187). Beyond the war there are the further references to Stella's early marriage and divorce and to the inheritance of Mount Morris and the marital tensions of Francis and his wife. Closer to the action of the story there are the flashbacks to the first meeting of Stella with Harrison at the Francis' funeral; there are tantalizing hints of a visit by Harrison to Mount Morris before the beginning of the action, no doubt on some secret military contact. It is then coincidence, as the text points out, that Harrison, attending the funeral, should meet the lover of the man whose treachery he has discovered in some other context. The novel is not afraid of coincidence; it is another major coincidence that when Harrison takes Stella out to dinner to pressure her into accepting his advances, they should run into Louie, who has been attempting to pick up Harrison on the evening when he first made his offer to Stella. Coincidence simply formulates conspicuously what is implicit in the whole pattern of the novel: that actions are conditioned by the past and by various strands of the past reaching back over various lengths of time; a crisis is the precipitation of factors that have accumulated in character and social institutions. It is no doubt true, as Lassner indicates, that many of Bowen's protagonists live through a "demystification of the past" (1990, 147); but if this is so, demystification is not denial: crisis is not a negation of the past but a concentration of it.

Crisis is one of the key concepts of the novel. Explicitly, Harrison's conduct is said on one occasion to show crises of "emotional idiocy" (40). The moment in question is one of tension in which Stella, angry at his revelation about Robert, his insistent presence, and his meddling with the objects in her flat, shows sudden irritation and stares at him closely "in the intimacy of her anger." The narrator then comments: "There is actually little difference as to color in the moment before the blow and the moment before the kiss; the negligible space between her and him was now charged, full force, with the intensity of their two beings" (40). The two characters are concentrated in time and space, and the whole novel can be seen as a similar enterprise in concentration of character and history. As Stella, during her visit to Ireland, reflects on the puzzle of Harrison's visit to Mount Morris, the narrator comments that "this book-dark darkening room, through which imperceptibly the current of time flowed, held truth sunk somewhere in it, as the river held the boat" (164). Harrison was present when Francis sank a boat in the river; it will be raised, later, by her son, the new owner—after the truth about Robert and Stella has been elucidated. Time is an alternation of loss and restoration; it flows "imperceptibly" to those who are within it, subject to its delusions. Lassner comments on Bowen's elision of the distinction between continuity and transience (1990, 123); a passage such as this beautifully displays this elision. But time is still perceived by the narrator and the reader.

The perception of time that the characters do have is often that of lack of time, of haste and pressure. The forty-eight hours leave is typical. So, more centrally, is Harrison's "foreclosure" (226) on his contract with Stella. Conversely, Stella taunts Harrison with his "not having time" to win her over: "But a woman takes time. I could take twice the time you've got" (132). Louie, finding that Stella and Harrison in the restaurant are trying to "decide something," reflects with her usual good-natured vagueness: "Still, even that takes time" (228). Time is a matter of deadlines. Cousin Francis's widow tells Roderick that there is at Mount Morris a special Persian rose "only ever blooming for a week, and no sooner are they open than they die. So you must look for them at the right time" (208). Especially acute is the night in which Robert and Stella recognize the doom of their relationship, the night in which Robert discovers that "my time's run right out" (279): "Now it was a question of counting the last of the minutes as they ran out into hours, the last of the hours as they ran out into tomorrow, which was already today, as they never had" (262). Already today; it is two in the morning. The conversation between the two is intense as they ask what they have meant to each other, how deception and concealment have come between them, as they do not ask what is to happen next. Their love survives, "for the time being," only because it is outside the chain of moral responsibility, cut off from time that is in fact ever more insistent. They have been, Robert has said at an earlier point, "about due to take this knock" (190). There is a vague fatalism here, based on the feeling that things cannot last.

Against finality, there is, occasionally, hope. Relieved of the immediate anxieties of London during her stay in Ireland, Stella is able to enjoy without reserve the beauty of the moment, "the peace of the moment in which one sees the world for a moment innocent of oneself." The phrase is a curiously contorted one; the moment is both the dominating factor and part of what one sees; the innocence is awkward and perhaps illusory. "One cannot remain away," the text admits in the next sentence. And yet Stella thinks of this as "a unique day: the very day in which— who knew—something would intervene to save her" (170). Something does happen; "there cannot be a moment in which nothing happens," the narrator asserts, two paragraphs later. But what happens is the news of a British victory, and it appears to have no impact on Stella's individual fate. On her return from Ireland, in fact, she immediately tells Robert of the charges against him and so plunges deeper into disaster. The rich expectancy of this moment, its "breathless glory," has been destroyed, interrupted, by conflict and politics—which have always been a condition of it—and the next chapter ends with the aftermath of Stella's brief escape, as she returns amidst the fatigue and delay of a long and difficult journey. Her hope is reduced to "the hope that she might speak soon" (173). Hope about one's own future actions is strange; hope seems to comprise some element of hopelessness.

In fact, her "speaking" is delayed by the fact that Robert proves to be accompanied by his heartily inefficient sister. The latter greets her with the cheery phrase, "How-d'you do, Mrs. Rodney? You must be dead." Since the disembarcation of the train passengers has just been described through Stella's eyes as the "arrival of shades in Hades, the new dead scanned dubiously by the older" (174), the greeting may seem to Stella all too apt, and ideas of abandoning hope may be in the air. The scene is characteristic of a whole side of the novel that contrasts with the sense of urgency that we have seen so far; there is much in the novel that is concerned with inertia, indifference, and delay. At its best, inertia means a euphoric acceptance of life as it is, and as it develops. So, the relationship of Robert and Stella has been an unformulated acceptance of the provisional,

> a submerged decision to go on as they were, for that "time being" which war had made the very being of time. War time, with its makeshifts, shelvings, deferrings, could not have been kinder to romantic love. . . . [They were] happy to stay as they were, afloat on this tideless, hypnotic, futureless day-to-day. (95)

Happy until the "testing time" comes: when Harrison calls. Inertia is seductive, as well as dispiriting. It may be silly when Robert's sister tells him, when he tries to get his family to sell their old home, that "it's no good rushing things. . . . Better take everything one by one" (244). But it may not be *just* silly: when Robert asks Stella to marry him, she too clings to the status quo and implies that such clinging is the reason they have not yet married: "Why not wait till we see what's going to happen next? We always have" (189). Robert's defense of his promptness in proposing is that "one cannot time feeling" (189). The conversation comprises a debate between promptness and delay, in which Robert stands for change and Stella (like other characters in the novel) for stability. Robert, in the final truthful conversation, defends his betrayal of his country as a refusal of the past. He has preserved his individual past; he has in the family home a large collection of photographs of himself in youth that maintains a lasting self-image. But if he preserves his individual past, he sees nothing to preserve in the national past. The defeat of Dunkirk has revealed to him—as he claims—the failure inherent in the English upper class, their lack of true commitment to any country; it has left him with a private love, for Stella, but no public love. And this he sees as the heredity that has wounded him, as he was literally wounded in the defeat: "I was born wounded; my father's son" (263); the excitement of spying "bred my father out of me, gave me a new heredity" (264). The implied need for attachment to nation and earth clearly echoes the Nazi ethos (and other forms of nationalism), and the combination of individual will and novelty with a desire for control and order echoes the style of fascism. Robert sees the war as "the beginning of a day. A day on our scale" (264). For Stella, hope can only be more personal and more speculative; her world is a private one; her country is one of place and also of time, of continuity, the fullness of which she has paradoxically felt because her experience of place and people has been enriched in her love for Robert.

The simplest and most unreflective faith in historic continuity is attached to the Mount Morris theme: Cousin Francis has left the house to Roderick, "requisitioning" him as the future, "fit[ting him] into a destiny." This is an "egotistic creative boldness with regard to the future" (168), which Robert, quite consistently with his own attitudes, has denounced as "a racket of that old lunatic's" (153). And Roderick accepts his destiny, going to visit the widow, finding some uncomfortable truths from her about her own marriage but also some revealing ones about his parents' marriage (which Stella herself is not eager to revive, calling them "ancient history"), and going finally to visit the cemetery where Francis is buried. Near the end of the novel, Roderick becomes the audience of the story we are reading. Told the truth about Robert by his mother, he at first regrets his youth but then sees it as an advantage: "Or are you telling me, then asking me, because I *am* young, and so ought to last on later into time? You want me to be posterity?" (289)

But he sees the uncertainty of this. Facts disappear; time erodes them. Art survives: "By the time one is able to understand it [Robert's death] it will be gone, it just won't be there to be judged. Because, I suppose art is the only thing that can go on mattering once it has stopped hurting?" (290). The sense of decline, of the unreality of inheritance and the insignificance of action, is certainly strong in the book. The novel ends with deep irony on inheritance. Louie emerges to the foreground in the last chapter, Stella fading away into marriage with a character not previously known to the reader. Louie has been worrying that she has become pregnant while her husband is away in the army. The problem vanishes when the husband dies, and as the novel ends, she is persuading herself that the baby is coming to look more and more like her husband. In the last lines, she holds him up to see three swans flying westwards: symbols perhaps of hope, freedom, and progress, but if so symbols to be read with caution. What is really dominant here is simply "the baby's intention to survive" (318), an intention that is clearly that of his mother too. Kenney, it should be said, regards Louie's intention to survive as the "only consolation in this novel of the '*desiccation*' by war, of our day-to-day lives" (1975, 75–76). Louie is attuned to the future, Stella to the past. Louie is comic, Stella tragic.

Life goes on; evil has been excluded in the death of Robert and, in a more muffled and puzzling way, in Harrison's abandonment of his sexual extortion. Stella's narration of this abandonment has led to a "fading out," "a sort of confession of why so many stories, now that she came to tell them, had no ending" (276).There is something inexplicable in the story, something unintelligible in the character of Harrison, a limit to communication and to conclusiveness. The key passage is the one in which Stella and Harrison go out to a nightclub for a meal, and he tells her that he knows that Robert has been tipped off—because he has changed his behavior, thus strongly implying his guilt—and indicates that the crucial moment has arrived: unless Stella immediately yields to him he will denounce Robert. At this moment Louie appears. She has wandered into the nightclub by mistake, confusing it, in her usual inefficient manner, with another one where she has arranged to meet a friend. As a result of this she is as solitary and intrusive as she was in the first chapter, and her clumsy manners and appearance intensify the oddness of the meeting. But she acts as a distraction, and as she desperately attempts to make conversation, Harrison tacitly relents, so that when Stella asks him to confirm, in terms veiled from Louie, that "a friend is out of danger," he simply instructs the two women to leave the club together. The scene is a strange one, prolonged and almost futile on the surface: it is dominated by Louie's chatter and the reader's sense of how alien it is to the conflict of the other two. But not only by that; the reader also senses the ordinary humanity represented by Louie, her sense of sexual relations as a matter of companionship and good will ("People to be friendly, that's what the war's for, isn't it?"), and the cryptic clarity of judgment in Stella's comment on her relations with Harrison. For her, this "may be still be the first of many more evenings, but what will they be worth?" (231–32). The action may seem to be stagnating. But from this state of expectancy, of readiness for change, of bleak contemplation of an inescapable and urgent dilemma, a decision is somehow precipitated. What exactly it is, we do not yet know: Stella has to ask Harrison what has been decided—more precisely, no doubt, whether he will insist on sexual payment for Robert's escape—and gets no answer. Why it has been made we do not know either; Stella later speculates that she has hurt his feelings or called his bluff (274–75); Harrison himself cannot remember, later (310). Perhaps no more has happened than that the confrontation of Stella and Harrison has been softened by Louie's kindliness and vulnerability, that tension has been dissipated by plain sociability.

The author provides several chapters on Louie's career, both before and after this climactic moment, which go to offer an image of a way of living through the war that is simpler and more accidental than the heroine's—and that invites less respect or engagement on the part of the reader.

And what, in the novel, has been achieved overall? Roderick regrets that his own response to Stella's story has not given it "enormous meaning like there is in a play of Shakespeare's" (289); the Irish servant Donovan remarks that, for the relations of Harrison and Francis, "there was nothing to show in the end of it all" (304); Stella tells Harrison in their last meeting that they should "learn how to be survivors" and that this means forgetting (307); she wonders if there is "no right *or* wrong to it after all" (309); the war itself appears, in the final pages, to be approaching "a moratorium as to everything" (316). Louie has been said, at the beginning of the novel, to have little sense of things "getting or failing to get her somewhere"; "her object was to feel that she, Louie, *was*" (13); "she saw then and now on the same plane," without "stereoscopic vision" (15). This looks like a condemnation of her superficiality, her childishness. But the clearest opposition is with the more or less antipathetic male characters: Robert with his new order and Harrison with his forte for plans (309). And perhaps the novel itself demonstrates that all events *are* on the same plane. Stella resembles Louie and differs from Harrison because she is, in her own phrase, not "a worker-out" (231); the novel tends to passivity, and so to indiscriminacy.

The individual, moreover, may lack a meaningful past, may be left like Stella and Robert in the fairytale atmosphere of love and war with a "short unweighty past" (92). Stella reflects, on visiting Robert's home, that "she, like he, had come loose from her moorings" and that "life had supplied to her so far nothing so positive as the abandoned past" (109). But when later at Mount Morris she wakes to find that "her place in time had been lost" (169), the effect seems to be something of a liberation. Mount Morris as a whole is "out of time"; Stella imagines that she has reached "another time" rather than another country (156). And throughout the novel there is a fascination with the distance from action implicit in timelessness, in the arrest of motion, from the sense of Regent's Park as an "hourless place" at the very beginning (6) to Stella's flat, with "the look of no hour" as she faces the catastrophe of Robert's deceit at the end (268).The change here is major; the opening conveys Sunday idleness and unchanging good weather; the end conveys Stella's nocturnal desperation, her "insupportable nervous blankness of mind," her inability to face action or change. This pause has been anticipated, in the near context, by Stella's "arrestation of memory" as Robert briefly vanishes from her mind (260) and by the comment that "all love stood still in one single piercing illusion of its peace, now peace was no more" (263).What they have in common is the recognition that the significance of events can come in the intervals between events. The illusion of peace echoes the "mirages of repose" (86) of the dense vegetation of bombed London, or, soon after this, the moment, as Robert and Stella first get to know each other,when she comes to feel the force of his character and his concern for her, a moment like that in the cinema when "some break-down of projection leaves one shot frozen, absurdly, on to the screen" (93). Absurd, verging on travesty as the text has just said, but nonetheless a moment of recognition, of concentration. Knowledge seems to be in the momentarily unchanging gaze.

All this concern with the passage of time is reflected in the writing of the novel itself. This shows an acute sense of pace in two respects. On the one hand, it is often slower than one might expect, suggesting the reluctance of the characters or of the narrator—through aesthetic fascination, disproportionate self-indulgence, lack of imagination or of purposiveness—to press on with the action. Alternatively, chapters or sections may show a sudden change in pace, as events start to press in on the leisurely advance of the story. A single example of each will perhaps suffice.

Chapter 7 starts with Stella returning from a day spent with Robert at his family home, a day of general futility narrated in entertainingly comic style and marking a considerable lull in the tension of the book, since the whole Harrison-Robert conflict is necessarily in abeyance. Chapter 7 starts from the moment they return to London and Stella walks home from the station while Robert goes on duty; the tight link of chapter sequence suggests a certain immediacy of action. Since the chapter recounts a lengthy meeting with Harrison, it might have been expected to raise the tension again and perhaps to lead to some step forward in the characters' relationships. In fact, not much of the kind happens. The chapter starts with a fine sense of Stella's unease in a strangely still London; it is Saturday evening, and London is a place of "suspicious listening, surreptitious movement and leaden hearts." With this there is mingled a comic disproportion as Stella remembers the parcel entrusted to her by Mrs. Kelway on the grounds, no doubt erroneous, that post offices in London are open on Sundays. She approaches her flat and notices someone waiting for her. So far, this is material for Hitchcock or Graham Greene, the familiar tension of isolation, anxiety, alertness, handled with a sharp sense for the worrying emptiness of the blacked-out streets and for the rare, disturbing event, the lovers glimpsed in doorways, Stella's eye nervously searching out her own door. But here the excitement vanishes. She recognizes Harrison and addresses him casually, banally: "Been waiting long?" She invites him in, and he makes himself at home, calmly observing, "You know, this is very nice." The initial conversation is not much more inspired: told that they have been spending the day in the countryside, Harrison asks if they have been "making the most of the last of the fine weather." There are hints that they are not just strangers making conversation; even the "last of the fine weather" in the context of the book's sense of autumnal constriction is not just phatic communion. When Stella, tired by her day, comments incidentally on Harrison's laughter, the implication is that she is getting used to him, almost getting used to his intimacy. And the banality of the conversation is itself a sort of teasing: can two people in so tense a situation find nothing better to talk about? We ask, and we wait. Before too long, in fact, the conversation assumes a Jamesian tone, apparently flat utterances being pointed up by economical authorial comment: "Harrison's grin at that was so unequivocal she could only like him. Swiftly he ruined that—'One thing one can see you've been doing, Stella: you've thought things over.'" Stella, expectedly, replies, "Thought what over?" The skill—such as it is—of this verbal fencing is to avoid directness, to avoid decisiveness, for as long as possible. And so the conversation continues with reflections on dreams, on certainty and speculation, on the cast of mind of men and women, which leads Harrison to remark, touching accurately on one of the major temporal features of the book, if in uninspired terminology, "I rather took it you'd rather leave the thing in the air." After some five pages of such conversation, a piece of information is given: Stella tells Harrison that she has not informed Robert of his intervention. He already knows. Harrison now offers to fetch Stella a glass of milk, and she reflects for over a page on her marriage, some twenty years ago. Harrison returns with the milk; they talk of his mother, of Cousin Francis, of the coincidence of Stella "turning up in two different stories." And then there is a brief period of intensity: Stella, abandoning any politeness, says that it was a pity they met. Harrison, with a directness that astonishes her, calls it "the very hell," and she responds, with "her own kind of violence," that she too has suffered, not from unrequited passion but from gratuitousness: Harrison, she insists, cannot reasonably complain that the contact he has engineered "had, after all, no point." This is a chapter about pointlessness; it reveals how painful such futility can be, but it also demonstrates pointlessness in action as tedious, rather ridiculous, but allowing also a gradual growth in acceptance and understanding. This section of the conversation ends with Stella formulating the accusation that Harrison "succeed[s] in making a spy of me"—of making her like himself, just as later she will recognize that Robert too, the alien spy, is like Harrison. Indeed, "it was Robert who had been the Harrison" (266). Futility means uniformity. And there for a time conversation fizzles out. Harrison looks out of the window, notices that it has started to rain (it really is the end of the fine weather), and prepares to leave. Stella looks out into the night, a peaceful interlude in which the two are speechless, anonymous, "depersonalised speakers in a drama which should best of all have remained as silent as it essentially was" (134). Their conversation has been inessential; what has mattered is their being together, in a situation of unshared desire. The situation has not been resolved or allowed to lapse; it has been left in the air. Harrison's visit amounts to little more than an assertion that the story is still there. The reader has read with at times a sense of frustration that these people sound so much less interesting than they should, less interesting than is promised by Stella's intelligence, or by Harrison's mysteriousness. For a time they do sound interesting, and the reader wonders if this precision in defining their situation is going to lead to any will to change it. It doesn't. The chapter becomes timeless. At the beginning, Robert is eager to be on duty by nine; at the end, Stella reflects that she hasn't heard a clock all evening: "It might be any hour" (135); Harrison consults the luminous dial of his watch and doesn't tell her what it says. Time is standing still; the relation of the two people is, for the time being, immutable.

A chapter that contrasts very strongly and, it seems, explicitly with this is the final scene between Stella and Robert, chapter 15. Chapter 14, like chapter 6, concerns a visit by Robert to his family and ends with him catching a train back to London. But chapter 15 begins in midconversa-

tion, even in midexchange: "'What if I am?' he repeated." "What if I am
a spy?" is up to the reader to supply. Robert and Stella are sitting at first
in the glow of an electric fire and then in darkness (this is a novel of sen-
sory deprivation). Their conversation throughout is precise, undisguised,
free of cliché and formula, often eloquent; it is a debate on the nature of
patriotism and on the relation of their personal loyalties to their national
loyalties. Robert draws the curtain to look at the night—as Harrison has
drawn it to look at the rain—and Stella sees him as not human. He
continues to explain himself and she to lament her own exclusion from
his deepest activities and his adoption of the "specious, unthinkable,
grotesque" Nazi cause (264), and she reflects on her love of the country
she has known with him. Robert looks at the luminous dial of his watch
(Lee notes the echo as a sign of claustrophobia) and broaches the question of whether he will have any part in the future. Fearing that he is
watched by Harrison, he leaves by the roof, the narrator reminding us of
his stiff knee. The chapter ends in midexpectation, recording that no
sound can be heard from anyone waiting in the street. The next chapter
begins with a reference to "Robert's fall or leap from the roof" (281).

   This chapter has not been like the one previously discussed. It does
not involve any discrepancy between passionate feeling and banal
communication. It is the climactic chapter of the novel and is worthy of
this function. It maintains a high emotional tone, showing us two characters who feel strongly and articulate their feelings powerfully, sometimes
rhetorically, and whose feelings are complex in the mixture of continuing
desire and resentment, of need and hostility. Because of this complexity
of feeling and of the exhaustion of emotional intensity, there are fluctuations in the contact between them: fluctuations from speech to silence,
from explanation to argument, from anger to laughter. What does not
change, until near the end, is that, despite Robert's belief in the new day,
the past tense dominates. They talk of the past; they seek to understand
what they have been. Robert raises the issue of his future with the utmost
tentativeness and gets only another question by way of answer: "I shan't
have any part in it—I suppose, now?" "Why do you ask me?" (267). But
then the business of getting away interrupts, and the pace and scope of
the narrative change. It is dealt with a little clumsily, with odd detail, as
Stella makes sure Robert has his cigarette lighter, and the language slips
to the colloquial stiff upper lip: "What a laugh on the roof!" Passion and
action are incongruous with each other; it is the passion that lies behind

the suicidal action, but the nature and quality of the act are lesser, more accidental, more matter-of-fact and rapid; it is a thing to be got out of the way quickly, even a thing the author hushes up completely, recounting it only through the garbled and biased intermediary of newspaper reports in the next chapter. And although this is the climax, it is far from the end of the book. Two chapters follow, in which ordinariness resumes. Full knowledge of passion and guilt are rare and special. *The Heat of the Day* shows how little the formulation of such knowledge can be integrated into the current of time.

Henry Green: *Loving*

LOVING starts, "Once upon a day" and ends, "Lived happily ever after."
It is a fairy tale, except that the *"day"* warns us that it is not quite an
ordinary fairy tale. It is a fairy tale because it takes place in wartime, but
in Eire, "where there is no blackout." Just as Stella Rodney finds neutral
Ireland to be an escape from time-ridden Britain, so do the characters of
Loving, the owners and servants of a big house, find themselves remote
from the activity of the war. The master, Jack Tennant, is away for much
of the story, being in the British army, and his wife and mother visit
England at one time to see him. The English servants who occupy the
foreground of most of the story talk about the possibility of a German
invasion of Eire and debate whether it is really to be feared or not, but
this has an air of bogey-man unreality, not very different from their
anxiety about the native Irish, with whom they have little contact. They
consider the possibility of returning to England; the bogey-man here is
the recruiting officer who will be waiting for them at the quay-side. They
have chosen escape, irresponsibility, and so isolation and a certain timelessness. Ireland is a place of inertia, "a sort of lotus land, seductively
beautiful but morally unhealthy" (Stokes 1959, 101); it has "a timeless
present that makes past and future irrelevant" (Holmesland 1986, 113).
North goes so far as to claim that the novel, unlike other works of Green,
shows no interest in the passage of time: "It is as if the passage of time
had been erased by placing the entire novel in the romantic fairy-tale past
of *Caught* and *Back*" (1984, 142).

But things do happen in *Loving,* as they do in fairy tales; quite a lot of
things, in fact, although they may seem fairly trivial: a peacock is killed,
buried, and dug up by a dog; a maid steals some peacock eggs and some
waterglass; a ring is lost and recovered, after the visit of an insurance
inspector. The most obviously important thing is that the lady of the

house, Mrs. Jack, is found in bed with a neighbor, Captain Davenport, and hastily leaves Ireland for a time, only to return and resume the relationship. The timing of these events is often extremely vague. The opening paragraph continues: "From time to time the other servants separately or in chorus gave expression to proper sentiments," and, after the placing in Eire, a new paragraph starts, "Came a man's laugh." All this is obviously theatrical: the chorus of proper sentiments gives only a vague background, and "from time to time" implies something of its desultory nature. The man's laugh is the start of the action. Shocking, improper, since it occurs by the deathbed of the butler Eldon, it introduces his successor, Raunce, who is about to steal his whisky. By the end of the book, Raunce will take the place of Eldon not only in his status but also in his sickliness, and that "living happily ever after" will be a teasing unreality by comparison with Raunce's gradual growth in responsibility and sensitivity and the text's gradual growth in realism.

From this imprecise opening, the progress of the events continues, often with equal imprecision.Things happen "another morning" (30), "some days later" (95); "a few days passed" (157), As if fearing that even these indications are imprudently specific, the narrator starts another section, "It may have been a few days later" (64). And yet we do also find in the novel quite a few precise indications of sequence, signs of will and urgency: "two days later" (10), "that afternoon" (53), "Later that same afternoon" (58), "at dinner the same day" (87). At the opening of the book, when Raunce steals the whisky, Eldon is alive. Two days later, he is dead and about to be buried. Raunce asks in the same breath, "What time's the interment?" and "How long to go before dinner?" But even before the interment, he has already asked Mrs. Tennant for Eldon's position. "Two days later" means "only two days later" and is an assertion of Raunce's shameless ambition.

The novel, that is, presents unashamed and specific desires in an atmosphere of unreality or remoteness. This entails multiplicity of time schemas. People are concerned with their own plans; these may chance to coincide with the plans of others. The coincidence is sometimes manifest through a particular sort of link between scenes, which, like so much in the novel, is reminiscent of the theater, or perhaps of the cinema. A case occurs in the third chapter, which includes an account of Edith and the other maid, Kate, in their bedroom. They are relaxed, chatty, sensual; the conversation ends with their reflecting with half-hearted nostalgia on their remoteness from England. And then Kate remarks on the sound of the birds outside: "Edith looked out. A great distance beneath she saw Mrs. Tennant and her daughter-in-law starting for a walk. The dogs raced about on the terrace yapping which made the six peacocks present scream" (24). Kate's vague reference to the "birds" anticipates the peacocks, whose constant presence will form one of the leitmotivs of the book, and these are plausibly aroused by the dogs, who are a normal part of country life. The plunging view onto the terrace indicates the size (and social status) of the building and at the same time marks a change of focus, directing the reader's attention to a new conversation, between Mrs. Tennant and Mrs. Jack, which now continues. There is nothing to indicate that the maids' conversation is complete; the reader is simply shown another conversation that has equal right to his attention. And which is very different: it is carried out in the dialect of the upper classes, grammatically and phonetically correct, understated and brief of utterance, with an appearance of urbane self-discipline and empathy ("I mean there's no shooting or fishing yet. He'd get very restless poor dear"). It follows the norms of polite concern for other people, but it hints at a certain tension: Mrs. Tennant faintly suggests that she is not quite convinced by her daughter-in-law's concern for her absent husband. This discussion too comes to an end in a somewhat haphazard way. Having reached the goal of their walk (not, in fact, identified, despite its marble pillars, it proves forty pages later to be a ruined temple, and forty pages after that to be "a complete copy of a Greek temple"), they turn back and "began a talk about underclothes." The hints are that all this is *bavardage*, conversation for the sake of filling time and masking the potential hostility of the two women. The next paragraph takes us back to the maids: "But Kate and Edith were not to get out of the Castle without difficulty" (27). The *but* obviously does not relate to the discussion about underclothes, or indeed to any sentence formulated in the text; it must imply that the two maids—during the period of the ladies' walk, during which they have "dressed for the afternoon"—have formed the wish to go out; in other words, it pretends that the former scene has been going on although the reader has not seen it. What prevents them going out is the discovery of the housekeeper, Miss Burch, weeping at the death of Eldon; the discovery reinforces the display of real personal warmth on the part of the maids, especially of Edith, who stays to comfort Miss Burch, and it also brings the chapter full circle, since it began with Miss

Burch showing to Raunce her regret for Eldon and her resentment of his own succession. The upper classes have their own lives, in which the servants are quite important as distraction, entertainment, or annoyance. A sequence from this other world has been intercalated with conspicuous skill into the presentation of the extrovert and generous but narrowly repetitious world of the servants. All this is beautifully done, but it is also somewhat outrageous; if we expect connections between scenes to relate to the purposes of the characters, as seems to be the case in traditional authors such as Trollope, there is something scandalous about a connection based on mere spatial proximity.

There are other ways of showing congruence of time that are just as blatant. A scene that counterpoints two groups from the servant world takes place in the ninth chapter, the one that begins with the discovery of Mrs. Jack and the captain *in flagrante delicto.* Kate is becoming intimate with the Irish lampman Paddy. A primitive to match the wildest English fancy, Paddy speaks unintelligibly (except to Kate, who can translate) and never washes or combs his hair. In a scene of nicely judged eroticism, Kate combs his hair for him while complaining with apparently genuine distaste at its condition; she ends by promising to make him look like the captain, laughing at the name, and then giving up, saying, "Look. . . . I'm fed up. You take hold and finish" (91). The text then cuts to the cook, Mrs. Welch, and her nephew: "'I'm fed up with you,' Mrs. Welch said to her Albert at this precise minute." And Albert explains why he is not with Edith, who is separated from Kate with her future lover Raunce and the mistress's children. There are parallels here, based on the usual intimacy of the two maids and perhaps also on a sense of women caring for and controlling males; but there is also a feeling for the way the multiple social links of a large household are in fact breaking down into couples and are held together only by a "precise moment" (a phrase in which Mengham, reading with insufficient irony to my mind, finds an expression of "pedantic assertiveness") within the space of an afternoon.

The life of the servants is very much dominated by a predictable timetable—which includes the timetable of their meals. Raunce ends the first chapter by announcing that since it is ten to three in the afternoon it is time for his siesta and that he should be called at half past four. Lunch is late because Raunce cannot sit down to carve until ten past two. On another occasion, the children are to be taken out for a walk at half past two but in fact go at a quarter to three. No work is usually set for the afternoons, though the sense of "the day's work" is strong. There are organized alternations of work and inaction that parallel the way Raunce's persona is split into the officious solemnity he shows in the public rooms and his spontaneous crudity in the servants' quarters behind the green baize door. During working hours, the servants interact in a restrained and indirect manner, often under the eye of the masters; in the privacy of the afternoon, idleness, pleasure, and sensuality are indulged. The quality of life in the novel changes when the masters are all away and the separation of the two sides of the door is lifted, to the scandal of some who are outraged that Raunce should sit in incomplete uniform with Edith in the drawing room. But even then it appears that it is the afternoons that are set aside for games, picnics, and flirtations.

If routine is strong and much of life therefore predictable, there is also much that is surprising. These surprises operate in two directions. On the one hand, surreptitious pleasures are liable to interruption from authority; on the other, the orderly pattern of decorous intercourse is liable to be interrupted by sudden outbreaks of emotion.

The finest example of an interference by authority is perhaps the strangely beautiful scene—aptly noted by Stokes as "one of the most deservedly famous passages in Green's work" (1959, 163) and which Holmesland sees as "an instant impression of eternity, a momentary bliss that surmounts time and decay and shatters the stagnant tranquillity of history" (1986, 124)—in which Raunce interrupts the two maids, who are dancing with each other:

"The little bitches I'll show 'em" he said and suddenly opened.

They were wheeling wheeling in each other's arms heedless at the far end where they had drawn up one of the white blinds. Above from a rather low ceiling five great chandeliers swept one after the other almost to the waxed parquet floor reflecting in their hundred thousand drops the single sparkle of distant day, again and again red velvet panelled walls, and two girls, minute in purple, dancing multiplied to eternity in these trembling pears of glass.

"You're daft," he called out. (62)

This is very complex, in the shift of point of view: "whirling whirling" seems to present the sensibility of the two women themselves, or at least

of someone who strongly identifies with them; the image of the chandeliers seems much more remote. And it is complex in tone, from the crudity of Raunce's bullying to the fine, surrealistic image of the "trembling
pears of glass." The complexity is what makes the moment important; it
allows a quite simple contrast, between the authority of Raunce and the
women's enjoyment (which conceals a contrast of authoritarian hetero-
sexuality and sensual, easygoing lesbianism), and it also brings together
some perspectives that are complementary though not easy to consider
together: the grandeur of the surroundings—accessible due to the
absence of the owners, itself the result of illicit sexuality—and the heed-
lessness of the maids, the power of Raunce and the possibility of aesthetic detachment, the immediacy of physical rapture and the multiplicity
and smallness of vision; in short, the subjective body and the objective
body. In any case, the sense given is that there is a truth of the person, or
of the potential of humanity, which is not exhausted by action but may be
sensed in vision.

The static scenes have naturally been commented on by critics
(Mengham 1982, 128; Holmesland 1986, 129). There is, of course,
something paradoxical about them: it seems as if the author is attempting
something better not done through language, which is inherently sequential, temporal, but through a visual form such as the painting or the pho-
tograph. Or the cinema; the slowing of action to an entrancing pause is a
common move in films, which are both visual and sequential. And this
perhaps brings out the full import of the procedure. What is conveyed
here is not just the fascination of a certain moment for narrator or character but the recognition that this fascination arises as an act of abstraction
from the concerns of the story; the text, or the film, chooses to abandon
its normal pace in order to dwell upon the beautiful, the revealing, the
pathetic or disturbing, but it shows that its choice is constrained by the
unavoidable return to plot and change. And this return is the result of the
crude power of Raunce their superior, hostile to all pleasure but his own.
The scene is an invasion, and North rightly stresses that the plot is largely
driven by such invasions (1984, 153). Raunce even relents and invites
them to play their record once more, but they refuse, unwilling perhaps to
accept their pleasure as a gift of power. Edith replies, "It's over now";
experience is again partitioned—into times of freedom and times of
control. The scene will be repeated. The two girls play Blind Man's Buff
with the children of the house and the youth Albert, an underling of

Raunce's. Albert's presence, with his adolescent fascination with the
sexuality of the two young women, adds a powerful, erotic quality to the
scene. The text carefully follows the pace of Albert's searching as he is
blindfolded, his heightened senses, his hearing strained for female
giggles, his imagination of the unseen but fantastic scene, his final sudden success and the pause that follows it: "He went slow. He could hear
feet slither. Then he turned in a flash. He had Edith. He stood awkward
one hand on her stomach the other on the small of her back" (114). The
two kiss, as required, formally, by the rules of the game, though for
Albert at least this is more than a formality. The game proceeds. And
then things change:

> But there was an interruption. As Edith knelt before the child a door in the
> wall opened with a grinding shriek of a rusty hinge and Raunce entered upon
> a scene which this noise and perhaps also his presence had instantly turned to
> more stone. (115)

From languor to immobility; the text economically contrasts the hesitation of timid pleasure with the Gothic paralysis imposed by power.

A like stilling of activity and feeling seems elsewhere to transcend or
alienate authority rather than to manifest it. At the end of the sixth
section of the novel, Kate and Edie go to visit the Irishman Paddy, who is
responsible for the peacocks (and with whom Kate will later have an
affair). They find him asleep, and the section ends with the maids seeing
through his window—amidst a curious soundlessness—first the peacocks
themselves and then Raunce replacing them as he drives them away. On
the face of it, this is not a very decisive conclusion. They see at the end
of the section what they have often seen: the peacocks and their immediate boss (and suitor). The difference is that they see them through glass.
But this difference, the isolation from experience, the momentary
strangeness of the familiar, has its impact on the characters. The last
words of the section recount a response that may seem disproportionate:
"The girls stood transfixed as if by arrows between the Irishman dead
motionless asleep and the other intent and quiet behind a division. Then
dropping everything they turned, they also fled" (53). The scene is left
practically empty; there is an arrest of life, which acutely designates a
certain emptiness and vulnerability of emotion, especially of erotic
feeling, of which Green often shows himself aware. The reader is offered
the scene as immobilized spectacle. The passage is a fine example of the

"constant sense of remoteness and estrangement" that Gibson finds in Green's work (1990, 118). On the one hand, the moment of peace, distance, and beauty contrasts with the meanness and grotesqueness of the actions narrated earlier in the section; on the other, it echoes a whole set of references to peacocks (including another disturbing episode, referred to within this section, in which a peacock is killed by the cook's nephew and concealed in the larder). These references provide local color (peacocks are not uncommon in Irish farms and estates) and more significantly a sense of chilled, luxurious beauty that evokes the diffuse, erotic atmosphere of the novel as a whole. This particular climax is thus a condensation and highlighting of the overall sense of longing, admiration, magic, which in this novel is associated with the feeling for a free and elegant life. The two men here, *between* whom the girls stand, are symbolically important. Kate is to take the Irishman as a lover, and Edie is to have Raunce; the passage hints at how far the realities of love will approach and how far they will miss the glamor of the peacocks, and at how far strangeness and fear form part of the nature of love.

These are images of a peaceful emotion being interrupted by authority, or the specter of authority. The reverse also happens. The smooth running of the day may be interrupted by oddities arising more or less directly from the private passions of the characters. One such scene, involving Raunce and Edith, has been strangely interrupted. Raunce is attempting to persuade Edith that he has fallen for her, though in a feeble and "hangdog" fashion, in which his professional status appears as a vaguely paternal spirit. She is not entirely uninterested but responds with "excitement and scorn," "You tell that to all of them Charley." This incompetent idyll comes to a stop when Edith exclaims, "Why Badger you dirty thing whatever have you got then?" The dog Badger then appears, carrying the body of a peacock, and it is explained that this bird has been killed by the cook's nephew, buried, and disinterred by Badger (an apt name for one who digs). The characters constantly, if superficially and without great conviction, fear German invasion; they have in fact been subject to invasion by this British child who has brought death, disorder, and concealment with him.

A more startling surprise occurs with the discovery of the mouse, which closely precedes the magical vision of Charley through Paddy's window and contrasts strongly with it. There is in the drawingroom of the castle a map with illustrations of the neighboring countryside. It so

happens that the illustration for Clancarty, the captain's home, shows a
naked couple. On the map is a pointer connected to a weathervane over-
head, and this has stuck, pointing precisely to this image, which Mrs.
Jack finds distinctly embarrassing. Raunce is contemplating the pointer,
working out a way of defrauding his employers by purporting to buy a
new spring for it. The two illicit desires, Mrs. Jack's adulterous love and
Raunce's moneygrubbing, coalesce in a scene in which she attempts to
move the arrow but breaks it, an event that he greets with cheerful defer-
ence, since it gives him the perfect excuse for a purchase. With Edith's
aid, he finds a panel covering the mechanism of the pointer. The surprise
is elegantly handled:

> He put his head forward to peer. He saw two shafts which met to be joined by
> three gear wheels interlocked. And caught between those teeth, held by the
> leg was a live mouse.

> At this Edith let a shriek with the full force of her lungs. A silence of horror
> fell. (46)

Green presents with fine mimetic force the "peering," the careful
discovery of the mechanical arrangements, before suddenly showing,
through the inverted sentence with its odd punctuation, the living crea-
ture that is a victim of the machine. This also rapidly turns to Gothic
horror. The scream is part of a well-worn joke about women fearing
mice; but the alternation of scream and silence and then, after this moment of stillness, the bustle of others rushing up to help and intervene
gives a more solemn emphasis. As it should; the scene sharply brings
together eroticism and cupidity, routine and cruelty, with a suddenness
that is both comic and revelatory. And it suggests a symbolism of life and
mechanism that may be pertinent to the mechanistic life of a highly organized community.

A more frequent display of suddenness comes from bad temper. Many
of the characters are subject to annoyance; there is Raunce's irritation
with Albert, to whom he speaks in a "sort of shout" (70), Mrs. Jack's
"searing rage" (73), Edith's "flash of rage" (109, also 129), Raunce's
furious "shouting in passion" (152). These rages do not last. Emotional
life in the castle is in many respects superficial, if unpleasant. The story
thus tends to relate small fits of excitement, which the characters themselves hardly take seriously and which the reader takes seriously only

insofar as he or she can see them as symptoms of emotional impoverishment (in the case of Raunce), of an immaturity that is being gradually overcome (in Edith), or of a gap between public appearance and lasting passion (in the case of Mrs. Jack). Upper-class status, one notes, means respectability, planning, and deviousness.

There is, as this implies, a certain amount of long-term planning by the characters in the novel, as with the ladies' planning for Jack's leave some time in advance and Raunce and Edith's planning for their marriage (which includes Edith's "saving herself" for the wedding night). But these are also connected with very sudden decisions: Mrs. Jack's decision to go immediately to England after her discovery, and Raunce's decision to go to England for the wedding, without even giving in his notice. Both of these are somewhat complex in their effect. It looks at first as if Mrs. Jack is tearing herself away from the temptation of the captain; but he very soon follows her, and when she returns it proves she has seen "quite a lot" of him in London. Raunce's decision looks like tearing himself away from the lotus-eating temptations of Ireland for the stern duty of England, but it is done with his usual selfishness; the more conscientious Edith is eager to give a month's salary in lieu of notice, but Raunce is dismissive of such legalistic propriety. His decision seems to be made in a state of confusion brought about by illness, by the pressure of his mother who has at last replied to his regular letters, in terms he dare not show to Edith but presumably denouncing his cowardice in staying away from the war, and by a faint state of panic.

There are also gradual developments in character, indicative of a deeper shift in the self, of a *Bildung*. The clearest example is in the slowly maturing certainty of the boy Albert, who announces not much more than halfway through the novel, during a picnic with the two maids, that he is worried about his mother and sister in the bombing of England and is considering returning to be with them. This picnic scene displays what is keeping Albert in Ireland; it beautifully conveys the mixture of sexual curiosity, rough teasing, gentle, rather timorous attraction and sincere communication, playfulness, and tedium that unites these adolescents on a summer's afternoon. A particularly fine detail is the moment when Edith leans over the pantry boy, lying on the ground, to tickle the sleeping Kate, who, as she wakes, pronounces the name of the Irish lampman:

Eyes welling, she looked direct into Albert's below her. He lay quiet and yellow in a simper. This brought her up sharp.

"Can't you even have a joke?" she asked. (135)

This acute, scarcely formulated confrontation of sexual invitation and sexual constraint hardly affects the working out of the action, but it is part of the growth of the characters. Before very long, Albert announces, to the fury of Raunce, his intention of returning to England to join the airforce (160). The placing of the announcement is typical. It takes place in the aftermath of a lengthy and highly repetitious account of the visit of the insurance inspector seeking to investigate the disappearance of a valuable ring. Although the point is not mentioned, Albert has foolishly but chivalrously attempted to take responsibility for the loss. Remaining gauchely silent during this part of the discussion, he looks grave, turns white, and when the possible German invasion is yet again mentioned, blurts out his decision. After Raunce's expostulations, Miss Burch, still preoccupied with the death of Eldon, again bursts into tears and has to be led away for comforting. Albert's decision arises from adolescent embarrassment, from a sense of being an outsider, and is soon obscured by the pathetic comedy of Miss Burch and the attempts to console her. But it is none the less a real stage of growth. The point is reinforced by a discreet echo; towards the end of the novel, the servants, led by Raunce, fall into prolonged hysterical laughter as they imitate the accent of the insurance investigator. All the servants, that is, except Albert; Albert merely simpers. He has found maturity and responsibility, as has Edith and even eventually Raunce. They have rejected the life of idle comfort and self-seeking. But that life has been a sort of education for them, and it is in the gradualness, the imperceptibility of their learning, that the novel finds its fascination.

Raunce develops through illness, which he diagnoses as dyspepsia, though the reader may be more pessimistic. In one way this illness makes Raunce more sympathetic, as it coincides with his increasingly genuine and tender love for Edith. In another way it is a loss; the monstrous egoistic energy of the man fades away. The novel, in this character, balances a scene of decline against a sense of growth and allows the nostalgia of repetition. Raunce twice has "a return of his old manner"; first (63) his authoritarian manner gives way to cheerfulness, but near the end of the book (216) his developing mildness gives way to irritation with Albert;

on the last page of the book, the dog Badger also has a return of his old manner, interrupting Edith and Raunce with exaggerated tail-wagging and seeming deeply ashamed of something. This time the tail-wagging dog is allowed to lie and its assumed crime is not investigated. It leaves, looking back at the butler "with a wild yearning look of grief" (228). The repetition is incomplete; Raunce has not rushed off with it in what might seem to be play or conspiracy, as he did earlier, and the dog's role in the book therefore ends in melancholy as well as in mystery.

The book is therefore quite appreciably concerned with sameness and with delay. Much of the comedy—and much of the poetry, the two largely overlapping—is concerned with things that recur or that produce their effect long after they occur; this is a static and repetitive world. A nice if small example is the telephone messages. Albert answers the telephone (98) and returns with news of a telegram for Raunce. Raunce reprimands him emphatically for not writing down the message, although Albert in fact appears to remember quite convincingly the seven-word message, "Staying on for a few days Tennant." Two pages later, Albert again answers the telephone and returns with an illegible message written on a scrap of paper. Raunce expresses despair, and Albert recites the message from memory. It proves to be from Mrs. Jack and has the same content as the last one. Over fifty pages later, Albert answers the telephone and returns with a message written out in block letters, which says "Returning Monday Tennant" (157). Slight as this is, it merits a few words of comment. First, it calls for a considerable span of attention on the part of the reader; a hasty reading might miss a great many such details. Second, it shows the beneficial effects of education; Albert has acquired a skill. Third, it shows the ongoing effects of power; Albert is obedient. Fourth, it is funny because it is disproportionate and inefficient; the small scale of life in the servant's hall means that structures of power are asserted through trivialities, and the reader has a constant awareness of storms in teacups.

One should add here the effect of delayed explanation. Mrs. Welch, the cook, is eager for her assistants never to speak to the Irish tradesmen who come to the castle to deliver goods, and she institutes an elaborate system by which these have to ring a bell to indicate they have been and to allow the young women to collect the goods after their departure. It appears, very near the end of the novel (213), that they have been leaving gin for Mrs. Welch, who is thus able to collect it unobserved. In the same spirit we can note the delayed result. Raunce finds that his predecessor, Eldon, has been making a profit by charging for sashcord that is never installed (42); a few pages later, after the startling mouse incident, Miss Burch—an admirer of Eldon but obviously herself too honorable to know about his dishonest maneuvers—expresses fear that one of the maids might break her neck because the broken sashcords are "a proper death-trap" (48). The reader sees something that neither Raunce nor Miss Burch sees, has the pleasure of putting things together after an interval; the disposition of events changes retrospectively, becoming funnier and more sinister.

Stokes comments accurately on the domination of scene over summary in Green (1945, 70), and this corresponds to his increasing preoccupation with dialogue in the critical essays collected in *Concluding*. *Loving*, like all Green's novels, is a novel of conversation. It is largely a novel of banal conversation, which is infuriating insofar as it does very little to advance the plot.

A characteristic conversation occurs on the occasion of the loss of Mrs. Tennant's sapphire ring. This event is in itself a startling one, which starts a chapter with some degree of éclat. Miss Burch enters the servants' hall for elevenses, announcing that "she's mislaid her big sapphire cluster" (64). The specialized vocabulary and the lack of name give a sense of a closed society, and indeed the narrator goes on to comment that there was no need to ask whose ring was lost, since Mrs. Tennant was prone to losing things. This comment first supplies the information not given by the character and, second, mutes the importance of the surprise; although Miss Burch is looking worried, it is not clear that she need to be, given the habitual carelessness of her mistress. And indeed everyone else reacts with indifference; Raunce jokingly dismisses the remark and turns the talk to the missing gardening glove. Miss Burch, however, a page later, is "still on about the ring" (the colloquial idiom, with its hint of arrogant dismissal, implies that this is Raunce's point of view) and suggests that the drains will have to be opened to search for it. The topic is dropped. The passage turns to Mrs. Welch discussing the IRA and ends with her lamenting her lost waterglass. Later in the day, Miss Burch and Mrs. Welch revert to the topic of missing waterglass and ring, with anecdotes of rings lost and found at Brighton, suspicions and allaying of suspicions, criticism of Raunce and Mrs. Welch's proposition that the plumbing should be opened up, to which Miss Burch replies,

"Just what I said with the cup of cocoa this morning." Mrs. Welch adds, "'Ave they so much as glanced at those drains in the last twelvemonth?" Over a hundred pages later, when the disappearance of the ring and its various later appearances and disappearances have become generally upsetting, Mrs. Welch comments, in conversation with Mrs. Tennant, on "a terrible stench of drains." She attributes this to the Irish tendency "never to clean things out" and repeats her remark: "A terrible stench of drains and me that had thought we were going to have them all up while you were away with Mrs. Jack" (177). Mrs. Tennant feebly echoes, "The drains?" and Mrs. Welch introduces the idea of the "lovely cluster ring," though at the same time she pours scorn on the idea that it might be "down the plumbing." Mrs. Tennant helplessly tries to put a stop to this obviously distasteful conversation, and Mrs. Welch asks what she would like for lunch, advising her not to think twice about the stench of drains. From this point on, she harangues her employer about the missing ring, the missing waterglass, the missing peacock's eggs, the IRA, and Raunce's amours with Edith until Mrs. Tennant comes to the hypothesis that she has been at the gin. Mrs. Tennant leaves and meets Raunce, who tells her that the ring has been found. Mrs. Welch's verbose repetitiousness on this occasion no doubt is to be traced to the gin, but there is nothing exceptional in characters being repetitious or obsessive, or in their using a slightly skewed rhetoric. A prominent and more charming example is Edith's frequent recurrence to her narrative of her discovery of Mrs. Jack and the captain, in which the reader can see a sort of possessiveness and a sort of innocence. The effect of such repetitions is usually funny because of the self-centered eccentricity it implies in almost all the characters, who have little interest in the concerns of their colleagues but a strong wish to dominate an audience—however reluctant, as in Mrs. Welch's case—with display of their own concerns.

This means that to a considerable extent the novel appears to stand still; many of the characters are incapable of change and seek only to maintain the status quo. They therefore have no business to address and no motive to deal with things in a businesslike way. The reader may be delighted with such complacency of speech, such disregard for the norm that information should be important and new. The narrator encourages relaxed enjoyment by the lengthy depiction of such fruitless discussion, the reproduction at length of Raunce's laboriously composed, clumsy, and hackneyed letters to his mother (whereas the obviously forceful letter from the mother is not reproduced), and by conspiratorially slipping into the vocabulary of the characters. An early example is Raunce's encouragement to Albert to help him in stealing the whisky: "'A spot of john barleycorn is what you're in need of,' Raunce went on, but the boy was not having any." The popular idiom is neatly ironized by the failure to contract "was not," and the oddity halts the reader's processing of the conversation for a moment. Broadly speaking, the novel is composed of much trivial inaction, some hasty and dramatic surprises, some moments of static beauty, and an almost imperceptible process of growth. The balance of these things can perhaps be most clearly felt in Raunce's final vision of Edith, on the last page of the work:

> For what with the peacocks bowing at her purple skirts, the white doves nodding on her shoulders round her brilliant cheeks and her great eyes that blinked tears of happiness, it made a picture.

> "Edie," he appealed soft, probably not daring to move or speak too sharp for fear he might disturb it all. Yet he used exactly that tone Mr. Eldon had employed at the last when calling his Ellen. (229)

The moment is visual and poetic. The colors, the leading of the eye in from shoulders to cheeks and eyes, even the extraordinary and precarious moment of a person with doves actually on her shoulders, all suggest the description of a painting. The discreetly varied verbal patterns of "peacocks bowing" and "white doves nodding," even perhaps the phonetic echoes of "peacocks-purple" and "doves nodding—shoulders" add to the static quality of the scene. Time is frozen. Raunce recognizes this and respects it. For once, the reader is in agreement with Raunce, as both wish to preserve the stillness of the scene, the fascination of the visual. In Green's work there is, according to Gibson (1990, 135), both a rejection and a perpetuation of aestheticism: rejection because the moral life matters, the right to individual integrity, and perpetuation because the reader is invited to see moral commitment as a spectacle. But there is still a gap between reader and character, for the phrase, presumably from Raunce's consciousness, that "it made a picture" is crude enough to suggest a simple and naive artistic sense different from the feeling of the narrator's own evocation of the picture. The reader needs to be aware of a change in Raunce, who has "disturbed it all" often enough before this; his aesthetic appreciation is new and estimable. The conclusion of the text then is the integration of a timeless scene into personal change. Raunce attains unselfishness. But this unselfishness is deathly, for it identifies him with Eldon. The text manifests circular time, broken in the most implausible way by the departure for England, in the one brief paragraph that succeeds this description. The final scene is a manifestly fictive one, in other words; the discovery of timelessness is a renunciation of action and desire, in which style supplants conflict and change.

Graham Greene: *The Heart of the Matter*

GREENE uses the format of the thriller in many of his serious novels; the genre, as Allott and Farris point out, had trained him to write with speed and economy (1963, 162). Indeed the distinction of serious novels and entertainments is not easy to maintain, since the works that have criminal or espionage plots tend to claim some more general significance, and the novels about adultery, drink, and politics tend to be formulated in terms of mystery and pursuit. In particular, they tend to be written in terms of tension. The essential thrill of the thriller is waiting, knowing that some event of major importance is likely to happen at any moment and wondering which moment it will be, or even whether some moment will avert it altogether. This creates a very special sense of time in fiction, or in cinema—superbly illustrated in many passages of Hitchcock. Nothing actually happens, but the attention of the reader or viewer is stretched to the maximum in case something *does* happen. This means that the surface of the work has to be concerned with the ordinary, the routine, the predictable or inevitable, but that this ordinariness has to be tinged with threat or promise. The tension is raised if the threatened or promised event is of major importance: identification of the criminal, arrest, death. Or, in the case of Graham Greene, damnation. Greene has the advantage, for a novelist, of believing that it is possible to earn eternal damnation in a moment of time. Specifically, Scobie, the hero of *The Heart of the Matter*, is damned because he takes Holy Communion without having previously confessed and been absolved.

Scobie is living in a West African country (apparently Sierra Leone) during the war. He has long been married and feels pity and concern for his wife, Louise, but there is little comfort or obvious affection in their relationship, which has been strained by aging, by the discomforts of colonial life, and especially by the death of their young daughter three years previously. Louise leaves the country for a prolonged break, and in her absence Scobie starts an adulterous relationship with a younger woman, Helen Rolt. Again his attitude is largely made up of pity, as he first sees Helen when she is brought ashore from the ordeal of spending forty days in an open boat after her ship has been torpedoed. On her return, Louise asks him to attend Communion with her. He does not wish to confess his adultery to the priest, which would require him to renounce Helen, or to avoid Communion, which would require him to reveal his guilt to Louise, and therefore he has—or so we are invited to feel—no alternative but to commit his deadly sin.

The pace of *The Heart of the Matter*, as Lewis justly enough points out, is part of the "handsome telling" of the story, which he compares, a little maliciously, to that of Robert Louis Stevenson. The pace is "leisurely but never slack" (Lewis 1987, 26). More seriously, Eagleton recognizes Greene's "flawed and tired respect for a pragmatic negotiation of everyday life" (1987, 99); life is effortful and weary. The thriller dimension is perhaps most clearly shown in the scene of Scobie's damnation itself (CE, 255–64). On the day of her return, Louise has proposed that they should go to Communion together the next day, a Sunday. Scobie does not go to confession but instead visits Helen to explain the theological position to her (and to the uninstructed reader). On Sunday morning, he has postponed the issue—being a lover of delay—by pretending to feel ill, taking a glass of brandy to relieve his symptoms, and then declaring that since he is no longer fasting he is disqualified from Mass. The key chapter begins with the proposition being renewed: "It was the moment he had known would come" (256). His previous avoidance of the issue has been mere temporizing. The reader watches as he approaches the inevitable, with some bravado. He makes an excuse and drives away, blaming God. Specifically, he blames God for forcing a decision on him, "suddenly, with no time to consider" (256). He has been avoiding the issue for a long time, but now he can no longer separate his secular—or apparently secular—feeling for the two women from the framework of dogma to which he has been blinding himself. For some time he debates within himself the "right answer," which he presents as a selfish one: the strategy of confessing his adultery and renouncing it, thus abandoning the vulnerable Helen to her own resources and to the advances of the predatory Bagster (who is assumed to be a worse adulterer than Scobie), and the "ordinary honest *wrong*

answer," namely to abandon Louise, forget his "private vow," abandon
his job—and presumably the church. Two points are worth special
emphasis: first, the choice is regarded as having implications about the
timing of its results; second, it is regarded as a trap. A merit of the right
answer is that it is the long-term one; it is reasonable to assume that
Helen, having survived her ordeal in the boat, will also survive love and
despair—as Scobie has already done, with the death of his love for
Louise. Catholicism, reason, selfishness, duration are contrasted with the
immediacy of unselfish feeling, and the choice between them is a trap.
The term (elsewhere used more literally of, for instance, Scobie's relations with the wily trader Yusef and of Yusef's with his rival Tallit)
seems to imply a contrast between Scobie's actual life of constraint and
responsibility and some imagined freedom. The inevitable, in other
words, is unwelcome. And now the reader watches Scobie entering the
trap; he goes into the confessional, vaguely hoping for a miracle, and
doesn't find one; the priest methodically considers his sin and asks him
to avoid seeing the woman; Scobie refuses and is denied absolution. He
leaves the confessional with a sense of hopelessness; "It seemed to him
that he had only left for his exploration the territory of despair."

The novel has entered a new phase. Scobie's life is radically transformed, and the next morning this transformation will be complete. The
day starts with a rejection of further delay: Louise wakes him to take him
to church, and he reflects: "What was the good of another delaying lie?
. . . I am damned already—I may as well go the whole length of my
chain" (261). The decision has virtually disappeared; Scobie is simply
noting what has already happened. And now the text enters a phase of
minute accuracy and expansiveness; the words of the Mass are quoted
and Scobie's passionate reflections carefully analyzed and then cited
verbatim. The form of the ceremony of course entails a steady advance
towards the crucial moment of taking the wafer: "Father Rank's whisper
at the altar hurried remorselessly towards the consecration." Remorselessly—from Scobie's viewpoint, the order of Mass is a torment for
which repentance might be expected. And Scobie grows increasingly
aware of his irremediable state: he has abandoned the hope of peace
"forever." Momentarily he clings to the possibility of an escape; as
Louise asks if he is feeling unwell, he is tempted to leave the building, to
delay the decision yet again. But he resists the temptation. He goes up to
the altar with Louise, reflecting that "only a miracle can save me now,"

and no miracle takes place. In the last paragraph of the chapter, Scobie—
still dreaming of "some incredible interposition," but knowing it to be
incredible—takes the wafer ("the time had come") and offers up his
damnation to God, knowing the "eternal sentence" as it takes effect. All
this adds up to a powerful scene of tension between Scobie's genuine
feelings of responsibility, his conflicting conviction of the truth of the
Catholic doctrine of sacraments and punishments, and his wish to avoid
decision, his wish for changelessness. He is torn throughout the scene
between the logical certainty of inevitable doom and the emotional
longing for miraculous escape or for postponement.

Scobie's feeling for time, in other words, is largely that of obligation,
of the need simply to continue. He passively undergoes time, like a prisoner. Scobie, the policeman, decorates his office only with a pair of
handcuffs, which may seem to symbolize his own captivity to the routine
of his life as well as a threat for wrongdoers.

Scobie's patience is perhaps ultimately a paradoxical resignation to the
feeling that time passes too slowly, or, more radically, that time as such
is a curse. He reflects, in extraordinary fashion, early in the novel, that
life is too long: "Couldn't the test of man have been carried out in fewer
years? Couldn't we have committed our first major sin at seven, have
ruined ourselves for love or hate at ten, have clutched at redemption on a
fifteen-year-old deathbed?" (52). The outline of human life is remarkably
simplified, since it appears to consist essentially of a test that we can
expect to fail. Everything else is secondary and therefore tedious. A lot
lies in that "therefore," but the result appears to be that there is a further
test, namely, that of surviving nevertheless. The novel thus praises
stamina (156); Helen Rolt and her fellow passengers impress Scobie and
the reader simply because they are still alive. In Scobie's own case, habit,
routine are what constitute stamina—and deny fullness of sensation.
"Comfort, like the act of sex, developed a routine," the author comments
of Scobie's relations with his wife (39). But routine has a charm. "Who
wanted," the author queries, referring not to Scobie but to Wilson, "at
any given moment to change the routine of his life?" (250). It is a seductive and dispiriting charm: even in church, Scobie is prey to "the awful
languor of routine" (175). And yet routine is close to what Scobie most
longs for, peace. "All he needed was peace. Everything meant work, the
daily regular routine in the little bare office, the change of seasons in a
place he loved" (60). It is Louise—and with her the whole burden of

personal relations and the challenge of change—that robs him of peace. Scobie has an aspiration to timelessness that is at least an escape from the continuing pressure of events. He "vaguely" tells the commissioner, his superior officer, at the beginning of the story that he wishes to stay in the colony because "it's pretty in the evening" (9). The explanation looks inadequate; it is somewhat elucidated a few pages later when the narrator comments that "in the evening the port became beautiful for perhaps five minutes. . . . It was the hour of content" (19). Characteristically, on this evening Scobie is "just too late" to benefit from these five minutes, but the sense of content and beauty indicated here—which appears to be essentially secular—is something that never leaves him and appears to be bound up with his moral concerns. What concerns him is peace, but a peace that cannot be wholly aesthetic, that must be united with responsibility. He attains peace, for instance, by shipping off Louise to South Africa (110), but the peace is an unreal one because it is bought from Yusef. The importance of the concept of "peace" in the novel had been emphasized by Mudford (1996, 11); the reality of peace appears rarely. We see it, for instance, in Scobie's dream as he is on his way to investigate Pemberton's suicide; it is "a dream of perfect happiness and freedom" in which he walks calmly with Ali. Awaking, he reflects that he could be wholly content with Ali if only he had arranged for the happiness of Louise (which, the text emphasizes, is impossible). "Without me you'll have peace" Louise tells him (60), and he replies angrily, "*You* can't give me peace" (61). Peace can be given by the Lamb of God at Mass. Louise bitterly implies that Catherine, their daughter, has given him peace by dying. The vision is a disquieting and lucid one. Greene's works, as Allott and Farris acutely observe (1963, 28),are melodramatic because they depend on the disruption of routine—Greene feeling routine to be hatefully reductive. In this, he is far from unusual. The special feature of his writing is that he seems to detest both the routine and the departure from it.

In a passage from an earlier version (Greene 1948, 262), perhaps omitted as too explicit, the pattern of time is powerfully formulated by Wilson in the scene immediately preceding that of Scobie's damnation. "In human love there is never such a thing as victory: only a few minor tactical successes before the final defeat of death or indifference." The novel does not assert this view in too facile a way. Wilson is, it seems, about to achieve his ends. Early in the novel, an Indian fortune teller, who seems oddly well informed about his secret mission to spy out diamond smuggling and about his secret love of poetry, prophesies that he will get his man and that he will win the lady of his heart (67). At the end of the novel, with Scobie's death, it seems very much as if he has done both these things and so has actually attained a victory. The novel thus appears at last to lead to a major and significant change: the defeat of Scobie and the triumph of Wilson. Its art is precisely to persuade the reader that this is not the true pattern, that life is not a zero-sum game in which one person's loss is another's gain, but that we may all be losing.

People may seek to control the impact of time on them by planning. But planning is seen as either ineffective or somewhat disreputable. Scobie tells Wilson, "I have always been a planner. . . . My plans always start out well" (84). Specifically, he is planning on this occasion for Wilson to have dinner with him and Louise, thus playing into Wilson's hands both as regards his purpose of spying on Scobie and as regards his attraction to Louise. The plan will not end well. Later, after first making love to Helen, he plans the moves of his incipient adultery, "like a criminal" planning an "undetectable crime" (186). His adultery is detected, and he ends his life planning to make his suicide undetectable. He is again unsuccessful, since Wilson notices the falsification of his diary that is intended to prove that his death is natural.

The suicide is a long-drawn-out affair, proof of Scobie's patient persistence. His first encounter with suicide, quite early in the book, is the death of Pemberton. Hearing that Louise is returning from South Africa, with inevitable complications, he reflects, "I don't want to plan any more." He longs for peace as an escape from planning, and he envies the dead. Taking aspirin for nausea, he contemplates poisoning himself and reflects that this is an unforgivable sin (though one he would like to see forgiven). In the next chapter, he participates in a conversation in which a doctor recommends a more discreet form of suicide than that adopted by Pemberton, the form that Scobie himself will in due course take, and he feels he is "embarking now on a longer journey than he had ever intended" (227). The destination of the journey is not specified, only the point of departure, the desolate past: "If he looked back he knew he would see only a ravaged countryside." The first-time reader has the sense perhaps only of an indefinite lostness; the second-time reader knows that the end of the journey is death and that it involves a cautious, thorough, dishonest planning.

On two major occasions, Scobie is decisive; in two moments, he takes possession of his past and future. First, he tells Louise that he can afford the ticket for her to visit South Africa (108); then he chooses death (297). He wants happiness for others and peace for himself. These two decisions are as near as he can get to achieving these things. He wants an unchanging state; the drift of the book is to imply that the only state that is unchanging is that of damnation, and that ordinary calm or happiness are essentially precarious and incomplete. The decisions themselves are impulsive. Scobie knows that he cannot really afford the ticket. He has been worrying about it for a considerable time, and this worry has added to the nightmarish atmosphere of his inspection of Pemberton's body and his almost hallucinatory encounter with Yusef on the same occasion. "Slowly and drearily" (107) he has decided to refuse Louise the trip, on the grounds that he cannot accept the temptation of a loan from Yusef, with the compromises that this would entail. When Louise tells him—ambiguously—that she knows of an opportunity to get a ticket but does not expect him to take it, he suddenly tells her to accept: "He spoke rapidly—he wanted the words out beyond recall." The commitment is irrational, a moment of weakness rather than one of strength. Near the end of the novel, after Louise's return and his acceptance of damnation, he calls on Helen, to say good-bye. She too is ambiguous in her response: she renounces his love, promises to go away, and—ironically—congratulates him on acquiring peace as a Catholic free from the demands of a pack of women. But she also expresses her sense of loss and ends by asking to "go on as we are." Scobie, while all this is going on, prays to God to kill him before he hurts God again (as he had in taking Mass without absolution, as he had in allowing the murder of the Christ-like Ali), and he clings to his promise not to abandon Helen; he is at once faithful to his past with Helen, a man of his word, a man of continuity, and also eager for an end. And the section ends with Scobie asking for time to think but not taking it: "He leant over her and closed the door of the car. Before the lock had clicked he had made his decision." This is the decision to commit suicide, and though it is only gradually revealed, the decision has actually been as sudden as the first one, as simple and irrational, as destructive and escapist. There are limits to Scobie's endurance, though these limits are strangely bound up with the competence and rationality with which he is to live out his remaining days.

But these rapid decisions occur in a context of slowness. The theological interest of the book lies in Greene's implication that this knowing self-condemnation is an act of love and so particularly saintly. Its psychological interest lies to a considerable extent in the representation of Scobie's hesitations and uncertainties. So, the third and last book of the novel is largely preoccupied with Scobie's rediscovery of Louise as she returns from the south. She is new to him both because he sees her not simply as a responsibility but also as a person wronged by his love for Helen and entitled to impose decisions on him, and also because she has matured, become more self-reliant and decisive, whether because of her absence or because she recognizes the change in him. From this point on, he carefully plans his suicide (a preparation that occupies ten days, each meticulously and boringly recorded in his diary). Because the final sense is of an act that is not fully voluntary, the feeling is of a gradual, resisting slide towards it, not of a decision but of a series of small approaches to the end, of a gradual emptying of selfhood. Greene's theological point depends on a sense of Scobie's motivation, of the kind of feelings that impel him to destroy himself. I am not clear whether this motivation is at all relevant for the Catholic, who should perhaps see in Scobie's conduct the violation of a number of divine laws. For the non-Catholic reader, it is certainly easy to feel some respect for him, since he is obviously not a mere adventurer but a sensitive and responsible character. This motivation is presented especially through his delay in deciding and his thoroughness in implementing his decision. Slowness comes to look like gravity. There is still an important gap here: he dies, finally, because he cannot bear to hurt Helen by breaking off their affair (though she is already quite frustrated by his scruples and apparent coldness). If anything, we should like even more reflectiveness, we should like him to hesitate more explicitly over this choice. What in a sense we have is a displacement of anxiety from the crucial decision to a diffuse indecision. Greene, in special reference to *The End of the Affair*, quotes a phrase of Von Hügel on "the purification and slow constitution of the individual into a person" (WE, 136). Some such slow constitution is taking place here; the paradox is that there is, after all, a decisive moment.

Greene's style, his rhetoric, reflects the conception of time as bleak endurance. Largely it seems to be concerned with the precise and impersonal recording of happenings. The extreme form of this, to the point of caricature, is found in Scobie's diary, which contains such things as "Louise left. Y. called in the evening. First typhoon 2 a.m." (128). "His pen," the narrator comments, "was powerless to convey the importance of any entry." The second point here in fact refers to a meeting with Yusef in which the trader seeks to gain intimacy and personal advantage on the basis of his loan to Scobie. Events are without importance in the diary; in the text of the narration, their importance is usually implicit, the text to a considerable extent emphasizing physical sensation, external acts (especially conversation), and feelings of discontent, while often leaving intentions and decisions unexpressed. The opening section, for instance, starts not with Scobie but with Wilson; the first paragraph describes his "bald pink knees" on the ironwork of a hotel balcony (so this is a place where people wear shorts) and continues with his new mustache and his lack of interest in the African schoolgirls he can see, all signs of the newcomer to the colony (as the narrator, himself an old hand, points out). Other characters are placed in the scene: the schoolgirls (involved in typically Greene style in an "interminable task," namely that of trying to wave their curly hair), some clerks, the Indian fortune teller, some merchant officers, and some schoolboys—the extras of a tropical setting. A boy brings Wilson some gin, and a new character appears: a white man, Harris (to be a moderately prominent character later in the book), with whom a conversation ensues. In the course of this, Harris points out Scobie passing beneath, and a brief description is given of him through Wilson's eyes. All these items in the text are an impersonal record that could easily be filmed, for instance. They convey an impression of discomfort in the heat, of menace (the vulture that is noted when Wilson, vulture-like, first sees Scobie), of moral degeneracy (the boys pimping), of resentment (in Harris's conversation). To these externals the text adds a strong sense of Wilson's emotional life, through inner presentation: he "dreams," he feels "almost intolerably lonely," he contemplates going to read a book. A section of more remote authorial comment indicates that he likes poetry but does not publicly admit it, and another intrusion points out that he does not realize that his first view of Scobie is going to be important and memorable. All this very effectively creates the atmosphere of an idle and uncomfortable tropical day; what it does not do is identify directly the issues that the novel is going to discuss. Wilson's role as an outsider and his ill-mastered romanticism will prove to be major elements in the development of the story, but there is no indication yet as to the impact they will have; the text signals heavily that his relationship to Scobie is going to be important but does not indicate how.

Parallel to such blank narration is a special sort of dialogue, and one effect is that the reader can congratulate himself for his perspicacity in seeing through it. The form is familiar from thriller films. A case in point is Scobie's first narrated encounter with the shifty Syrian trader Yusef. Scobie discovers that Yusef's car has broken down and offers him a lift; there is some teasing about Good Samaritans (Scobie is a Christian, Yusef a Muslim); Yusef admires Scobie's car and speculates on its price, Scobie insisting that it is not for sale; Yusef inquires about Scobie's rumored departure, complains about his business, offers Mrs. Scobie the present of a roll of silk in gratitude for the lift he is getting, and so on until finally he speculates that Scobie will not find any smuggled diamonds in the ship he is to search tomorrow. All of this just could be affable conversation, passing the time during a chance encounter. But there is also a complicated play of power and friendship: Yusef is seeking to seduce Scobie by demonstrating his superior knowledge, hinting at Scobie's difficulties in his career, offering money and gifts as a potential bribe, while Scobie, without explicitly commenting on Yusef's purposes, resists them by insisting on his role as the upright policeman eager to do his duty and condemn any hint of crime. This advances the plot, slowly. "Dialogue in a novel as in a play," Greene comments (WE, 20), "should be a form of action, with the quickness of action." Certainly here it is action, but it is hardly quick action. The conversation lasts some five pages, a whole numbered section of the chapter, and on the face of things does no more than get Scobie some way home from his previous engagement. The reader is eager to see some major change in Scobie's sense of himself, especially since Scobie's tense relations with his wife and with the other British inhabitants of the colony have just been shown, with some intensity and much sympathy. If so, the reader may be annoyed by all this negotiating. But negotiating with other people is precisely part of the business of living. Hence the need for disguise and persistence. Scobie is coming to terms with someone who is very peripheral to the British colonial vision of order and who is viewed with much well-founded suspicion by officialdom, and he is seeking to maintain the correct distance from him. In fact, the distance he finds is not quite the correctly formal one. He finds himself liking Yusef, accepting his frank human imperfections, and this liking is the beginning of an enmeshment that will lead to contamination and deep guilt. Greene's sympathy is obvious, and in part it is based on respect for the devious perseverance and determination of his hero. The delay that makes up the texture of the novel here constitutes both part of Scobie's ordeal and part of his achievement; it is a sign of the weary patience through which he approaches damnation and sanctity.

A crucial moment in the novel is the death of Pemberton, a scene in which Scobie is separated from his wife, is closely concerned with Ali, meets suicide for the first time, and finally falls prey to Yusef. The chapter starts with "*the* police van" immobile (the *in medias* opening is very common in Greene). It is immobile for a long time until it crosses a ferry, with the expectation of more ferries and more delays. Scobie and Ali exchange a few words about their rate of progress and Scobie's headache. This section includes a large amount of Scobie's private thoughts, which begin as a dream of happiness but rapidly are dominated by worries exacerbated by fever. The text insists that his present activity is secondary: "It was not Pemberton that worried him now—let the dead bury their dead: it was the promise he had made to Louise" (92). The promise to get the money for a ticket to South Africa: Scobie's interest is not in what he is doing but in what he can't do. They arrive at the mission, where Pemberton's body is, and Scobie has a theological discussion with the priest there (first briefly described, with his drab surroundings) and then views the body, the suicide's life being captured by such things as lists of the books in his room and a description of his dead face, the method of suicide, and the text of the suicide letter. The tone is impersonal but for the occasional poetic note such as the remark on the "peculiar innocence" of the early morning light and Scobie's mental comparison of the weight of Pemberton's body with "a child's bones, light and brittle as a bird's." A child's: perhaps his dead daughter; Scobie's mind reverts readily to loss. Finally Scobie goes to sleep watched by Ali, has dreams that reiterate his financial worry and imply an identification of himself with Pemberton, and receives a visit from Yusef. Here the plot starts to edge forward: from stalling Scobie's inquiries about his relationship to Pemberton, who has committed suicide because he is excessively in debt to the Syrian, Yusef carries on to offer Scobie friendship and money. Scobie now refuses both and returns to his dreams, waking at last "to the small stone room like a tomb" (105). What has happened here is that Scobie's helplessness has been illustrated, a temptation offered and rejected, and suicide condemned, as a sin, but also comprehended, as another sort of temptation.

The chapter, in other words, has shown the reader (in an extremely skillful blend of impersonal description with development of theme and character) a period—lasting some hours—of abstraction from commitment and change, a period in which dangerous possibilities are opened up, and has amplified the gravity and allure of these by the strain on the sense of personal identity brought about by illness and contact with extremity. Greene, in an easy phrase, is a master of atmosphere; more precisely, he is a master of inaction, of sensitivity to anxiety and discomfort, a master of the displacement of concern, by which here Scobie's wish to placate Louise is transmuted into his wish not to yield to Yusef. The course of time in *The Heart of the Matter* is thus an alternation of moments of sudden decision and long periods of delay and evasion of action, the joint effect of which is the methodical futility of Scobie's death.

The chapter has a further function: it shifts the focus of the book from the specific discomforts of life in a colony, in a secondary position and with a discontented wife, to what it suggests is a fundamental feature of life in general, its vulnerability to the overwhelming pressure of shame. This most precisely, of course, touches on the guilt involved in contracting unmanageable debts, as Scobie will reluctantly do immediately after, and thus it anticipates Scobie's own suicide at the end of the novel. More generally, it creates an atmosphere in which despair can be regarded as always potentially present, and—for any character, however ordinary or immature, who is not unambiguously saintly—where despair is normal or even a creditable sign of sensitivity and responsibility (Scobie is ambiguously saintly; the book hints that his despair is his sanctity). This is a fallen world; this episode allows Scobie to show extended pity for its fallen condition.

Scobie has to cope with Louise, Helen, Yusef, and the ship's captain, who first of all calls for his mercy in allowing an illicit correspondence with his daughter in Germany and then proves to be involved, as the authorities have long suspected, in the diamond smuggling racket. Each of these elements of his life seems to move uncontrollably at its own pace. So, Louise disappears for a long period in the middle of the book but returns more demanding and preoccupying than ever; Helen is sporadically visited by Scobie, and her mood fluctuates according to her total situation, and with her mood her expansiveness and the demands she makes on Scobie's time; Yusef appears unpredictably, and his affability makes for long, unstoppable conversations; the ship's captain appears only on the two occasions of his ship's arrival, and the length of contact is determined by the official procedure of searching. But there is also a general focusing of anxiety and self-judgment, notably with the episode of the death of Ali. Ali is Scobie's native servant; he has worked for him for many years and is trusted by him more than any other individual. He is then well placed to notice sensitive matters such as Scobie's adultery and the diamond sent by Yusef as a reward for collaborating in smuggling. Moreover, rumors start to accumulate to the effect that he is closely connected with Wilson's agents. Towards the end of the novel, Scobie visits Yusef and talks with exceptional openness about their relationship, about his connection with Helen, about the smuggling, and is then made to send for Ali and to wait a long time for his arrival. He never arrives because he is murdered on the way, freeing Scobie and Yusef from the danger of betrayal but revealing to Scobie his love for the murdered man. Many threads of the plot are coming together here, and as the plot moves towards cohesion, so the themes also come into a pattern, as Scobie reflects while he waits, with less patience than he usually displays, on his damnation, now become "as unimportant as a habit," his corruption, his adventure with Helen. The section is a long one (unusually, the section coincides with the chapter); it is uneasy, at times tense, at times disproportionately absurd, as Yusef with apparent sincerity appreciates the dramatic skill of the Royal Ordnance Corps Shakespearean productions. Yusef is patient; he welcomes the wait: he views it as a rare opportunity to deepen his acquaintance with the much admired Scobie and to display his bonhomie and worldly wisdom. And all this culminates in a sacrifice, the death of Ali through Scobie's guilt mirroring the death of Christ through human faithlessness. A prolonged meaningfulness has been attained; it will eventually dissipate in irony and anticlimax, but the vision has nonetheless been formed. The chapter ends with an eloquent formulation of Scobie's loss of innocence, as the broken rosary he has sent as a token to Ali enhances his reflections on his distrust of Ali and his own untrustworthiness. The chapter ends with Scobie's words, "I loved him." His final words will be, "Dear God, I love," and the reader will have to guess the object of the sentence: God or Ali, both betrayed by Scobie. The chapter ends, that is, with self-knowledge, transcending the legalistic aspects of Catholicism. What has led up to such self-knowledge is a period of waiting, of inaction, in which there is a strange tension between male intimacy and solitude.

The novel appears to be hopeless. But it is perhaps no chance that the Portuguese boat that Scobie has to search is called the *Esperança*. The boat represents temptations that appeal to his weakness and to his strength. He sympathizes with the captain because his illicit letter is (apparently) an unsophisticated and pious expression of his love for his daughter in Germany, while the smuggling for Yusef is the result of blackmail about his own love for Helen. In other words, his guilt is the result of his capacity for pity and responsibility and a sign of his moral worth. To this extent it is a sign of hope, and the book elsewhere hints at signs of hope. Confessing his sins to the priest soon after his first meeting with Helen, Scobie complains of a feeling of emptiness, which the knowing reader may see as an expression of the sin of accidie. The priest, with brisk optimism, comments, "That's sometimes the moment God chooses. . . . Now go along with you and say a decade of your rosary" (176). The drama is in the contrast of Scobie's hesitation, his unwillingness to conclude, with the priest's businesslike promptness, his wish to get on to the next penitent and to discourage Scobie from brooding. But simple and thoughtless as his response may be, it suggests a vision that is important in the novel, as in other Greene novels—a vision, however, which makes the novel as a genre problematic: the vision of the overriding grace of God, which makes human effort, emotion, or choice secondary.

Scobie may be redeemed despite himself. This comment of the priest's is not quite the climax of the chapter, which ends by lingering on Scobie's distaste for God's excessive accessibility. The priest's advice is a hint that the story may be heading in a different direction from the one that appears most clearly. A later chapter reverts to the same technique. The Portuguese captain tells Scobie that his daughter is praying for him, even though she is "married outside the faith." Scobie, with his usual self-destructive caution, comments that the prayers said by someone who has excluded herself from the church don't count, and the captain, suddenly becoming a voice of at least conceivable authority, replies with a note of hope: "No, but when the moment of Grace returns they rise, . . . all at once together like a flock of birds" (235). And the text goes on with

Scobie returning to his normal duty of searching the cabin; seeing himself in a mirror, he wonders if his face is that of a person whom other people pity. The closure of a chapter on self-reflection occurs elsewhere in Greene. The emphasis it places on self-discovery, the analysis it offers of time as leading up to a series of small and speculative self-recognitions, is characteristic of Greene's orientation as a writer. But we cannot forget the captain's "absurd and touching" gesture of hope; the moment of Grace may come.

Whether the moment of Grace ever does come for Scobie, the book is of course too discreet to say; the account of his last moments with his longing to serve some victim, someone in need—perhaps the dead servant Ali, but perhaps someone else—and the final echo of his saint's medal as it falls to the floor, certainly leave open the possibility that it does. And the text, even more curiously, also carefully leaves open the option for another character. This is the non-Catholic, even at times anti-Catholic, Helen Rolt. Left to herself at the death of Scobie, she appears doomed to the insensitive attentions of Bagster. But Bagster leaves after a brief quarrel, and as he leaves she asks him if he believes in God and says that she wishes she believed herself. Then she touches the other pillow on her bed—the one, presumably, used by Scobie—"as though perhaps after all there was one chance in a thousand that she was not alone, and if she were not alone now she would never be alone again" (318).

Put rationally, the memory of Scobie protects her against less serious and considerate men. Put less rationally, Scobie is a saint whose martyrdom has inspired in her the wish for conversion. Either way, the chances are low but nevertheless worth mentioning at Helen's last appearance, in the last section but one of the book, to indicate that Scobie's life is not entirely wasted; the end of the novel, two pages later, will be to assert Scobie's love of God. The hint is that perseverance redeems Scobie; perseverance in pity, responsibility, and sin has been a test of his saintliness.

Purposiveness in *The Heart of the Matter* is replaced by impulse and resignation. These, perhaps, manifest the purposes of God. That such an interpretation is conceivable is the effect of the rhetoric of the text. This is dual. There is a verbal rhetoric, composed of bold metaphor, of hauntingly repeated words, allusions, scenes; and there is a temporal rhetoric of surprise and delay, composed of alternations of protracted helplessness, desperate and hasty action, and precarious stillness. This temporal dimension of the rhetoric may be precisely what is familiar to non-

Catholic readers and makes the text seem plausible to them. They may recognize the texture of many lives in the experiences of discontent, boldness, and longing. The more specifically Christian pattern of guilt and loss gives a conclusive form to such a texture, but some readers may find more conviction in the texture than in the form.

L. P. Hartley: *The Go-Between*

THE Go-Between is the memoir of an old man looking back at his childhood. But the memoir does not cover the whole of Leo Colston's childhood: he looks back at a period of two and a half weeks, from Monday, 9 July 1900, to Friday, 27 July 1900. The period is special, a holiday period that the twelve-year-old Leo spends with his schoolfriend Marcus at Brandham Hall, the country house rented by Marcus's prosperous family. It is a period in which the normal routine of school and family is disrupted; his previous life is indicated for the most part incidentally or schematically; only the immediately preceding months are narrated in any detail, since they give the essential background to certain events of the story proper: his reputation as a magician, the illness that breaks up the school early and that will recur for Marcus, so leaving Leo alone and irresponsible. His later life, comprising some fifty-two years, is dealt with much less informatively: he has survived and avoided adventures. These weeks of 1900 concentrate the interest of the novel, and, it seems, of Leo's life.

But even within the set period, there is a good deal of concentration. The nineteen days of the period are carefully traced; each day is named and dated, and the reader is never in any uncertainty as to the date of the events recounted. Leo's "minute ordering of time into segments," as McEwan points out, is "a consciously diagrammatic feature of the novel's design and helps make the reader more conscious of the problems of time in fiction" (1981, 138). How Leo spends each day is also carefully indicated by reference to his old diary, the finding of which is explained in the introduction. But some of these days pass in relative imprecision; others receive close and detailed attention. The former contain few if any marked incidents, and Leo passes them in waiting, finding out, entertaining himself; the latter involve incidents, often

142

depicted with close attention to detail and especially to the feelings they evoked in the boy, and usually involving a perceptible shift towards some radically new situation. Ultimately they all lead to catastrophe; in the short run, they comprise the recognition of problems and attempts to cope with them. So, the first four days, 9–12 July, are dealt with in some twenty pages and involve Leo's discovery of the house, his getting to know the family and the guests, and his discomfort in having only hot clothes to wear in the unforseen heat. Friday and Saturday, 13–14 July, start to demand more attention. On Friday, which he notes as the turning point of his visit, he is taken by Marcus's elder sister, Marian, to have new cool clothes bought for him in Norwich, the nearest large town. He has become the center of attention, and he remembers it. There is also a delay on this day, to which he pays little attention at the time but which slightly slows the pace of narrative: Marian leaves him alone for an hour while she apparently goes to meet someone else (so perhaps he isn't really the center of attention). On Saturday there is a bathing party, at which Leo looks forward with some interest to seeing Marian in her bathing costume, is disappointed in its capaciousness, but again gains her attention by offering her his own, dry bathing costume to protect her clothes. Again there is a disruption; the party is somewhat concerned by finding that the bathing spot is already occupied by the local farmer Ted Burgess, whose physical fitness, self-satisfaction, and prowess in bathing are stressed. The reader will eventually discover that the delay on the previous day was also caused by Ted Burgess, but for the time being, the sense is of Leo's gradually burgeoning fascination with the adult body.

The next day, Sunday, is the first one on which a great many things happen, and indeed this is the day that makes Leo a go-between. Marcus is found to be ill; Leo has a moment of closeness with Marian, as she slights her suitor, Lord Trimingham, a scion of the aristocratic family to which Brandham Hall belongs, and apologizes to Leo for an instant of forgetfulness. After a conversation with Trimingham, he leaves the house and meets Ted Burgess at his farm. Ted gives him a letter that he hands to Marian in conspiratorial secrecy. All this occupies three chapters, of somewhat varying length, and some thirty pages (more than the whole of his stay so far). The day is memorable for a number of reasons: it involves the potential for change (seen in, for instance, Leo's discovery of the world outside the house), it involves closer contact with adults, by whom he is treated with proper consideration and politeness, and it gives

Leo the chance to be indispensable to Marian. Freed from the obligations of childish friendship by Marcus's illness, Leo's life is expanding, and the rhythm of narration expands with it.

The next day, Monday, 16 July, is less exciting and merits less attention, though it does end with a certain degree of intimacy with Marian, albeit of an awkward kind. Asked to bring her to play croquet with Trimingham, Leo finds she is recalcitrant, but even so she shows him some affection and partakes of some revealing conversation about the merits of Ted and Trimingham. The next three days are passed over quite rapidly, in a single chapter of some ten pages, which however ends with a crucial discovery. On Friday morning (20 July), he is carrying a letter from Marian to Ted (for the fifth time) and discovers it to be a love letter. This discovery gives a strong conclusion to one chapter. The next is occupied with Leo's visit to Ted and a quite intense quarrel that ends with Ted's promise, as a means of appeasing him, to tell him the facts of sex. The day is obviously a memorable one: a shock and a quarrel, a closer knowledge of both adults, and information that forces him to reassess what he means to them, what they mean to him, and the morality of the triple relationship.

Saturday, 21 July, is the longest day yet, in narrative terms. It is taken up with a cricket match between the hall and the village. The length of the section (three chapters) is in part an indication of the normally leisurely pace of the game, in part a tribute to a community ritual in which social hierarchy is made flexible and so confirmed and in part a recognition of the large part that sport occupies in the imagination of schoolboys (Leo's first embarrassment in the novel, while he is still at school, arises from an excessive interest in another game, namely, football, which leads to his being bullied for his disproportionate comment in his diary). The section is also long because, in addition to the game, there is a concert in the evening. More centrally, Leo is a star on both occasions; he ensures victory in the cricket match by catching out the best batsman of the village side, Ted Burgess, and his singing at the concert is acclaimed as the most moving performance of the evening, overshadowing Ted's. This prominence is emphasized by two things: first, the delay brought about by the lengthy narration of the hall innings, which is necessary only because it sets up a target score that the village side has to match, creating great tension in the second of the sequence of chapters as the scores grow so close that everything turns on the last ball; second, the fact that Leo's success is unpredictable, since he is not actually a member of the team but only a substitute (or "twelfth man") and because he is not expecting to sing and has no music with him. But the sequence ends with a new shock: Leo's triumphs are shaded by his sudden discovery of Marian's engagement to Trimingham—with, he naïvely thinks, the end of her contact with Ted. The whole section is finely composed, beautifully conveying the child's excitement and wonderment, his acceptance of a slow and ritual pace, his integration into the public, respectable activities of adulthood, his sense of decorum and of belonging, and it ends with a note of questioning, as Marian's apparent choice of respectability seems not quite to satisfy Leo.

For a while the pace slows. On Sunday morning, Leo relaxes; he is happy at his successes and interested to converse with Trimingham, though the conversation turns out to be about duels for the sake of a woman. But then comes another, greater shock; despite her engagement, Marian sends him with another letter to Ted. Leo is angry with her and shows his resentment to Ted when he sees him, Ted responding with sudden anger. The letter and its delivery occupy a chapter by themselves, a chapter of above average length and marked by intense and emotional writing. The story has changed fundamentally; morality has really entered the picture. Leo feels himself and the lovers to be guilty, and his guilt transforms the book. The discovery of guilt is sudden (for the boy, if foreseeable for the adult reader); at a moment of triumph, of high self-esteem, Leo suddenly conceives of himself as a mere instrument, excluded even from the hidden knowledge of sex, which Ted actually refuses to provide. The day will continue with lengthy anticlimax, making this Sunday (22 July) the longest single day in the whole book. Leo writes to his mother, attempting to get her to send for him to return and revealing something (but not enough) of his worries; has tea; resists Trimingham's request to take a message to Marian; has a conversation with Marcus, largely in French, in which he boasts of his familiarity with Marian's movements and learns that she is intending to buy him a bicycle for his birthday on Friday 27 July; and after some hesitation decides to let the letter go to his mother.

A long and full day. A lot of things have happened, some of them very dramatic and upsetting, some ordinary or merely tantalizing (as with the bicycle that he will not get if he succeeds in leaving early). All are important, though in different ways. First, there is the attempt to escape;

this will give tension to the next few days, as Leo persists in uncertainty, torn between the excitement of an illicit adventure and a wish for peace and decency, and it will give a special complexity to the cataclysmic birthday, which is characterized from the beginning as an inescapable risk brought about by Leo's failure in diplomacy with his mother, as well as a new period of prominence and glamour. Second, there is the learning process that Leo undergoes as he is told of the link of duels and sexuality, of death and honor. Third, there is the deepening of his relation to Marian and Ted by anger, resentment, and self-judgment. Fourth—unknown to Leo—there is the way he reveals to Marcus information that will eventually be used against him by Mrs. Maudsley. And finally, there is the dangerous approach to the erotic as he and Marcus overhear the conversation of lovers (no doubt of Ted and Marian) during their walk together. It is partly obvious why the old Leo remembers these things and recounts them in obsessive detail: partly, at this stage of the novel, they amount to an insidious preparation for disaster; partly they form a protracted anticlimax after Leo's triumphs of the previous day, in which he rediscovers the primacy of the adult world, the world of guilt, and attempts, very insecurely, to adapt to it.

The next few days pass quietly, not least because Marian is away getting the bicycle. Leo is preoccupied with his futile waiting for his mother's letter, he hears from Ted and visits him to say good-bye, he has a conversation with Trimingham, partly on Ted's possible enlistment in the army, partly on the Dutch paintings in the smoking room that Leo finds disturbing in their sensuous and uncritical acceptance of life. The section ends with high emotion as Leo's mother refuses to withdraw him, as Marian returns, and as Leo and she discuss with great intensity the two men in their lives, Marian declaring in tears that she *has* to get married. These three chapters of standard length have taken us up to the morning of Thursday, 26 July. They differ in structure to some extent from previous chapters because the chapters do not coincide with the days, each chapter covering parts of two days (thus somewhat disrupting the orderly categorization of time in the novel so far), and because there is little sense of climax until Marian's sudden outpouring of her feelings to Leo. Leo is thus favored with a greater level of intimacy with her than he has yet known, and perhaps greater than most of the other characters enjoy. The scene leaves him with a glow of reconciliation and appears to be the high point of the book so far, as far as this relationship is concerned.

The rest of Thursday occupies another chapter and is of importance symbolically rather than practically. After reflecting thoroughly on the relation between Ted and Marian, Leo, recalling his success at school as a magician, decides to cast a spell to separate them. The spell involves a magic decoction of the atropa belladonna, or deadly nightshade, that he has discovered growing in a shed at the back of the house. Leo leaves his room late at night, goes out in the frightening darkness to the shed where the plant is growing, finds it has grown to huge proportions, and in a state of panic and seduction uproots the whole plant. The excursion to the shed and especially the struggle with the plant are described with a strong sense of atmosphere and detailed presentation of the boy's imaginative response. The final image of Leo "lying on my back in the open, still clutching the stump, staring up at its moplike coronal of roots, from which grains of earth kept dropping on my face" indicates the closeness of attention and the imprecisely erotic tone of the description. The night-shade has always exercised a fascination (Bien [1963, 179], perhaps a little too simply, identifies the belladonna with the beautiful woman, Marian). Even early in the book, the first sight of it has occupied a prominent position in the story and given a slightly disproportionate climax to a chapter during Leo's first days at Brandham. There is something strange about Leo's preoccupation with the plant; the reader is very likely to see this battle with it not just as part of his "magic" procedures to avert the specific evil of Marian's affair but also as an expression of his own excitement and guilt about the matter. In narrative terms, this indicates the state of Leo's feelings on the next day, which is the culmination of the whole story. It is not clear that if Leo had been in a different state of mind on Friday anything different would have happened, as far as Marian and Ted are concerned; but perhaps the shock for Leo himself and the long-term emotional disruption might have been less. Beyond that, this is a rhetorical delay; the reader's attention is being kept back from the culmination of Marian's deviance and diverted to Leo's discovery of physical pleasure and excitement. The result is partly to ensure that this is read as a book about Leo, not one about Marian; a book about emotional education, not one about deceptiveness.

Friday, then, is the conclusion of the story and properly involves fairly lengthy narration. But at first not much happens: Leo gets up, the foot-man commenting on the mess left by his magic, reflects on his recent experiences in the light of his new maturity at the age of thirteen, and

receives letters and presents. All this occupies one chapter of normal
length. The weather is described (now dull and threatening rain after the
overwhelming recent heat), Leo reflects on the experiences of the past
three weeks, he receives a number of presents, including two ties, one
acceptable and one not, and an outing is planned but does not take place.
The pace, that is, is leisurely, with a high ratio of reflection, description,
commentary, incidental conversation, to real change. The following
chapter raises the tension and the number of incidents. Leo is entrusted
with a letter by Marian. While it is still in his possession, he is questioned
by Mrs. Maudsley, who ingeniously cuts through his prevarications. It
appears as if at any moment the truth of Marian's conduct and of Leo's
complicity may be revealed, but the moment passes, and tea ensues, Leo
again being treated as an honored guest and a somewhat artificial atmosphere of celebration being created. Candles are blown out; the event is
meticulously narrated. This joviality grows thin in waiting. Marian is
expected to be delivering a special present (which we know to be the
bicycle) but does not appear on time. Attempts to make excuses for her
miscarry and, in the great climax of the novel, Mrs. Maudsley hysterically forces Leo to accompany her to the shed where the atropa belladonna grew. Suddenly destroying the state of expectation, "her body
... bent and trembling, and her face unrecognizable," she decides that
"we won't wait" and rushes Leo violently to the meeting place. And here
they see Marian and Ted in sexual intimacy. Leo faints. The chapter ends
with a brief note that Ted has later shot himself. We have waited a long
time; waiting, for activity, for clarification, for knowledge, for release,
has been the characteristic quality of the novel. Its ending is a hysterical
denial of the charm and precarious tranquillity of the summer.

Waiting has in fact dominated the latter part of the novel. The last
major change is Marian's engagement, announced in chapter 13 (of
twenty-three, apart from the introduction and conclusion). The effect of
this is to make Marian's conduct unmistakably guilty. Already discred-
itable in the eyes of her family, if they had known about it, if only
because of the class difference, it becomes a major obstacle to social
order once it threatens her marriage to Trimingham (a marriage between
the rich bourgeoisie and the old aristocracy), and it becomes, even in
Leo's unsophisticated eyes, an act of disloyalty as well as of self-indulgence. From this point on, Leo's aim is to extricate himself or, better
still, to undermine the relationship. And his attempts are wholly ineffec-

tive. The latter half of the novel presents the spectacle of a set of fumbled attempts to escape, attaining drama, direct or symbolic, on a number of occasions. These, moreover, have been counterpointed with the routines of childhood or of country life, walks, games, meals. The catastrophe has been waiting until it is precipitated by the birthday and Mrs. Maudsley's growing suspicion and nervous tension. Real change is suspended. The second half of the work is concerned with a period of time that is special for Leo because its fullest meaning is in the lives of other people, to whom his attitude is ambiguous, comprising both deep attraction and disapproval, and whom he cannot control. The last day is characteristic of the movement of the book as a whole; it is composed of inaction, of routine, of politeness, of self-reflection, alternating with moments in which Leo has to painfully defend himself against Mrs. Maudsley, once with partial success, once with complete failure.

The Go-Between is dominated by the slowness of change, by a cling-ing to the status quo, by fear of discovery and confrontation, but where the interweavings of social contact finally get the better of a long-held secret (thematically, the family's wish for clarity defeats the lovers' wish for concealment). The overall pattern of the novel is that Leo first of all gradually becomes fascinated by Marian and suddenly discovers her sexuality (in reading the letter); then gradually asserts his own maturing and independence (especially during the day of the cricket match) but suddenly discovers Marian's guilt and his own involvement; as a first reaction confronts Ted with hostility; after further delays gains additional intimacy with Marian (as she tells him of her need to marry), and after shorter delay, occupied chiefly by the belladonna episode, discovers the full depth of guilt. There is then a patterning of gradualness or delay and of suddenness. Leo partly undergoes the processes of learning through patient instruction (especially from Trimingham, with his kindly interest and his constant readiness to explain matters of propriety or of history, but also from Marcus, more intimidatingly instructing Leo in the lifestyle of the rich, and from Ted with his embarrassed and clumsy accounts of the importance of sex); partly he learns through unprepared and emotion-ally intense revelation, which is always shocking and finally disastrous. The early shocks produce anger or panic; the final shock produces catatonia. The novel has chosen as its central consciousness a sensibility that is limited by Leo's place as an outsider and by his immaturity; in addition to the self-regard and inflexibility of mind from which many of us suffer on occasion, Leo is held back by an ignorance of sexual matters that we might now think extraordinary and by a general timidity and sickliness. All these things mean he can take in information only at a moderate rate; as he does so, his personality is strengthened: he grows in self-confidence, ease of manner, awareness of his own feelings. But the story of the novel is that of knowledge being forced upon him, and this destroys his personality.

A powerful example of the destructive impact of surprise is the scene in which Leo discovers that the letters he has agreed to deliver are love letters. This is characteristic both of the clear articulation of surprises in the novel and of its sense of the moral and psychological complexity that results from a child's exposure to adult emotion. The adult reader may have had little difficulty in guessing that Marian and Ted are lovers (despite their social disparity) and that the letters between them are intended to make assignations. But they do not reveal this to Leo, and instead make vague references to "business," which Leo seems to receive with indifference or mild curiosity, certainly not with any skepticism; he is contented to be of service to the lovely Marian. But one day, in haste, she gives him the letter unsealed. As Leo sets off to deliver it, there is a lengthy analysis of the schoolboy code of honor that permits people to read unsealed letters. This analysis is written in a style of meticulous accuracy, convincingly combining the simplicity, righteousness, and lack of nuances of early adolescence with the elaboration of legalistic scruple that goes with a certain type of childish intelligence and also with an acute sense of the dilemma as analyzed by the narrating intelligence of Leo after fifty years, still preoccupied with this moment of knowledge and contamination. All this makes for a passage of slow, restrained, cautious writing, tending towards a patient restatement or modification of feelings, as here: "There might even be something about me in the letter—something kind, something sweet, that would make me glow . . . gloat" (117). Kind or sweet, glowing or gloating; there is an excess of precision about these soft and harmless emotions. Not so when Leo does at last start to read the letter, which begins

Darling, darling, darling,
Same place, same time, this evening.
But take care not to—

The rest was hidden by the envelope.

And there the chapter ends, with Marian's obscure anxiety and the remaining veil of decorum in the envelope, still not removed, replacing that sudden, urgent moment of passion. The discovery is unmistakable; for the reader it is a release (though the continued masking by the envelope reminds us of the continued furtiveness of the affair). It is the discovery of a delayed truth and an accession to adult feeling, so long concealed by the intelligent but blinkered vision of the child. The climax is very marked; coming near the center of the book (this is the end of the ninth chapter of twenty-three), it will raise the general emotional tone of the narrative; Leo will become ever more curious about the facts of sex and the relationship of the lovers, and will become acutely aware of a sort of companionship and rivalry with Ted, notably in the cricket match and the concert, Leo's songs of death defeating Ted's songs of love (165)—as eventually Leo will precipitate Ted's death. The tone in which this heightened sensibility is conveyed is, at first, bathetic; the next chapter starts with the words, "Not Adam and Eve, after eating the apple, could have been more upset than I was," and continues with much talk of "spooning," "soppiness," and sea-side postcards. But the Adam and Eve reference, despite the banality of "upset," does focus on the loss of innocence that is the essence of the book, and the scene with Ted that occurs when Leo does deliver the letter begins quite strongly to show a new gravity and willfulness. Leo has not quite grown up in a moment, but the centrality of that moment in the process of growing (or falling) is made manifest.

The child seeks calm. He delights in the time when the weather—and his emotional life—are "set fair," when he experiences a "guaranteed serenity, as of a landscape by Claude" (223). He loves the heat earlier, with "the sense of suspended movement that it gave or seemed to give, reducing everything in nature to the stillness of contemplation" (56). He loves the moment outside time, as when he delights in the task (again quasi-erotic) of rubbing oil into Ted's cricket bat: "The rhythmic rubbing half soothed and half excited me. . . . I belonged to the present, not to a ruined past and a menacing future. Or so I felt" (185). He is capable of contentment, then, though that last remark hints that the contentment is illusory. But he is also capable of eagerness for change, as when wrestling with Marian he "wanted to go on to a conclusion" (268). He has been avoiding a conclusion for a long time; one is soon to be forced upon him. Indeed, it is anticipated in the very next paragraph by the intrusion of Mrs. Maudsley. It seems as if stability has gone on long enough.

The novel as a whole has an outstanding feeling for different sorts of time, as McEwan points out (1981, 139), contrasting the regular, clock-measured pace of a leisurely holiday with a double movement of delay and suddenness. It sets the will of Marian to retain the present situation—her affair with Ted Burgess—against Leo's recurrent attempts to escape from it. One should add that the situation is not one of simple repetition: Leo is increasingly aware of the difficulty of his situation and of his unhealthy complicity. Nevertheless, there is essentially here a double pattern of repetition: the repeated carrying of the messages and the repeated efforts to escape. These latter are doomed in a way verging on the absurd, as with the kindly but obtuse letter from Leo's mother, while the former clearly call for much tact and charm on the part of the lovers in their attempts to maintain Leo's support. The pattern of the book is repetition and sudden collapse: the reader has known that the summer must end—the period of nineteen days is mentioned early and the date of Leo's departure from Brandham Hall has been set from the beginning, even though it has been extended by Marian's wish for continuation and the number of complicating factors (Marian's engagement to Trimingham, the prying of her brother, Leo's friend Marcus, the neurotic tension of Marian's mother) should lead the reader to some sense of instability; but the instability is repressed for much of the book. So, as late as chapter 18, Leo—while waiting for the letter of release from his mother—enjoys two of his happiest days: "For the first time at Brandham Hall it was like family life, not like a party" (212). He continues to be fascinated by Marian, to regard Ted and Trimingham with curiosity and respect. He continues to enjoy the sophistication of Marcus (and is tempted by it to hint misleadingly and calamitously at his own sophistication in knowing what Marian is doing). It is only when he learns of his mother's refusal to withdraw him that he resolves to take action, and the results of this are not at first apparent. His action is incompetent (he attempts unsuccessfully to impede the lovers' meetings) or symbolic (he uproots the deadly nightshade). These appear to be continuations of his repeated escape attempts, like the previous ones in their impotent challenge to the adult world. It is Marcus's malice in giving away his claim to secret knowledge and the mother's nervous acuteness of observation and brutal determination in investigating and intervening that brings about the real change, the final revelation of the lovers *in flagrante delicto*. Suddenness is moral failure; it is the state of inconclusiveness that makes for moral tension and moral seriousness, however naïve and uncomprehending.

Even before the catastrophic, culminating moment, Leo's life has been evolving, not just gradually but through a series of suddenly enforced reevaluations. Soon after his arrival, in unseasonably heavy clothes, "suddenly I caught sight of myself in a glass and saw what a figure of fun looked" (48). When Marian loses her temper as he attempts to refuse to carry any more letters, Leo reflects that she has first of all transformed him into a popular hero, transfigured him, created him, and now "like an enchantress [competing effectively with Leo's own magical claims] she had taken it all away" (179) as he suddenly comes to believe that her interest in him was wholly exploitative. A little later, Marcus's claim that she considers him to be "green" again has the force of a disillusioning revelation, and he responds with anger and betrayal as he boasts of his secret knowledge of her whereabouts. In the final hours at Brandham, Leo is shocked by the adults who remind him of the Dutch paintings in that they "had forgotten themselves" (276). Leo is always very aware of himself, but the awareness—and therefore the self—change suddenly and radically.

The deadly nightshade is disturbing not just because it is associated with the sexual and the illicit but also because it is a symbol of confused growth. It is fascinating and repellent because "there was no harmony, no proportion in its parts. It exhibited all the stages of its development at once. It was young, middle-aged, and old at the same time" (204). This compression of development is what threatens Leo himself. He is on the boundary between childhood and adolescence; much of the humor of the novel arises from the clash between his childish naïveté and his adolescent curiosity and sensual excitability. But the tragedy, the distortion of personality and potential, arises from the same things: the book hints at a process of gradual discovery, of gradual maturing, of an acquisition of knowledge and responsibility, and it shows the overriding of these by uncontrollable revelations.

A similar confusion, one might fear, threatens the whole text of the novel. The narrator of the novel, it might seem, is "young, middle-aged, and old at the same time"—or at least old and young, since Leo's middle age seems to have been more than usually insignificant. But the distinction is very nicely held; if the narrator is sympathetic towards his younger self, he is ironic too, the childish illusions being neatly pointed out for gentle mockery. One may recall the very elegant joke about Marcus getting a joke wrong. It should turn on a pun on "war-mongers" and "awe-mongers" (211). The joke has little enough point anyway, and Marcus has himself missed it, though regarding it as both "very funny and very rude," and he ruins the punch line by giving it as "awe-inspirers." Leo, after this discouraging beginning, is bewildered even by the correct line; he meekly tells the more worldly and experienced Marcus that he can't "quite" see the joke and only gradually brings himself to laugh "quite heartily"—by which time it appears that Leo has got the joke and Marcus hasn't. The point of all this is, of course, that the adult reader and the adult writer can see what the two boys can't; the children are placed outside the society of writer and reader.

But most importantly we find that the writing of the text itself, as Bien rightly stresses (1963, 172), is a sort of delayed and gradual discovery for the old Leo. He discovers as he recounts the experience of his youth the qualities of which he was not wholly conscious at the time and the logic that bound together his experiences. This process of discovery is meticulous, and this largely accounts for the characteristically very slow pace of the narrative. The first numbered chapter, for instance, does not get Leo as far as his arrival at Brandham, which one might reasonably regard as the beginning of the story. To prepare us for his arrival, we have a general description of: Marcus (without his name); the character of Leo's mother and dead father; the social attitudes of public schoolboys; the state of mind of Leo and of his mother after his magic triumph; the outbreak of illness and a detailed description of the departure of the boys from school, with, *inter alia*, a close description of Leo's trunk and tuck box, the weather, and other circumstances of the previous year, a letter of invitation, and preparations for departure. On one level, all this could have been omitted without harm to the story. On another, it is a slowing device, which makes the onset of novelty more gradual and therefore contrasts all the more obviously with the later sudden onset of knowledge and especially the sudden collapse of the whole episode of Leo's fainting. But it also conveys two aspects of the old Leo: one is that he is fascinated to retrieve in detail the sensations of his past, that tuck box "which still showed, by a patch of darker paint, where my initials had been painted over [my father's]"; and the other is that he is eager to define for himself explicitly the feelings and character of the people involved, especially those things not previously made explicit. The chapter thus ends with a failure of communication between himself and his mother, with the old Leo's wish to work out what might have been said: "And I suspect that she had something special to say, which the room would lend weight to, but she never said it, for I was too near to tears to be open to practical or moral councils" (35). Curiosity is what constitutes the tone of the narrative here, a curiosity to define everything that happened or might have happened. Leo is discovering the truth about his past, not simply recording it. The process of discovery is strongly stressed, from such a simple thing as his failure even to recall Marcus's name (25) and his rediscovery of it when he remembers the terms of the invitation to stay with him (32), to the rather more drawn out business of the southwest front, which adds a delicately humorous strand to the text. A guidebook that he consulted before going to Brandham Hall (and transcribed into his diary, which is why it is still available to the novel) particularly stresses the southwest façade. Leo has no memory of this, having been more interested, as he says in his opening chapter, in the rear parts of the building (and we are later to find out what sinister attraction the rear parts have). Even as late as his narration of the day of the cricket match, the old Leo cannot visualize the southwest front, though he recalls the brightness of the moon as he approached it while conversing with Marcus. The last words of the book tell us how "the south-west prospect of the Hall, long hidden from my memory, sprang into view" (296). This seems to be, then, almost a Proustian novel about the recapture of the past. But there is a difference: L. P. Hartley's memory is in part an active, moral force; it is not purely aesthetic and aleatory, as Proust's is. Leo starts his story because he finds the diary by chance—but also because he is convinced that "my secret—the explanation of me—lay there" (22). Having told the story, up to the fatal Friday, he hopes to put away his memories. But writing is not enough; months later, his memories have not "settled," and he attains harmony only by the steps recounted in his epilogue: he goes back to Brandham, meets Marian again, and promises to intercede for her with her grandson, who seems to feel some inherited guilt; he promises to be a go-between for her again. He is, in Bien's words, used precisely in the context of the southwest front (1963, 178) "an advocate of love." He intercedes voluntarily, if a little reluctantly, and out of something like pity for the elderly Marian, rather than out of infatuation with her; he relives as moral agent what in the course of his narrative he had relived purely as memory. There are facts "beyond the reach of memory and gleaned from outside, from living sources" (283) that are needed to formulate fully "the explanation of me."

William Golding: *Lord of the Flies*

LORD *of the Flies* is a novel that works by compression. Within the scope of a story about schoolboys wrecked on a coral island, it claims to say something about the nature of humanity, good and evil, rationality and irrationality, democracy and totalitarianism. Not only are the location and number of characters strictly limited by the circumstances depicted, but the happenings are restricted by the author's sense of the inevitability of moral decline in a state of anarchy. Essentially, the boys, finding themselves alone on an island cut off from civilization by nuclear war and the accident to their plane, start by seeking to retain civilized order: they maintain orderly debates, in which the speaker is denoted by holding a conch, they build shelters, they light a fire to attract the attention of any passing ships, they explore the island systematically for shelter. But tension is already apparent in the conflict for leadership between Ralph, the voice of a rather unintellectual British decency, and Jack, the voice of British brutality, who is the leader of a choir who obey him automatically and whose chief interest—unfulfilled for some time—is in hunting and killing the wild boar on the island. There is a potential for decay also in the widespread tendencies towards idleness, play, uncleanliness, undiscipline and self-pity. "Boys will be boys," Kermode neatly comments (Page 1985, 57); the novel is an examination of boyhood at its worst.

Attitudes to time are intimately connected with the decay of order and with its ideological implications. Certain characters represent a stoical or liberal gradualism; their aim is to build up institutions through which civilization may be maintained; they believe in regularity, planning, thoroughness, and restraint. It is the casualness with which the fire is maintained that leads one to insist that they "put first things first and act proper" (50). Jack's supporters—who, tragically, come to be the majority—stand for fascist impulsiveness; responding directly and immediately to the pressures of the moment, to the desire for excitement or the fear of the alien, they live a life of intense suddenness, in which the only predictable thing is the carrying out of their short-term resolutions, such as their hunting of the humanistic hero Ralph. The fascist life, Golding acutely observes, is a life of play; it has the freedom of play and play's lack of long-term purpose or perspectives; it is a life of spontaneity. And the novel, sympathetically adopting the suddenness of rhythm character-istic of such a social sensibility, presents some of the attraction, as well as the overwhelming evil, of irrational violence.

The novel relates one day in which the boys seek to establish order after their landing on the island (with a brief reference to what seems to be the previous night) and then traces, with great economy, the downfall of the children's community. Gindin puzzlingly claims that "Golding provides no clock sense, no particular indication of how many or how quickly days and weeks pass" (1988, 25). In fact, there is, after the first day, a very clear indication of how the days pass: they pass quickly. There is an unspecified time between the arrival and the beginning of decadence, but it is long enough for their hair to grow much longer and for their clothes to get thoroughly dirty and start to wear out. Decadence is precipitated by two things: Ralph's anger when Jack and his hunters, excited by actually killing a pig for the first time, let the signal fire go out, and the arrival on the island of a parachutist who is killed on landing and whose dead body, in the strange movements caused by the air in his parachute, is taken by the boys to be a strange beast, possibly of some supernatural kind. These events take place on the same day. It will be referred to here as day 3, after day 1, the day of arrival, and day 2, a day shortly before the boar hunt, which is described as a time of increasing discontent and anxiety. Over the next five days (4–8) the islanders become savage; the bulk of the tribe turn away from Ralph's moderate and law-inspired leadership to Jack's brutal domination, in which hunting is the central act, celebrated in ritual dances of reenactment. In one of these, another boy, Simon, a solitary and mystic, is killed, in Maenad fashion, as a symbolic substitute for the boar. Needing a lens to light a fire, Jack's followers steal the glasses belonging to Ralph's friend Piggy, a liberal, rationalist, and intellectual, and when he seeks to retrieve them, he too is killed. The novel ends with the boys hunting their erstwhile leader Ralph, potentially to the death, but in the course of the hunt, they set fire to the undergrowth on the island, and this ironically does what the

smaller and deliberately lit fires have failed to do: it attracts a British ship
that takes the boys off the island and returns them to civilization. The
events are rapid because the implication of the book is that civilization is
superficial, cruelty is natural, and once direct social restraints are lifted,
the principles of order and decency do not hold out long against inherent
evil. *Lord of the Flies*, that is, depicts the helplessness of the good; speed
and simplicity of narration correspond to absence of inner conflict.

The space accorded to each day varies very considerably. Day 1
involves discovery of a new situation, of new people and a new place; it
involves discussion and the making of practical arrangements; it includes
the first attempt to kill a pig. It ends disastrously with a large-scale fire in
which a boy dies (anticipating the final fire of the book, which thus has a
disturbingly neat symmetry). The chapter evokes a world without
civilization, a world in which the reader's cultural assumptions are
immediately invalidated. Boys meet in an incongruous tropical scene,
play, tease each other, start to plan for orderly life and for rescue, and in
the teasing some malice appears (Piggy objects to being called Piggy, but
the others persist), in the meetings some sense of difference is manifest
(the choirboys appear in perfect uniform and paramilitary order). The end
of the chapter is ominous: Jack fails to kill a pig but violently asserts that
he will succeed next time:

> Next time there would be no mercy. He looked round fiercely, daring them to
> contradict. Then they broke out into the sunlight and for a while they were
> busy finding and devouring food as they moved down the scar towards the
> platform and the meeting. (34)

The scar is the one made by their plane in crashing; the chapter end
neatly recapitulates the beginning of the novel when Ralph is seen
moving along the same scar, and so signals that something is complete.
What is complete is the bringing together of a crisis with a need for
order, of the pleasant imperative of food and the vicious love of aggression, of sun and democracy with killing and rivalry. The chapter
announces both the programs that will make up the plot of the work and
the symbols that will structure its interpretation; it tells the reader to
expect an adventure and a fable.

Day 1 occupies forty-five pages. Only one other day has as much
prolonged attention: day 3, the day on which the descent into violence
starts. Again there is a great deal of activity, much conflict and debate:

the pig is killed, it is discovered that the fire is out, Ralph reproaches Jack for this negligence, the hunters feast on the meat of the pig, Ralph calls a meeting and gives a lengthy and carefully considered speech on the need for order, the youngest children complain of the presence of a beast, and their claim is discussed until Jack ostentatiously breaks up the meeting. The parachutist is carried to earth and his body is noted in terror by two boys, Sam and Eric, who have been appointed to keep watch over the fire. And there the day ends, in the middle of a chapter that will resume with the news of the "Beast" being broken to Ralph the next morning. All major characters or groups of characters have participated, older and younger, moderates and irrationalists; there has been action and talk, formal debate and informal conversation, planned activity and the incursion of the unknown. It is a full day, which has involved everyone in the movement towards catastrophe and located that movement in the whole texture of their physical and mental lives. The reader has been able to reflect at length on the thematic significance and possible results of the events of the day, and especially has been made aware of the extremity of the characters' feelings: feelings of antagonism in the case of the older boys, of panic in the "younguns." The day receives as many pages as day 1 (after a mere eleven pages for day 2, which has simply denoted the beginnings of Ralph and Simon's concern at declining standards of behavior and Jack's hostility as he continues to attempt to hunt). The next two days show a concentration of activity: days 4 and 5 occupy twenty-nine and thirty-four pages, respectively, and include, first, the boys' searching of the island for the Beast and, second, Jack's abandonment of the democratic forum, the gradual desertion to him of the majority of the other boys, and the Dionysian celebrations in which Simon dies. Now the line of battle is drawn: Ralph and Piggy, with Sam and Eric, are a hated minority, and the remaining days rapidly account for their martyrdom at the hands of the majority, days 6 and 7 occupying sixteen and fifteen pages. Day 6 sees the theft of Piggy's glasses, day 7 his death and the threat to hunt down Ralph. Day 8 is the actual hunting of Ralph, stopped short of death only by the chance arrival of adults. This last day is a climax to the book in terms of tension and excitement; Ralph's desperate position gives him special intensity of observation and reaction, which means that the chapter is full of incidents, of threats recognized, and forms of escape decided on and carried out. For eighteen pages, then, the reader follows with sympathy and anxiety his apparently hopeless stratagems, before the brief three pages given to the barely comprehending naval officer and to Ralph's final lamentation.

The effect of the pages devoted to the last day is complex. They constitute a close-up of suffering; the book leaves as its final imprint on the reader's mind the sense of the vulnerability of life, the sense of fear, distrust, desperate persistence in self-protection. Second, this is a new kind of cruelty. Simon has died in a wave of mob hysteria, and Piggy as the victim of a psychopathic whim; Ralph is the victim of a whole community, acting under obedience and in a state of high organization. The presentation of cruelty thus approaches the encyclopedic; it is not difficult for the reader to recall comparable acts in individual crime and in the history of totalitarian societies. But the presentation is not only systematic, it is also intensifying, as conscious evil becomes endemic in the society. It is no longer a case of individuals escaping social restraint; society itself is now a destructive force. Third, the length of the description of the hunt contrasts with the brevity of the conclusion, with complex and uncertain results. The reader experiences a sense of relief as Ralph, "tensed for more terrors," in fact suddenly sees not another person, threatening or otherwise, but a uniform, a white-topped cap with the insignia of the navy, a white drill suit with epaulettes, gilt buttons, the symbols of established power. But the evocation of authority is too brief and sudden to eclipse the reader's long exposure to savagery, and it may even seem unreal, artificial, a gesture by the author to the "happy end." Indeed Gindin (Page 1985, 65) views the ending as a gimmick that undermines the seriousness of the whole work, but he appears to retract the charge elsewhere (Gindin 1988, 29–30); presumably the sense of artifice is not indisputably lacking in seriousness.

This is not a happy end; at most, it is an end in which knowledge is gained or formulated, because Ralph weeps, in a fine rhetorical conclusion, the more impressive for its incomprehensibility to the bewildered but good-natured sailor, for "the end of innocence, the darkness of man's heart, and the fall through the air of the true, wise friend called Piggy" (223). Much could be said about these dignified words; here it may suffice to say that the lines summarize a shaping of time: a process, the end of innocence, a permanent state, the heart of darkness (Page 1985, 105, notes the very apt echo of Conrad), and a loss, the death of the rational. Ralph has had long enough to look back on his fears and to rapidly attain a new understanding with Jack; he has attained an overall perspective on his story and he feels it to be a discovery, an education. He has moved from innocence to experience. But the logic of the novel is to ask whether the innocence was ever really there.

The novel, that is, ends on a memorable and complex climax. It has been structured throughout on a series of very marked chapter climaxes (often but not always coinciding with the ends of days or at least of recognizable portions of days). To list these would largely be to list the stages in the normalization of violence: Jack's timidity at killing a pig at the end of chapter 1, his fear of the "unbearable blood," soon is succeeded by the accidental death of a child by fire at the end of chapter 2. By the end of chapter 4, Jack is actually celebrating the bleeding of a dying pig. In the final chapters, the climax is very strongly imbued with violence: the death of Simon in chapter 9, slightly distanced by nature, time, and aesthetics as the very last lines of the chapter identify him (not recently named) and describe the island being liberated of his body as it is carried out to sea by the tide; the night raid on Ralph and Piggy in chapter 10 and the loss of Piggy's glasses, leaving him helpless; the death of Piggy in chapter 11 and the threat to torture Sam and Eric, who are the last boys to desert Ralph. But although a crescendo of violence is strongly implicit in these climaxes, there is also a certain distancing; the moment of violence tends to be just before or just after the end of the chapter; the text frames cruelty in a context of moral contemplation. So, chapter 11 ends with Roger, the sadistic torturer who is abetting Jack and is immediately guilty of Piggy's murder, advancing on the two boys "as one wielding a nameless authority." The phrase is a rich one: he wields his authority as if it were a weapon, such as he might be imagined to be about to use on his victims. But, more suggestively still, what is the authority and why is it nameless? Is it the authority of Jack's totalitarian regime, nameless because it has no legal or contractual base? Or is it the authority of the fear inspired by crime, which no one dare name because authority is believed to entail goodness? The latter is perhaps supported by Roger's earlier recognition of Jack's "irresponsible authority" (176); the chapter climax is the culmination of a process of learning evil.

The rhythm of the novel thus includes the alternation of states of struggle and endeavor with moments of ever-worsening destruction, but the latter are then shadowed by moments of contemplativeness. In earlier parts of the novel, it is precisely such moments of contemplation that may form the climax to a chapter. Chapter 3 (day 2, the start of the action proper) is largely concerned with the growing tension between Jack and Ralph, and the larger part of the chapter ends with them looking at each other, "baffled, in love and hate" (60). (Their love, incidentally, is a theme much hinted at but that never quite comes into focus.) But this section of the text also includes Simon's quasitheological intervention to the effect that this "isn't a good island," and the chapter ends with Simon isolated in dense vegetation, immersed in the play of light and the soothing coming of darkness. A later chapter inverts the implications of this; chapter 8 again ends with Simon alone in the same place. By now he has become physically sick, his mental state is strained, and he is viewed by the other boys as insane. This time he contemplates something specific: the pig's head that Jack has left on a stick as a sacrifice to the Beast. The bloody head attracts flies, and the text refers to it in biblical terminology as the Lord of the Flies. The title of the book makes clear the symbolic importance of this episode: the Lord of the Flies speaks to Simon, in tones derived from the real figures of fear within his childish experience, from a school bully or a tyrannical schoolmaster, as the voice of human evil (of original sin, no doubt, for the Christian reader), the voice of that inescapable part of himself that corrupts life on the island. The chapter ends with the Lord of the Flies threatening, in childish terms, to "do" Simon; the next chapter ends with his being "done," being murdered by mass hysteria. Meanwhile he has, in fact, liberated the island from the imaginary Beast by freeing the dead airman from the parachute that has given him the appearance of life. But this liberation is ineffective, for the real Beast, the beast of evil within the person, cannot be eliminated, and the children pass from superstitious terror of the imaginary to a state of real, political terror. The two episodes of Simon's isolation, of his moments of aesthetic and existential contemplation, form major points of stillness in the book, skillfully placed nearly sixty pages from the beginning and just over sixty pages from the end to embrace the period when civilization appears to be still in the balance. Between them, they move the reader's perception of the island from freedom and beauty to vulnerability and degradation.

There is considerable skill in the handling of such climaxes, a skill that is significant in its control of distance and sympathy. As chapter 10, for instance, approaches a conclusion, there is a pause as Ralph imagines. The boys go to rest in their hut. The day is obviously coming to an end, and the reader has an uneasy feeling that after the atrocity of the previous day, the death of Simon, things are returning to an odd normality. But they are not quite normal; the children are uneasy, they "try" for rest. Piggy, when asked if he is all right, replies only, "S'pose so." And Ralph takes to his nightly game of supposing; he escapes into a fantasy of being transported by plane and train to Devon, where wild ponies would look over the wall at him. He is recalling a lengthy lull in action at an earlier point in the novel, where he has remembered an idyllic, almost sentimental experience of the English countryside, with ponies, snow (by contrast with the overwhelming heat of the island), cornflakes and cream, favorite books, a world in which "everything was all right; everything was good-humored and friendly" (123). On that occasion the memory was promptly disrupted by the violence of a boar hunt; now it has been lastingly undermined. The pony is all too wild for Ralph, wildness has lost its charm, and he prefers to think of civilization in the form of buses and lamps. The dream fades; the younger children start to call out, and Ralph and Piggy start to discuss the (remote) chance of being saved. This leads to some quite good-natured teasing as Ralph suggests that Piggy should write to his aunt and Piggy carefully explains that he has no stamp and no pillar-box. Ralph starts to sleep, but they are woken by the sound of someone outside. There is a brief interval of waiting until someone, frighteningly, calls Piggy, and then, suddenly, figures burst in and attack them. The attack is brief and confusing; it calls up all Ralph's energy and exhausts the sickly Piggy. After the departure of the enemy, the boys discuss the attack for a few moments, not without some satisfaction at their effective defense. And finally the text makes clear what has been at stake. Piggy first of all fears they have come for the conch, the symbol of political authority. But then he realizes they have come for "something else" and asks, "What am I going to do?" Why is he so at a loss? The answer comes in the last ten-line paragraph, which suddenly shifts away from the Ralph group to describe Jack and his henchmen triumphantly leaving—and carrying Piggy's glasses. The last line of the chapter allows the reader to grasp the full implications: without his glasses, Piggy is defenseless, and power has effectively passed to Jack. This, moreover, completes a neat circle; this section of the chapter has opened with Piggy lending his glasses to Ralph to light a fire and "wait[ing] to receive back his sight" (178). The rhetorical artifice of this is perhaps most obvious in Piggy's exclamation about "something else"; it characterizes Piggy's intellectual indirectness of expression, in this case an ironic understatement that controls his real despair. But there is more to it than that (as is further shown by the fact that we hear no more of the conversation of Ralph and Piggy and instead are suddenly shown the opposing party). There has been a moment of uncertainty for the reader, a presentation of anxiety without explicit object, before the changed situation is formally established. And the previous pages have done the same, on a larger scale: we have seen the boys insecure, seeking escape in private fantasy or in the partial relief of frank conversation; waiting has taken the form of fidgeting, sleeplessness, aimlessness. Waiting should be preparation for self-defense but can't be because the boys have no idea of what to defend themselves from; and the text, after lengthy concentration on this loss of purpose and the awkward growth in intimacy that goes with it, suddenly replaces waiting by a radical step towards defeat. Suddenness is characteristic of aggression; the Beast arrives suddenly, Piggy is slain suddenly, quarrels and waves of hysterical fear start suddenly. The pause is the time of moral awareness, of rational discussion, of satisfaction and contemplation.

Aesthetic contemplation and moral debate are a recurrent component of the novel and form a lull in action. As the boys assemble on day 1, for instance, they decide to explore the island; the decision is both practically plausible and a move in the traditional form of the adventure novel, and the ideological implications are brought out clearly when, in the course of their discoveries, Ralph proudly asserts, "This belongs to us" (31). This claim to human possession of nature appears in the middle of a lengthy, descriptive passage, occupying about a page. It starts with an incongruity. The boys are approaching the top of a mountain in playful spirit; as they reach one particular point, Ralph exclaims, "Golly!" This inarticulacy contrasts strongly with the author's own combination of meticulousness, sensuous apprehension, and imagination: the air "thick with butterflies, lifting, fluttering, settling," the island "roughly boat-shaped," and the almost separate fortlike rock that is prominent at one end of it, the coral reef like a line scribbled like a giant, the sense that the "boat" is moving in the tide. This will be followed by the boys' practical recognition that the island is uninhabited, their decision to move back to their starting point, and, with sudden spontaneity, the attempt to kill a pig. Action resumes; the pause has traced a moment of planning and preparation but also a moment of delight and fantasy; the boys seem to us richer, more interesting, because of the butterflies, the giant, the floating away of the boat. But the reader's empathy with them is limited by the "golly" and the "belonging to us," and later the whole episode will look very sinister. The play they indulge in as they climb is to push a large rock off the mountainside so that it smashes into the forest "like a bomb," or like an "enraged monster." This is a natural enough piece of childish delight in rapid action. But it is destructive action, and towards the end of the novel, Piggy will be killed by a large rock being pushed off the fort that they see, which then smashes into the forest, while the butterflies will recur frequently until they are driven away by the ugliness of the Lord of the Flies in the scene of Simon's dialogue with it. The boys think they are taking possession of the island; perhaps it is taking possession of them.The reader thinks the island is being held up for admiration; it is being made memorable as a stage for horror.

Moral debate also takes time. After Jack has "tempestuously" disrupted a meeting, Piggy, Ralph, and Simon talk about leadership, about order and irrational fear, about the temptation to yield to force. And Piggy shows himself acutely intelligent and explains where his understanding comes from: "I been in bed so much I done some thinking. I know about people. I know about me. And him [Jack]. He can't hurt you; but if you stand out of the way he'd hurt the next thing. And that's me" (102). Piggy, in effect, is predicting his own death. He can do so because he has been ill and so learnt to think. Thought is the opposite of action and is manifest in Piggy's lengthy, cautious, subtle speech. Ralph, the true leader, is active rather than thoughtful; the point is apparent throughout the novel in his very style of behavior. He is characterized by a businesslike promptness, while Piggy's movements are marked by slackness and dilatoriness (in his first speech in the book, he calls to Ralph to wait for him; two pages later, he explains that he is not allowed to run because of his asthma; the boys ironically note his reluctance for physical work). But the ideal leader has to reconcile action with rational thought. Ralph has demonstrated this in his long speech earlier in this chapter—a speech carefully planned in advance, systematically organized and lucidly argued, so that for the reader it marks a slowing of the action, a single substantial act occupying several pages of text. But it has been ineffective. Jack interrupts and, despite Ralph's assertion that he hasn't finished yet, complains that he has "talked and talked" and insists on his own turn. The child's span of attention is low; more generally, gesture and courage often command more attention than does argument.

There is in *Lord of the Flies* a kind of speech that is truthful without being reflective or rational, and so is brief, firm, confident. This is the prophecy. Simon tells Ralph that he is sure Ralph will get back to where he came from; challenged, he repeats his remark once, falls silent, and repeats it again. This is taken both as a sign of his "battiness" and as a gesture of friendship. His claim proves to be true. There is in the novel a logic that might seem to exclude it; the text defends reason as a bulwark against violence; it deeply distrusts one kind of unreason. But there seems to be another logic, a suprarational logic, in which Simon is a martyr, and the final surprise of the book confirms him as a prophet.

A lull in action ensues after the horror. When Ralph and his supporters meet the day after Simon's death, they are concerned to establish their innocence. This time Ralph is the more clear-sighted and insists that he and Piggy actually were present at the death ritual (and indeed the previous chapter makes it clear—with a slightly awkward distancing from the voice of the characters—that they were "eager to take a place in this demented but partly secure society" (167), the society of the murderous dancers). But Piggy insists that the death was an accident, caused by Simon's batty behavior, and is eager to ensure the cohesion of the new small society they form with Sam and Eric by suppressing guilt. Sam and Eric appear to be equally eager to deny their presence, and this leads to a conversation that starts by being suggestive of *Winnie the Pooh* ("Hullo. Fancy meeting you, Ralph") and goes on to parody the conversation of debs ("Was it a good [...] dance?" "We left early"). The perspective then changes from this urbane and comic dishonesty to the cruel Roger in the other camp. The reader has been disquieted by this incongruous vision of an ordinary evasiveness; he has been vouchsafed a view of irresponsibility together with a view of the inertia of social custom and language. But he is now to be shocked back into concern for the humane characters by a strong indication of the brutality they have to confront. The rhythm of the text, the low dynamism of the repetitious and second-hand phrasing of the discussions in which the boys disclaim guilt, is manipulating our feelings again, offering a respite from sympathy.

Some characters have density in time; Ralph has his ponies and his books; Piggy has his aunt, his former school, his illness (perhaps he has more past than the others because he is not an upper-class public school-boy like the rest and has more attachment to home and family, less hardness and peer orientation). Ralph and Piggy are also the boys with the strongest sense of the future and therefore of the need to plan for rescue. And it is Piggy who insists on maturity and stoic perseverance: "We just got to go on, that's all. That's what grown-ups would do" (154). Very pathetically, in a scene moving in its very oddness, which draws the text to a strange moment of concentrated stillness, is the small boy Percival Wemys Madison, who clings to the memory of his family address but has forgotten the telephone number. Against this, Jack has little background, and that only at school; he is proud of his singing ability and his control of his choristers. He has no great concern for rescue but only wants to be the chief, immediately. The point arises from the author's control of point of view; we never see Jack's inner thoughts, and this leaves us with the impression that he is entirely directed towards action and towards the near future; he is without a past, without long-term vision, without a home, and so without vulnerability.

The novel carefully observes the course of each day. The text is often extremely emphatic on the time of day. If we take day 3, for example, we find, first, descriptions of children playing and talking in sunlight. These occupy chapter 4, which obviously occupies a substantial portion of the day in view of the activities described (the boar hunt, the quarrel over the abandonment of the fire, the consumption of meat). In chapter 5, on the same day, Ralph is conscious of the declining sun as he plans his speech; he calls an assembly reflecting that "they had never had an assembly so late before" and notes the darkness of the island behind the assembly point on the beach. During the assembly itself, there is much stress on the setting sun and its level rays; Ralph regrets having called the assembly so late (98), and finally it collapses in darkness. The level rays of the sun will recur in the next chapter, at dawn, as Sam and Eric claim to have seen the Beast; the slanting sun will recur throughout the book, most memorably (204) as Ralph, on the last day before he is hunted, rests from his conflict with Jack.

Gindin comments on the symbolic sense of time given by such images of light and dark (1988, 25). The sense is a moral one. Night means irrationality; the Beast is seen in darkness (136), and it is said to come out of the dark (139); "As long as there's light we're brave enough" (138), one character comments, but children are afraid of the dark. Darkness is when Ralph, smitten with "the horrors of death," recognizes the gap that separates them all from the English schoolboys they once were, and sees himself as an outcast (205); it is the time when Sam and Eric are not ashamed to admit their conversion to the camp of savagery (207). Simon's death is a product of the darkness (though Piggy's takes place in bright daylight).

These references to time of day are often foregrounded by some exceptionally lyrical and metaphorical writing. A case is the return of light after the first sighting of the airman's body:

> The rays of the sun that were fanning upwards from below the horizon, swung downwards to eye-level. Ralph looked for a moment at the growing slice of gold that lit them from the right hand and seemed to make speech possible. (109)

The final point is very explicit: light makes speech possible; light is reason and liberates from the unspeakable terrors of night. But the previous lines also call for attention; they present the assembly as a theatrical occasion, lit from the right, the boys subject to the powerful and vigorous large-scale motions of the sun, to which they are carefully related as above or below. The world is subject to natural process and the text views it as spectacle and as nourishment (if the "slice of gold" recalls the fruit that is lavishly available) or as object of aggression (if the "slice" suggests their activity in cutting into the natural). The action stands still for a moment; the beginning of talk is marked, a ritual is beginning, solemnly, and that ritual is grounded in the aesthetic spectacle of the world in which people are secondary.

Throughout, people will be the victims of nature, and the text will at times pause to emphasize the fact. So, after Simon's encounter with the Lord of the Flies, chapter 9 starts with a substantial description of the upper air, in which heat is accumulating to the point where "the air was ready to explode" (160). Simon's condition is mentioned only after a paragraph, and the next two pages, in which he gives decent repose to the airman's body, the "poor broken thing that sat stinking by his side"—in which he demythologizes death but makes it a companion—closely relate his actions to conditions of weather and vegetable growth. The explosion will be the storm that breaks that night, and perhaps also the "explosion of violence," in a cliché that cannot be far from the reader's mind, in which Simon dies. The tropical world is one that hinders human responsibility, that impedes the assertion of a fully human (or humanistic) way of life, and the lyrical writing of the text clearly exposes the reader to the contagious temptation of lush, natural life.

Society calls for a precise sense of time. Symptomatic of the inertia of the stable society of prewar England, but also of the comforting orderliness of family and convention, is the fact that the children never adjust to the rhythm of their environment, where the overpowering heat might call for a siesta, but continue to keep to the "northern European" pattern of working, playing, and eating throughout the day, and find this tiring. They think of a certain time of day as tea time (129), although there is no sign of tea or muffins. Piggy longs for a clock, ineffectively (70). The chief, Ralph concludes, needs time-management skills; he has to recognize occasions, "and then the occasion slipped by so that you had to grab at a decision" (85). The conception is part of an important concern with the establishment of distinctions, of limits, in time as in space and in personality. Life itself is a continuum, in which there are no fixed identities; unfocused light can make a face unrecognizable through the confusing reflections in thick leaves; an advantage of the evening meeting (admittedly outweighed by the onset of darkness) is that at evening there is a single source of light and "the shadows were where they ought to be" (85). Dawn too does bring a sort of order: in it, "the maze of the darkness sorted into near and far" (108). But away from these privileged, transitional intervals, time seems to vanish.

Ultimately, the threat is that of entropy. Social order vanishes as distinctions vanish. The note is struck when Jack disrupts the evening assembly, which then "shredded away and became a discursive and random scatter" (100). Less explicitly, the concept is pervasive in the novel. Things "break up" (89, 154) or "go rotten" (102)—"it's no go," in the words of the Lord of the Flies (158). When Roger throws a stone in the neighborhood of another boy, it is a sign of potential aggression, as yet restrained (the stone is not thrown *at* him); but it is also "that token of preposterous time" (67). Already, quite early in the book, time is becoming unthinkable; the child absorbed in observing the endless processes of nature in the pools by the seashore finds the intrusion of another person—an act that inevitably implies a coming-together of people's different timeframes—something inconceivable. And later the sense of time and of definition will become ever more precarious, and sameness, haziness, indistinctness are the characteristics of the days: "This day promised, like the others, to be a sunbath under a blue dome" (113); pleasant, holidayish, but "like the others"; as the weather grows more intense, the sense of time grows more wearisome. When the sow, which

is itself "struck down by the heat" is killed, "the afternoon wore on, hazy
and dreadful with damp heat" (149). This sow's head is to become the
Lord of the Flies. As Simon is alone in fearful contemplation of it, "there
were no shadows under the trees but everywhere a pearly stillness, so
that what was real seemed illusive and without definition" (152). When
Ralph and his followers set off to the encounter that will bring Piggy's
death, it is in heat haze, things "shimmer" in the heat, there is an effect of
mirage. Piggy has declared that "life is scientific," but life here has
ceased to be distinguishable, measurable, explicable.

And here finally is the paradox of the book: *Lord of the Flies* seems to
be a book of great rationality, of clarity and economy, efficiently oriented
to an elegant fictional transposition of the horrors of history. The book
clearly segments time day-by-day and divides the night from the day, as
it divides what is humane from what is irrational, uncontrolled, formless:
fear, pride, mass excitement. The book looks like a fable, in which the
episodes come to take their place neatly and at the due moment. But what
makes it a challenging and haunting work is not the businesslike, onward
march to disaster and moral lucidity; it is the pauses, the moments of languor, uncertainty, bafflement, inconclusive debate, of fascination with
the immense and the indistinct. These are what speak directly to the
reader, these involve the reader in the seduction of the nonmoral, these
display the limits of order and of comprehension. The novel has shown a
domain of undiscipline, at first as lotus-eating idleness and playfulness,
as self-indulgence (an interesting comparison is with the idea of *la
souille* in Michel Tournier's rewriting of *Robinson Crusoe, Vendredi*).
After the darkness at the heart of human beings is revealed through anxiety, religion, and symbol, this self-indulgence quickly becomes deadly,
so that the children rush Gadarene-fashion to degradation. There is
something rather strange about the rhetorical composition of all this. On
one reading, the collapse of order at the end of the novel is a triumph of
human evil in the absence of rationality. On another, more literary and
self-conscious level, the collapse is a rational demonstration of evil.
Literary rationality and personal violence, strength of art and weakness
of will, go strangely together.

Some Popular Authors

Joanna Trollope

Joanna Trollope's *The Rector's Wife* is about a decision and an accident. The starting point of the story is that the heroine Anna, frustrated with the daily routine of a clergyman's wife and especially upset at the bullying her daughter endures at the state school she attends, decides to take on a job in order to earn money to send her to a private school. Her husband, Peter, is hostile to this decision; he has already expressed the view that it is inappropriate for a clergyman's wife to take on any employment at all, since this would be regarded by the parishioners as a derogation from her duties as a general assistant to her husband, and his opposition is not surprisingly all the stronger when she takes on the undignified function of filling shelves in a supermarket. His opposition makes a barrier between them, which adds to the separation Anna feels because he seems more concerned with his religious duties than with his home life, and she is tempted to abandon him for one of the three more glamorous and apparently more interested men she meets in the course of the novel: the saintly archdeacon, Daniel Byrne; his brother Jonathan, a gentle, tender, thoughtful, and articulate atheist philosopher; and the local rich man and sensualist Patrick O'Sullivan. She starts an affair with, of course, the philosopher, but does not decide for a long time to leave her husband. Finally, after yet another of a long series of quarrels, she goes out for a walk to think about her fate (the spatial sense is interesting: a certain gate that leads out of her garden into open countryside is regarded by her as a gateway to freedom and selfhood, but, a prisoner in her house and job, she doesn't go through it until the end of the novel). She decides to leave him. But, while she is out, a neighbor, sincerely but inaccurately, informs her husband that she is involved with O'Sullivan. The husband, no doubt very properly, decides to drive over to consult his clerical superior, the archdeacon, but is distracted from his driving by his jealousy and so hits a bus and is killed. This accident is the happy ending: Anna has attained the independence of widowhood without exactly being guilty or exactly making a decision.

The time sense of the novel is often concerned with the intolerableness of repetition. The opening words are, "As usual, there were five of them": five women waiting to meet their children from the school bus, and Anna will join them; the everyday routine of the housewife is seen as an imprisonment. Her daughter, Flora, has learnt during her day at school the word "intolerable" and applies it to most of her experiences; the novel appears to imply that most of the mother's experiences are profoundly frustrating (the word is one that recurs) but have to be tolerated, for a long time. So, the novel is concerned, on one level, with changelessness; not much, ultimately, can change. When, near the end of the book, Anna tells Flora that she might wish to live elsewhere, the child replies that she has to stay in the village: "That's what happens" (227).

And yet the novel is overall concerned with crisis and with the overcoming of a crisis as a path to maturity. Anna is extremely impulsive. She "plummets," for instance, "from fury to weeping" (91) and on another occasion feels a "spurt of fury" (164). But she is also very reluctant to act on her growing alienation from Peter, feeling "a strange diffidence . . . about leaving a situation I have been part of for so long" (161). The novel, that is, tends to a second decision (the decision to leave her husband) but never attains it. Anna's position is essentially unstable, since she neither accepts marriage as she knows it nor rejects it wholly, and this instability is what largely constitutes the texture of the novel. The essential events in it are a series of quarrels between Anna and Peter and a series of temptations offered by the various men she meets. The temptations, moreover, form a series of conversations; her future lover lends her a book for discussion, as if at a seminar, and offers her "a little mental exercise" (143). These, together with some conversations with female friends, help the heroine to understand her own character and help the reader to recognize the tension in her between independence and loyalty as well as to grasp the general point, a moderately feminist point about the male institutions that take for granted the subservience of wives. A characteristic conversation that helps to interpret the significance of the story is the one Anna has with her husband at the end of chapter 7 (117). Earlier in the chapter there has been tension; Anna has left the house and met the tempting O'Sullivan. Returning home, she goes to talk to Peter, who tells her that he does not understand her attitude, and that their joint commitment to God is all that counts for them. She asks if sacrifice, immolation, is all that matters, and the conversation is interrupted by a phone call about Brownies. The author nicely captures the way serious theological and moral concern is frustrated by the everyday, and she formulates a complex concern to which the reader, if at all conscious of the Christian tradition of sacrifice, should respond with understanding and respect. The crisis narrated in the novel, then, forms a fairly steady progress along three dimensions: marital frustration, the attraction of a new person (not just a sexual attraction but the attraction of being recognized as an individual worthy of respect and self-respect), and an intellectual—and to some extent impersonal—grasp of the situation. Some of the most memorable passages are not stages in conflict but eloquent defenses of female rights by Anna or other women. So, Anna recognizes her daughter's need for a new school (chapter 3), starts work (chapter 4), quarrels with her husband and leaves the house in angry tears (chapter 7), breaks down in tears during a reception for clergy (chapter 9), quarrels with one of the women who have usurped her housekeeping role at home (chapter 10), and participates in other scenes of extreme emotion. But she also speaks with dignity of her need for independence (69), her need to "occupy a space on this earth" (92), and in a fine climax to the whole novel, asserts that her adultery is less wrong than her husband's self-isolation: "The withdrawing of the essence of yourself, of your emotional and imaginative generosity, is what kills relationships. I never withdrew mine" (244).

There is also often a certain muting of the scenes of direct emotional confrontation. Muting is implicit, for instance, in the elision of one of the quarrels (126), which is not narrated but appears only in Anna's memory. A major change in Anna's emotional life is, of course, her first sexual experience with Jonathan (198). This is delicately narrated: the two have lunch together; their talk of childhood and relatives gently turns to talk of love; and they enter his bedroom, Anna asserting that she is not being seduced because she is fully willing for sex. This is the end of the section but not the end of the chapter, which returns us to the everyday anxieties of the characters, the next section starting immediately, "When Anna got home," and narrating a conversation with Flora about school, Anna's new happiness (and prosperity) showing itself in her offering her daughter a treat of Chocolate Hazelnut Spread (previously too expensive). Then we go on to worries: an unwelcome advance from O'Sullivan and a decision by Anna's son, Luke, to leave home. The change in her life does not wholly transform it; the multiple concerns of family continue barely altered. It is striking that explicit sexuality has actually been displaced into a fairly direct and somewhat distasteful account of Luke's adolescent experiences in the previous chapter; a link is established by his somewhat prurient horror at his mother's possible sexual activity.

Finally there is a change, of course. Anna's widowhood is presented as the acquisition of peace and acceptance, and she gains a new usefulness in teaching but also in offering support for clergy wives. She gains, that is, some quasibureaucratic distance from the category of "clergy wife" (thought she rejects the bureaucratic connotations)—a distance not quite unlike that of the author.

All this leads to a curious disproportion. The novel seems reluctant for things to happen; when they do happen, when decisions are made, it is suddenly, unpredictably, for reader and character alike. The reader risks feeling that the novel is as unreflective as the central character is (until, perhaps, the very end). Important questions are being skimped. Is the heroine right in taking on a job without even consulting her husband? Why does she take on a job far below her qualifications and then refuse promotion in it? (The point is raised by her elder daughter, a university student, but not fully discussed). Is her adultery justifiable, for someone who retains some imprecise acceptance of Christian values? A striking example of the rapidity of psychological movement in the book occurs after a quarrel, as Anna walks out into the garden. This is briefly described: "It was dusk-dark. The dark silhouettes of trees stood against a sky still lit by a dramatic glow from the western horizon, and faint mutterings from the branches indicated that it was not yet night" (111). The reader may perhaps recall Mrs. Morel in *Sons and Lovers* communing with the lilies after a quarrel with her husband. Here, Anna briskly, but in tears, puts on her Burberry and makes her way towards her next encounter, with O'Sullivan.

The central character is somewhat strangely composed of passion and inactivity. Presumably because her situation changes only spasmodically, the book often turns away from her for its main interest, which it derives from the accumulation of new characters, who add variety and afford a wide-ranging picture of a society. A lengthy section, for instance, shows Anna, wearied by the conflicts she is living through, going to stay with an old friend in Oxford (chapter 8). The section comprises a rather coarse satire of secular liberalism and female success (the friend being a successful novelist whose husband is subservient to her). It eliminates one possible reading of the book (that Anna should totally abandon her Anglican self-restraint); it also provides a lull, a possible period of recuperation—broken when she returns home to find, to her great anger, that some of the women of the parish have usurped her place with her husband by taking on her responsibilities for such things as cleaning the house—and doing it better than she does. The lull proves to be a new exclusion; it makes Anna almost as tangential to her husband as she has proved to be to Oxford.

The text is composed with extreme efficiency; the reader is constantly aware of the lucidity and coherence of the narrator's structuring of time and of the elegant concentration of events into a restricted period. A neat example is the third chapter. It starts with Miss Dunstable, a churchgoer briefly mentioned before, observing Anna digging in her garden, continues with various routine-seeming aspects of Anna's daily life—a brief conversation with a friend about the clerical vocation, distribution of parish magazines, during which she is seen by the outsider O'Sullivan, the school bus—and then change tone: her daughter has reached the stage where being bullied is literally intolerable, and Anna resolves to send her to a new school. She talks to her husband, who complains that this school is Catholic and, more significantly, expensive; tension lapses with the more-or-less comic presentation of a visiting grandmother, and a new pressure comes as Luke asks for money for a holiday trip. (Multiplicity of pressure is what constitutes character in this novel.) Finally, Anna sees Miss Dunstable again, who cheerfully calls out, "Action, action." And this is the conclusion; Anna sees this as a "a little revelation" and resolves to take action. The next chapter will show us—in its very first line, which introduces yet another character, the supermarket manager— what the action is. The circling back to Miss Dunstable turns these events—which cover several days—into a single unit, summarized by that moment of revelation.

This is a tidy book. It neatly follows the calendar, from spring through Easter (much anticipated and emphasized) to late summer (and in the last chapters to autumn, with an appropriate melancholy maturing), with apt references to seasonal flowers, to school terms, and to the activities of the church year, and with neat sequences such as that of Anna's training for her supermarket work: on the second day the warehouse, on the third the computer, on the fourth being left to work by herself. Scenes often start in midaction. So one starts with Anna in tears, facing her son (91), and goes on to explain their conflict and to promptly resolve it through their basic goodwill and the intervention of a friend, who closes the scene by driving away. Some scenes are neatly self-contained, as with the one following this, where Luke desperately turns to O'Sullivan for work, for which he has little qualification, and finds that O'Sullivan has the money and the social confidence to employ him and to keep him entertained with the trivial glamor of international faxes, a neat comic conclusion and temporary resolution. The scene and the chapter are real units here; time is parceled up into intelligible segments.

This is then, on the whole, a businesslike book, with a rather impersonal, calendar-based time sense. But there are hints of other scales. First, there is a strong sense of historic England, with its medieval church, and of the conspicuous and tasteless changes being brought about by modernization of the village (these changes producing some of the very few descriptive passages that slow the action of the story). Second, the book offers supernatural justification for the change it relates. The characters frequently refer to God's responsibility for their plight. So, in the opening chapter, Anna says to God, as she digs her garden, "I think You are a toad" (24; Christians will welcome the reverential capital letter). As her crisis deepens, the archdeacon comments, "Over to You" (192; the capital confirms the reference and the continuity of theme). Towards the end of the work, Anna ironically reflects on the badge she wears at work that reads, "Can I help you?" and remarks, "It wouldn't hurt *You* to wear one" (225). Up to this point God is providence or tyrant, the divine let-out. In the last chapter (its conclusive function marked out by unusual brevity), religion becomes a transcendence of time as weariness and tension, and becomes a vehicle of hope. Anna is seen speaking to her dead husband at his grave (and in the last words assures a malevolent yokel that Peter can really hear her), and she tells him of the tombstone she has erected, despite some opposition, which reads, "Pray for me, as I will for thee, that we may merrily meet in heaven" (284). There has been little enough merriment in her life; there may be some after it.

Ruth Rendell

The classic form of the detective story is this: a crime is discovered, the detective interviews a number of witnesses (and suspects), and finally he or she announces the solution. There are of course variations: second crimes, moments of danger for the detective or another character, announcement of false solutions, and the like. But the basic structure often remains readily perceptible, and there are many classics of the genre that make very little attempt to disguise it. The strength of the series of witness interviews is that it demonstrates two things: the detective's perseverance and his or her lucidity in seeing the truth through the mass of often irrelevant material accumulated in the interviews. The risk is the counterpart of perseverance, namely, monotony, and there are a great many routine stories that do fall into this trap. The skill of the accomplished detective novelist is to combine the steady accumulation of information with some shift in focus, approach, pace, or content that allows both a systematic acquisition of evidence and also a sense of the changing responsiveness to new situations that we (rightly or wrongly) tend to think of as characteristic of real life. Ruth Rendell's *Simisola* is a case in point. Essentially, the detective, Inspector Wexford, is presented with a puzzle: a missing person, Melanie, the daughter of a local doctor. He starts to interrogate people who might have witnessed her disappearance, especially those who were present in the Jobcentre (or employment bureau) where she was last seen. He is distracted by the discovery of the body of a young woman who works in the Jobcentre and sets about interviewing witnesses who may have information on this crime. Before this crime is solved, another body is discovered that is at first thought to be Melanie but then proves not to be. Wexford starts to investigate this too and discovers (of course) connections between the two deaths. Melanie is discovered, and Wexford carries on to deduce in the last chapters the connection between the two deaths and the person responsible for them. This already makes it apparent that on the one hand there is little escape from the sequence of interviews, but that on the other there is a considerable shift in focus as the problem being investigated changes: new crimes, and possible links between them. Wexford's usual manner is characterized by patience, thoroughness, and a clear sense of relevance. In one episode, he times the walk from the Jobcentre to the bus stop, notes the time of the buses, reflects on the temptation to ask for a lift while waiting for a bus, inquires of a neighboring shopkeeper whether Melanie has been spotted at the bus stop, and checks carefully how certain the shopkeeper is of identification. Police work is mechanical; it involves set procedures, designed to ensure thorough information, and the novel imitates these. Other kinds of novel do not aim at thoroughness; they aim at pertinence, at the telling detail. The detective story aims to give the impression of providing all the details.

This means that the interviews tend to provide a regular, repetitious sequence. But some provide more obviously important information than others, as when, for instance, one of the people interviewed reveals (99) that Annette, the first victim, a person of apparently very restricted private life, had been secretly carrying on for years a liaison with a married man—who now has to be interviewed in turn; or when the same witness later reveals that the victim's flat was unlocked, allowing entry to the murderer, at a time when it was thought to be locked (132). Such revelations reorient the investigation; there are new puzzles—of motivation or timing—and new possible solutions to choose between.

The author is, in fact, extremely skillful at introducing change economically and surprisingly, whether through the interview sequence or through some interruption of it. When change is taking place, it takes place without waste of effort or of words. Many scenes start *in medias res*. The novel, for instance, starts with Wexford waiting to see his doctor ("There were four people besides himself in the waiting room and none of them looked ill"), and many later chapters or sections use the same technique ("His phone rang at five past six" [20]; "It was going to be a fine day" [29]; "It had taken Barry Vine a long time to find Euan Sinclair" [43]). Other sections start with a generalization startlingly irrelevant to the previous material, which marks a change, displays the author's wisdom and prepares for a—usually quite rapid—resolution by shift to a new narrative scene. So the second section of chapter 1 begins, "Adversity is good for some marriages." Three short sentences later, we find the text is talking about the marriage of Wexford's daughter, whom he meets as he returns from the doctor's. Chapter 13 ends with Melanie's father declaring that the body is not hers. Chapter 14 carries on with no break in the action (the chapter break is a purely rhetorical device)— "Shock suspends everything. There is no thought, only automatic reaction, movement, mechanical speech" (207) and goes on to describe Wexford's humiliation and contrition at having falsely identified the body. As shocks are not uncommon at the beginning of chapters, so they appear also at the end of chapters. We have just noted an example; others are the discovery of Annette's body at the end of chapter 4, the indication at the end of chapter 7 that a rapist is active in the area, the discovery of what at first seems to be a blood-stained radio set stolen from the victim at the end of chapter 8, and the arrest of the person who stole it at the end of chapter 9.

The opening and closing of chapters with surprises tends to make the chapters to some extent self-contained, each being focused on the investigation of some specific piece of information. So, chapter 8 is fairly closely organized around the discovery of Annette's love affair, chapter 9 is chiefly of importance because it gives what appears to be a complete portrait of this relationship, and chapter 10 is partly concerned with the refusal of the lover's wife to confirm his alibi. But the chapters are by no means wholly concentrated on such topics. Chapter 9, for instance, also gives much attention to Melanie's parents and to the petty criminal who has stolen property from Annette's flat, culminating in his arrest. The text is concerned to convey the multiple currents of police activity while at the same time segmenting them to ensure emphasis and intelligibility.

A marked change of pace arrives as the end of the novel approaches, in accordance with the normal expectation of increasing tension at the end of adventures. Shock endings grow more frequent from chapter 18 on (a chapter that ends by linking the two murdered women for the first time). Shortly before the concluding movement is a signal that experienced readers will recognize as the beginning of the end. Chapter 19 (of twenty-four) ends with Wexford trying to remember a vital clue that he has heard but not fully registered; it appears to be going back on the positive progress of the previous chapter. In chapter 22, Wexford promises that the criminal will be arrested the next day, giving no indication of who this is, and also discovers what appears to be a major new clue, which is heavily emphasized: a certain witness has seen a suspect not once, as has been implied throughout the text, but twice. The acute reader may be able to solve the whole puzzle at this point; others at least recognize that this suspect has become a bit more suspicious. Also starting at this point is a somewhat extraneous element that adds excitement to the final sections: a march in protest against unemployment is to take place the next day, and Wexford's daughter is to participate. Chapter 23 starts with preparations for the march, the heat, the results of an election that has been running parallel to the investigation, and goes on to Wexford's explanation of the murder of Annette—identifying the person who actually committed the act—(the explanation arising from the double sighting just established) and his discussion of the second murder. The march then starts, visits the Jobcentre, and starts to get out of hand. Chapter 24 continues the action directly; in the course of the march, Wexford witnesses an attempt by the ultimate criminal—the person behind the henchman identified in the previous chapter—to kidnap a witness, the excitement of his arrest being added to by the confusion brought about by the marchers. A lot of things are happening in these last chapters. The most important of them is the sudden emergence of truth and justice from Wexford's insight; the heat, the crowds, the struggling add to the sense that things are changing quickly and in important ways. The novel has moved from talking to acting, and rapid and multiple events are a sign of that conclusiveness.

The prompt and regular pace of investigation and action is however slowed by other elements, especially by thematic concerns. There are, in fact, two related concerns, and they succeed one another in much the same way that the various mysteries do. The opening of the book is largely concerned with racism, Melanie being one of the few black people in a small English town, and her experience is profoundly affected both by the attitudes of the white people in the town and by her parents' defensive response to racism. Later in the book (after an anticipation about halfway through), the issue of racism is complicated by that of slavery, and specifically by the question of the importation into Britain of black people as unpaid domestic servants, an issue that proves relevant to the second murder.

In some points of the novel, the treatment of these thematic issues is an impediment to the action rather than part of it. There are, for instance, discussions between Wexford and his more conservative associate, Inspector Burden, on questions of racism, starting with the two-page conversation at the beginning of chapter 2 in which Wexford claims, "We're all racist in this country." Most conspicuous is the page-long quotation from a book on slavery that Wexford implausibly produces from his pocket towards the end of the story (348–49).

More commonly, however, the thematic concerns are impressively integrated with the action. In one notable episode, Wexford has formed a good relationship with Melanie's parents as he continues his search for her. When the body of a black woman is found, he sadly informs them and invites them to view the body—which is not hers. He is racist enough to think of black ethnicity as sufficient identification, and the parents are quite rightly outraged. Elsewhere, points on racism arise naturally in the situation. So, on first meeting Melanie's mother, Wexford thinks that "they all have such wonderful teeth" (22) and at once realizes the racist implications of his thought. And in organizing widespread inquiries to identify the body of the unknown black woman, Wexford reflects that it is in fact impossible to proceed for a black person in the same way as for a white one, if only because black people are conspicuous in a largely white society (230). These notes slightly slow the action, enriching its significance rather than distracting from the events. A very striking way in which the form of the novel reflects its thematic concerns is that the original problem of the missing person disappears altogether on page 301 in a more or less comic way, Melanie being unharmed and uncoerced, and leaves the reader to worry about the two deaths, the pathos of which has been made very clear. The full truth does not emerge until the last page of the book, page 378; over a fifth of the novel comes after the solution of the original problem. It may seem to the reader that the missing-person story is wholly a digression, with the unusual feature that the digression appears before the main story. In fact, her adventure has been in some ways tangential to the motivation of the real crime, as becomes apparent only at the very end. The reader should expect such a relevance, on the grounds of the normal coherence of novels, should retain some flexibility of mind, and he or she should recognize the picture of a coherent society, one in which the main thematic concern of the novel—racism, which affects both Melanie and the second victim—is pervasive.

Overall, the novel shows a fairly steady progress towards identification of the criminal and the exposition of some important social issues. The coherence and vitality of the text is ensured by a number of lasting factors of suspense that demand the reader's attention. Most obviously, there is the title, which remains puzzling until it is explained in the last word of the book. There may also be trivial kinds of suspense: the first chapter has Wexford visiting his doctor to complain of having fallen over. This is not a terminal sickness (which might be the end of the book rather than the beginning) but a minor virus (from which we later find other characters to suffer). While he is waiting, he spots an arrogant and attractive woman among the patients; she will, we can reasonably expect, prove to be a character in the story. Meanwhile, we have the trivial curiosity of what will happen to her when she outrageously starts to smoke in a doctor's waiting room (the cigarette is confiscated by a nurse). More significantly, there is the rape theme: early in the book, Wexford and other police officers address a gathering of women on self-defense. At the end of the meeting, one of them passes him an anonymous note asking what one should do if one knows a relative to be a rapist. She does not then personally contact Wexford, and we have to wait to the end of the novel to find out who the rapist is and what his crime has to do with the murders. A similar but incidental tension arises with contradictory witnesses. The married man with whom Annette has been involved claims to have been at home with his wife at the time of his murder. His wife refuses to confirm this. Who is lying? The reader is kept waiting for several chapters before discovering that the lover can be eliminated from the inquiries since his wife is simply seeking to embarrass him out of anger and resentment.

This means that at many points in the novel the reader needs to be expecting various things: new information relevant to any of the three dead or missing women, information on the rape, proof of the reliability or unreliability of witnesses, and so on. The large number of apparent digressions place a further demand on the reader's concentration. The whole meeting on self-defense, which occupies some seven pages, as well as some preparatory material (87–94), for instance, looks like a digression that creditably alerts readers to the need to be cautious but chiefly shows the normal, undramatic course of daily life in the police force and especially their responsible attitude and their effective teamwork. A more difficult episode to justify is the fête to which Wexford and his wife are invited (chapter 12). This gives them the chance to meet a lot of characters, some of whom will be important later either to the crimes or to Wexford's family life (itself a major retarding factor in the book); it gives the opportunity for a lot of enjoyable satire; and it constitutes a rhetorical lull. The chapter ends with the false news of Melanie's death; it appears as if violence has emerged from the most trivial suburban ordinariness, and it is all the more shocking for that. The illusion will be dissipated, but the sense of the immanence of evil within the everyday persists.

The author's wish to present a whole society (the small town of

Kingsmarkham, which appears in many of her other works) specifically takes the form of wishing to provide a wide range of interesting characters, the presentation of which may arrest the progress of the narrative. These may involve a certain level of psychological abstraction on the part of the narrator, who evokes what Barthes would call a "cultural code," i.e., a set expectation about psychological types, to place characters in relation to action or theme. So, the authoritarian Inspector Burden is shown to be unsympathetic to the unemployed amongst whom he has to make inquiries, rejecting the cliché, "There but for the grace of God go I":

> That he wasn't amongst them had nothing to do with God's grace in his opinion, and everything to do with his own industry, determination and hard work. He was one of those who ask the unemployed why they don't get a job and the homeless why they don't find a place to live. (49)

"One of those": the reader is reminded of a type, directed away from the strange and intriguing events of crime and mystery to his own daily knowledge of hardship and social distance.

This wish to convey a total atmosphere—not precisely focused on the major issues of the book—leads to a great deal of lengthy description. At best it has a meticulous, documentary quality:

> Someone had pretentiously named number fifteen Ladyhall Court. It was a gabled house on two floors built of the "white" brick which was the fashionable building material here in the 1890s. A screen of copper sycamores hid much of the ground floor from the road. (51)

There is a neat way in which detective writers integrate such descriptions with the progress of the investigation, which is the disguised clue. Passing, almost by chance, the house of one witness, Wexford admires its prosperous appearance, including the bars on the windows that he approvingly interprets as a precaution against burglars (135); many pages later (369), he points out that they have another purpose. The documentary quality is specially apparent in a lot of interesting but somewhat laborious exposition, either given directly by the narrator, as with the account of police procedures on the discovery of homicide (55), or allocated to a character, as with the account of the procedures for registration and interview at a Jobcentre. Rendell likes to know how things are done;

she impresses her readers though her humane curiosity about the details of people's daily routines. She impresses less when she seeks to communicate a personal judgment. At worst, her tone is hysterically rhetorical: "Anouk Khoori's hand on his arm, a beige-colored hand with purple vein branches, purple varnish on the long nails, lay there, in his fancy like some exotic crustacean" (266). There are also times when one might suspect that the author is being paid by the line:

> He smiled and uttered the usual archaism that was once an enquiry as to another's health.
>
> "How do you do?" (185)

Much of Rendell's writing then is leisurely, designed to show understanding rather than action or riddles. Overall, her aim is to combine regular progress to elucidation of a mystery with explicit reflection on the social conditions from which it arises. The result is on the whole admirably successful, within the normal expectations of the genre. What the novel shows, however, by comparison with the more sophisticated literary works we have previously considered, is that the quite perceptible gap between investigation (which proceeds efficiently) and interpretation· (which tends to be static)—which parallels the gap indicated by the word "arise" here, the gap between act and context—is itself an incoherence of the kind that more demanding authors have sought to escape.

Jeffrey Archer

Jeffrey Archer is one of the most popular authors in Britain today, and there can be no doubt that study of his work will reveal much of what the general public looks for in fiction. *First Among Equals* clearly shows many points that explain his phenomenal success. The novel is concerned with four men, from different social backgrounds and belonging to the two major parties of the time, who enter the British House of Parliament at the election of 1964 and after the vicissitudes of a political career—more elections, rivalries, promotions and demotions, personal and family difficulties—rise to be dominant political figures by 1991. It therefore appeals to widespread interest in politicians, in their private life, and in the competition between them; it avoids partisanship and presents the business of politics as an elaborate and subtle sport; it appeals to a popular interest in careerism and the spectacle of power. The imaginary events of the novel are skillfully intertwined with the real events of the period (whether it be the large-scale events of elections, wars, devaluations, changes in the electoral system, or the smaller events of the publication of books and the production of plays), and the author (who has himself been both a Conservative minister and a major party official) shows close knowledge of British political structures and prominent personalities (so that when a character meets the then Conservative leader Edward Heath in his Albany flat beneath a landscape by John Piper, the reader is ready to believe that Edward Heath really does own a Piper landscape). Readers of the time must have been specially interested in his prediction of the political future, since the novel appeared in 1984 (though the predictions have proved to be totally wrong). The author criticizes the personal character of some politicians, very seriously, but shows general respect for the political system and faith in it, and is critical on policy grounds only of the extreme Left that at one time sought to penetrate the Labor Party in a way that some observers felt to be threatening to the spirit of true democracy. Lord Archer accepts the sincerity and goodwill of his political opponents (to the point where the only fundamentally objectionable character of the four is a Conservative, whose measure of success might make some readers skeptical as to his party's powers of moral discrimination) and shows very proper feeling for the occasions where members of parliament show personal sympathy and admiration across party boundaries. His characterization is fairly unambiguous. Broadly speaking, people are fundamentally good or fundamentally bad. It is not difficult to decide which are which: the good are also likable and they are in the majority. This is a world in which hard work, serious judgment, and conscientiousness are conspicuous and rewarded. Most relevantly to our present concerns, there is a constant narrative drive that leaves the reader eager to know what will happen next, who will succeed and who will fail, how the characters will escape from their various dilemmas, and what ingenious new strokes they may play. The sporting analogy is essential; the reader wants to know who is going to win in the contest of political popularity and, to follow the fortunes of the players, needs to grasp the fairly complex principles of political strategy, of public image, of backstage manipulation, and of recondite procedure.

Here arise the issues that are usually central in more ambitious literary works (including, for instance, the political novels of Trollope), the issues of the relation of events to those values of human life that are essentially temporal. It has to be said, first of all, that the negative of Lord Archer's political generosity is that he has little feeling for questions of progress or retrogression, of adjustment to social or technical change, that are often thought to be the essence of politics. He is fair to all sides in politics because his values are basically the private values of honesty, kindness, and responsibility. Put more severely, he is a nonpolitical writer and has little sense (as a novelist) of what is at stake in politics, what issues of principle or of class interest are advanced by the selection of a nice or a nasty person as prime minister. But if his stress is on the individual, the reader may well ask what sense he has of personal development and of the options made available to an individual by a society.

In some respects, it must be said, Archer does show the consistency of characters' lives. Most obviously, he carefully traces careers, noting, for instance, the relation between increasing political reputation and the need to adjust to business or professional activity of comparable status during periods out of office. The titles of the various books of the novel, from "1964–1966: the back benches" to "1991: Prime Minister," clearly enough indicate the main framework of the story. Within this general development there are a number of individual, recurring themes. The future Labor leader, Raymond, is characterized by sexual problems; married to a woman for whom he has a good deal of respect and who contributes importantly to his political success but who does not inspire him with passion, he first of all resorts to a prostitute—with some risk of denunciation—and then is more seriously involved with two women in turn before finally renouncing such adventures and being reconciled to his wife. Simon, the sympathetic, Conservative figure, being of fairly modest social origins, is frequently beset by financial difficulties, and despite his conscientiousness, these too risk bringing him into public discredit. Andrew, the second leftwing figure (who is to leave the Labor Party), is concerned with family relationships; on the one hand, with his relationship to his father, who is a prominent Conservative, and on the other with his own difficulties in fatherhood, since he and his wife at first fear that they may not have children at all, then have a son who dies in a road accident, and finally adopt a daughter.

There is one major theme that gives an overall consistency to the events and society; it is a rather surprising one for an author who seems on the whole so well-meaning: the theme of blackmail. It is most strongly connected with the fourth (and nastiest) character, the Conservative aristocrat Charles. In one striking episode, Charles, having lost office in an election, wishes to return to his post as director of a bank. When the chairman refuses to reinstate him, he has his wife consult a disgruntled secretary. Using the information she provides about the chairman's paying his mistress out of bank funds and about his private deals with a Swiss bank account, Charles first of all forces his way back onto the board of directors and then takes over the post of chairman (16). Some years later, again returning from office, Charles wishes to take over again, this time from the person he himself has appointed to take care of the business in his absence. This acting chairman refuses to go and points out that there is nothing for which he could be blackmailed, but that there are things for which Charles could be blackmailed. If Charles is the person most connected with this theme, it nevertheless forms a constant thread in the whole work, from the prostitute who attempts to blackmail Raymond early in the novel, only to find that the British press, with its customary nobility, is not prepared to publish her allegations, to Simon's wife, a gynecologist, who—perhaps with the author's approval—threatens to reveal intimate information about Charles's wife if the latter does not abandon his underhand attacks on Simon.

In addition to his recurrent theme, a number of deliberate echoes and parallels give the sense of a coherent society. There is, for instance, the symmetrical ordering of the rivalries of Charles and Simon on the Conservative side and of Andrew and Raymond on the Labor side, and there is the neat and dignified repetition of Simon's apologies to Raymond. First, he taunts him in the House of Commons with not resigning from the government when it acts against his principles, and sincerely apologizes in a private letter when he discovers that he has in fact resigned (106). Much later, he wrongly accuses Raymond of taking up a certain issue purely for publicity and apologizes in the House when he realizes that he has actually been concerned with it for many years (352).

A very striking feature of the novel is the frequent recurrence of a particular event: the close-run vote. Virtually every election or parliamentary vote seems to end with a majority of one, sometimes after several recounts, or with a dead heat, as with the long-drawn-out conclusion in which the two major parties in the 1991 election gain exactly the same number of seats, the third party that holds the balance is evenly split as to which major party to support, and the government therefore has to be chosen by the sovereign. A particularly memorable occasion is the one in which Charles, preoccupied with his wife's adultery, spends the afternoon following her when he should have been in Parliament and gets to the House just in time to find that his party has been defeated by one vote (257). One hesitates to say whether this should be regarded as a coherent, structuring principle or as a sign of limited imagination.

Be that as it may, there are clearly continuing elements in the novel that require some degree of continuous attention and memory on the part of the reader and relate the happenings of the story to a vision of character and society. One should note that some of these have a rather blatant quality that suggests a somewhat artificial striving for continuity, such as the recurrent references to Raymond's colored shirts, given him by one of his mistresses, regarded as a sign of liberalism and unorthodoxy, and referred to whenever possible. More seriously, one has to note many factors that tend to atomize the events and characters.

First of all, things happen rapidly. Soon after his arrival in Parliament, Andrew meets the daughter of the minister of state for Scotland. The following day (after a triumphant maiden speech) he phones her and spends the night with her (36). It is then implied that he is to marry her. A chapter later (52), he meets another woman at a dinner, and although he does not speak to her at the time, they meet for lunch the next day and he immediately dismisses his first love. If love moves quickly, politics is not much less magical; a few chapters later (89), Andrew wittily scores a point against the opposition, and at once "had made a political reputation." Conversely, Charles makes one poor speech (97) and find his career in ruins (110). Still more fundamentally, it seems fair to say that Archer's deepest talent is for the anecdote, for the short and striking story that gives an occasion for wit or demonstrates exceptional qualities of courage, intelligence, or deviousness. A neat example is the story of Ladies Day at Ascot. Charles is invited to speak to a Luncheon Club in his constituency on 16 June. He refuses indignantly, in fact because it is a specially enjoyable day at the racetrack, and pretends that he is due to speak at an important conference (66). He goes to the race meeting, gets drunk, and is arrested for drunken driving. His court appearance is covered in the press, and the chairman of the Luncheon Club proposes a vote of censure on him—not for drunken driving but for lying about his commitments (80). A neat story of dishonesty unveiled, which is dealt with in a businesslike manner. It is spread over some fifteen pages (say, six thousand words) but itself only occupies about four pages, the rest of the space being taken up with the doings of the other characters and giving suspense to the story, so that the end—Charles being punished for what might seem the wrong offense—is an elegant surprise. Effective as this is, it is also a sign that the author is concerned with short-term conduct, and this concern has results elsewhere that are less impressive. One feature is the use of crude climaxes, as with the scene where Charles bursts into his wife's bedroom with the words, "I'm the new Minister of State at the Department of Trade and Industry," only to find her in bed with another man (177). Another is that stories fade away unresolved or are resolved by chance. Andrew's sudden abandonment of his girlfriend leads to the enmity of her father, the minister of state, who has considerable power to harm Andrew's career. Fortunately he dies of a heart attack after a few pages. Later, Andrew and his wife adopt a daughter who is black. In a pathetic scene, she is found scrubbing her skin with detergent to whiten herself after racist taunts at school (328). A few chapters later she reappears, being universally admired for her beauty and charm (381), and her race is not mentioned.

The simplicity of construction of such anecdotes is enhanced by the maintenance of strict chronological sequence throughout most of the book; there are few flashbacks and hardly any mysteries. A case where mystery is introduced shows how alien it is to the author's sensibility: the queen summons the four main characters (by now three party leaders and the Speaker of the House of Commons) and consults them on an undisclosed constitutional procedure she proposes to adopt. They agree to it, and it is rushed through Parliament on the eve of a general election. And then the election result is interpreted by an official—to the new king (444). So, that's what it was about! The mystery is one only for the reader; there is little feeling that the characters might need to learn by deciphering mysteries in their own lives.

It is, in fact, a book of great explicitness. Lord Archer likes facts; he also likes procedures, and he likes explaining them. A striking example is the account of the state opening of Parliament (124–25); the account follows the queen's arrival, by coach, her robing and taking her seat on the throne, the summoning of members of the Commons by the official

known as Black Rod, the Speaker's costume, the precise order of the
procession, and the like; fascinating information, no doubt, for anyone
who has not read a child's guide to the pageantry of the British parliament. Archer's love of explaining also affects his prose, as in the case of
Raymond changing his shirt:

> He took off his black coat and waistcoat, removed his white shirt and eased
> the stud on his stiff collar, leaving a small circle above his Adam's apple. . . .
> He quickly put on the new gift. The fabric had a pleasant soft feel about it. He
> started to do up the buttons. (204)

Shirts are going to be important, and they deserve some emphasis; it
seems that for Archer emphasis means elaborate instructions for use.

This very informative prose slows the pace of a novel that on the level
of events might seem to be extremely fast-moving. It can perhaps be
respected as a sign of decent, literal-minded clarity on the part of the
author, eager to ensure that no reader misses anything. But this precisely
shows the limits of Archer's fiction. His attention is close to the surface
of life; he has little sense that people's feelings or behavior may be difficult or uncertain, and he regards life largely as a game in which all the
cards are on the table. A revealing phrase occurs in the account of one of
Simon's triumphs. Simon has solved the Northern Ireland problem
("Ever since August 1969, when the troops had first been sent in, Parliament had been having another of its periodic bouts of trouble with Northern Ireland" [128]). He is injured by a bomb and unable to attend Parliament during the debate on his solution, but the debate is broadcast in its
entirety and he "sat up in bed listening to every word on the radio as if it
were the final episode in his favorite serial and he were desperate to
know the outcome" (309). In fact, the pressure of argument is so intense
that he is obliged to hobble into the Commons to conclude the debate
himself. Politics as a radio serial: this seems to be the model for *First
Among Equals*; short-term but repeated tension on issues of instantly
recognizable success or frustration. Jeffrey Archer brings much energy,
goodwill, and sympathy to this conception of storytelling, but it is one
that leaves things to wish for.

Conclusion

THERE seem to be four aspects of people's time-sensations that they find disturbing. They are concerned that moments of time are not continuous, that an experience may seem to be unrelated to the previous and succeeding times; that experience may be static or repetitious; that if there is change it may amount to decay; and that the pace of events may be too fast or too slow. In other words, people fear or resent fragmentation, stasis, decline, and pressure or boredom. The numerous books and articles on "time management" that are published would appear to respond to concerns of this kind, to the fears that one is wasting time, that one hasn't enough time, that one cannot cope with events at the pace at which they occur. The central factor seems to be the preparedness of the individual for the events he or she has to deal with; these to some extent are the events of natural processes (weather, season, the changes in the body) and to a considerable extent the events brought about by other people's actions and decisions. Implicit in these anxieties is a positive image of harmony between the individual and the forces of nature and society, in which one's purposes and strategies coincide with events. This harmony may include conflict: snow may fall, but I shall have had time to buy warm clothing; other people may apply for the job I want, but I shall have had time to prepare my application and to exploit my previous experience. The model of the game is an apt one; the rules of games allow appropriate reaction to the opponent's moves (and if the opponent is generous, I shall be allowed to play again if I wasn't quite ready). Ultimately, this vision of harmony is a myth of personal and cultural progress, which is very much part of the liberal, humanist tradition; it implies that people are able to meet challenges and opportunities in a spirit of efficiency, decorum, and due thoughtfulness.

Such a vision is assumed, largely, by the three popular works we have just considered; the structure is perhaps clearest in *First Among Equals*, which tends towards an animated curriculum vitae, and least clear in *The Rector's Wife*, where there is some sense of surprise and uncertainty. But in all of them there is a kind of problem solving: how do I attain freedom from my husband's profession? trace a missing person? become prime minister? There are steps towards attaining the desired end, and there are obstacles that impede them, and the steps and the obstacles succeed each other in an orderly manner, allowing the characters to summon up their resources of personal strength and social or institutional support. The spectacle is an interesting one; the novels display, with an apt balance of understanding and sympathy, people's competence in getting results they can be proud of. They show intelligence, thoroughness, diligence, team-work, charm, effective communication, resilience; these qualities are generally shared by characters and narrators (one could confidently rec-ommend both groups for responsible employment). This is a world one should be happy to live in, a world of shared expectations and regulated relationships. And to a large extent it is the world we do live in; the books are popular, no doubt, at least in part because readers recognize the life they know.

If we now turn back to the classic novel of the nineteenth century, such as *The Warden*, we do not find a wholly different pattern. There is a fairly clear issue: How does Mr. Harding defend himself from the attacks of the reformers? The novel deals lucidly and systematically with the resolution of this issue, step by step, move by countermove. And we enjoy the book for reasons not unlike those which make Joanna Trollope enjoyable, for its demonstration of decency, orderliness, proportion, and rationality. But things are not quite so clear as this may imply. First, of course, the question as we formulate it assumes sympathy for Mr. Hard-ing. This sympathy is not really in doubt in the novel, but there is at least some sense of the wrongness of his basic position and the weakness of his character. More seriously, our formulation of the question is deliber-ately vague: does "defend himself against the reformers" mean "defeat them" (as Grantly would wish) or "give in to them" (as actually hap-pens)? The uncertainty is part of the conception of the book, and its structure depends in part on the final—and much delayed—clarification of Mr. Harding's means of escape. Yet, more important (and clearly related to our last point), a great deal of the text does not seem to be about the changing balance of power as between Harding and Bold, Grantly and Towers. It is taken up with waiting and commenting: waiting for Sir Abraham Haphazard's opinion, for Eleanor Harding's response to John Bold; commenting on the *Jupiter*'s editorial and on the various decisions of Bold and Harding; most memorably of all, waiting for a whole day to meet the great Sir Abraham (in order, as it proves, to reject his advice).

The chapter on Mr. Harding's "Long Day in London" is an extraordinary one, if we expect the story to press on to a conclusion. It could easily have been omitted, either by having Harding make more efficient arrangements or by a phrase such as, "After a long day's waiting, Mr. Harding presented himself to Sir Abraham at the stroke of ten." But something would have been lost. One thing that would have been lost is the sense that Mr. Harding's resolution is one taken after mature thought, with a due recognition of the price to be paid for it. But perhaps even more important is the author's lingering in privacy. The London chapter for the first time shows Mr. Harding in complete isolation (the narrator explicitly comments that Harding does not choose to contact the acquaintances he has in London); it shows his seclusion, his seeking sanctuary from the pressures of friends and enemies alike; it shows him escaping from anxiety into sleep and dream, and being refreshed by the experience. And it is this side of Trollope that anticipates the development of fiction in later times. The chapter could almost be a short story like those of Katherine Mansfield, a story of waiting followed by arrival; it is faintly echoed by the section of *Mrs. Dalloway* in which Peter Walsh wanders around London immersed in his own worries and concerns (admittedly of a very different sort from Harding's) and falls asleep in Regent's Park. The author has chosen to delay the action because he has chosen to show his character away from the conflicting desires of other people; isolation means stasis. The author has chosen this; we read this chapter as emanating from a willed act of attention in which, as the author builds up to what is obviously going to be a decisive moment of the book, much anticipated by preceding conversations, he decides that what merits attention is not the changing situation but Harding's state of mind. And since we read it this way, we can interpret it in terms of a storyteller's motivation. Trollope—or his narrator—wishes us to see Harding as the harmless victim, to feel the right level of respect and sympathy for his vulnerability, his wish to escape, his temporary loss of the comfort of family and friends. He wishes to demonstrate, after the passion and force displayed in the action so far and before the formal solemnity with which the renunciation is declared and confirmed, that he is concerned with the private Harding.

Delay, in other words, in this novel, is a display of the author's chosen relationship to his character. In general, it would seem that fluctuations of rhythm in fiction express the kind of attention the author or narrator thinks the conduct of the characters merits. The point is very often implicit in the contrast manifested in the books between the actual, uneven development of narrative, with its compressions, its lingering, its inversions of sequence, and the regular mechanism of clock or calendar time; the storyteller judges the objective, impersonal time of the clock to be secondary to the importance, personal or moral, of acts, thoughts, and experiences. The rhythm of the novel is thus, in a sense, a characterization of the narrator who reconciles the demands of (more or less) clearly expounding a sequence of events with the wish to indicate the framework of values and sympathies that are pertinent to them. When the author's values are primarily those of effectiveness, he or she faces little tension in reconciling narrative with interpretation; when the values are those of some kind of privacy, there is serious tension at times, and this appears as ebbs and flows of attention.

The point is particularly clear in *The Go-Between*, the one novel we have considered in which the narrator is a character in the plot. The events of the novel very clearly follow an objective time, given by the duration of a holiday. They obviously tend towards some catastrophe because illicit passion is a matter of high tension and especially precarious in a conservative society, itself ill-assured of its class foundations. But the novel does not hurry on to disaster. The old Leo reproduces the fascinations of the young Leo, his learning about sex, class, and violence, his pride in achievement and his embarrassment at comparative poverty; and he lingers himself in fascination at his own memory, at his gradual rediscovery of events and his shifting judgment of people. The reader may well suspect—though the point is not explicitly made—that he is postponing the catastrophe, prolonging the idyll. All this adds up to a picture of how much the young Leo means to the old Leo, how far his self-image is changing as he sees his past afresh. There is irony in the presentation of the boy's naïveté, irony therefore at the dawdling pace of the book, and it is not always clear whether the irony is that of the old man or that of the author behind him. What is clear is that the pace of the book is an image of patient and acutely intelligent obsession, that slowness means self-awareness.

What is true of a dramatized narrator is also true, if less obvious, of the implied persona or distinctive voice of the narrators who do not appear as characters and whom it is tempting to identify with the authors. Obviously, the authors we have studied are very different from each other. What this book has been arguing is that the differences between them lie, to a considerable extent, in the way they balance, on the one hand, a more or less sympathetic and more or less leisurely entering into the situation of the characters, into their reflections, their sensations, their routines, their aimless or deviously purposive conversations, against, on the other hand, a lucid and businesslike tracing of a sequence of events, with a beginning, an end, and a series of recognizable, intermediate steps. This contrast is not dissimilar to that made by the Russian Formalist critics (e.g., Eikhenbaum 1978) between *fabula* and *syuzhet*, between the sequence of events and the manner of telling. It means that, on one level at least, the story that unfolds in a novel is the story of its telling, the working out of the narrator's strategy for reaching the end reluctantly. The classic, and hyperbolic, demonstration is in Sterne's *Tristam Shandy*, the subject of which is precisely the author's reluctance to advance his autobiography in any recognizable way, so that even his birth appears at quite a late stage in the text.

This perspective indicates why the temporal anxieties of everyday life, our concern for fragmentation, stasis, decline, or inappropriate pace, do not usually affect us when reading fiction. If such problems are depicted in the events narrated, the act of narration (almost) always proceeds in a continuous tension between narrative progress and intelligibly motivated, non-narrative distractions. Each episode of storytelling or of reflection or description adds to the persona of the narrator, makes the narrator more admirable as a manifestation of how we can deal with happenings, how we can integrate them into the ongoing texture of our experiences. So, reading fiction can give us an impression—which may well be misleading and temporary—not that life is pleasant, not that things happen in the right order at the right pace, but that if we have a properly mature attitude we shall be able to understand them in the right order and at the right pace, and that in doing so we shall be exercising a moral or emotional discrimination in the distance we adopt towards the fictitious characters—and perhaps, potentially, in the distance we may adopt towards real people.

This impression depends on the quality of the writing, on a rhetoric that is oriented to foregrounding either the way each event leads on towards a conclusion or the aspects of a situation that make it entertaining, curious, or pathetic enough to justify the degree of attention it is given. This is where things can go wrong, as with the job applications in *The Rainbow*, which readers may feel are neither contributing enough to the plot nor interesting enough in themselves to merit our lingering. Could Lawrence have made them interesting enough? I suspect he might, had he been sufficiently aware of his audience. The issue is a keen one for writers of popular fiction. Do we care where James Bond buys his shirts or what he eats for breakfast? We need some nonplot material of this kind to reduce the pace of events to a manageable level and to make us care which side wins, but is this the most effective kind of nonplot material? Obviously, Ian Fleming judged his audience soundly; at a time when consumerism and social mobility were developing, quite a lot of people did care about the signs of comfort and success. The interest, of course, may not be one that survives, or one that readers feel very pleased with in retrospect.

Among the authors we have studied, there is considerable variety in the personae implied by the distances they adopt towards their characters: from, for instance, Henry Green's humorous delight in the trivial to Lawrence's intense commitment to growth and discontent. The main dimensions of variation would appear to be: the consistency or variability with which the author addresses himself or herself to the characters' thoughts and sensations; the explicitness with which he or she indicates the shifts of attention; and the closeness of the attention granted, in terms of the immediacy of detail in sensations, thoughts, and language.

If, despite this variety, one tries to isolate typical models, one seems to find two basic postures (not wholly distinct from each other). There are authors who eschew selectiveness and who slow the action of the plot by parallel characters, by provision of context, by allowing the characters' purposes to gradually evolve; these authors tend to a rhythm of anticlimax in which nonplot material follows major events in plot. Examples are Lawrence, Woolf, Forster, and Henry Green. And there are authors who eschew conclusiveness and who slow the action by concentration on interiority, on private thought, on impressions, reflections, hesitations;

these tend to a rhythm of delay in which the nonplot material precedes the major turning points of the story. Examples are Bowen, Greene, Hartley, and Golding. Both groups, compared with popular fiction and with much pre-twentieth-century fiction, tend to reduce the importance of action and purpose. This makes the business of storytelling more conspicuous, and, presumably, more difficult; it presents the novelist as a person who *nevertheless* finds a story to tell.

If we wish to be still more speculative and to find a single pattern underlying the forms and sensibilities of many major modern novelists, it would lie in the opposition between peace and responsibility. Of our chosen texts, the opposition is most emphatic in *The Heart of the Matter*. Scobie longs above all for peace, which means isolation and memory. But he cannot attain it, for he has responsibilities—to his wife and to his job, at first; he even acquires a major new responsibility in his relationship to Helen. Coping with Louise, Helen, his superiors, his suspects, gives him a timetable, a series of deadlines. Time, one might say, is other people. The timetable is oppressive. Scobie attempts to escape from it, so that the dichotomy of peace and responsibility appears in the text of the novel as an alternation of action and waiting, and this produces developments that are conspicuously either sudden or gradual. The alternation of the gradual and the sudden is perceived by the reader as a hesitation between the outer-directed self and the inner-directed self, and this makes up both much of the excitement of the novel and much of its psychological plausibility.

Scobie is explicitly obsessed with peace, but the word appears quite frequently in modern fiction (as a number of the quotations in this book show) and often in particularly significant contexts. And even if the word does not emphatically appear, scenes of peace, or repose, of freedom from the pressure of the outside world, are often prominent. There are Mrs. Dalloway's waves of isolation and reflection, the periods of mystical, aesthetic, or scholarly contemplation experienced by Lawrence's characters, Stella Rodney's visit to Ireland. Or there are the moments of relaxed, aimless, and increasingly intimate conversation in Forster or Green. People and stories both seem to require an alternation of tension and relaxation. It is tempting to regret that authors appear to regard the private self largely as an escape from the public self, and to see in the work of Jeffrey Archer and Ruth Rendell a greater moral sobriety, a greater application to the seriousness of the world. What the more ambitious novelists show is that the great events of the world, the conflicts and betrayals, the moments of understanding and respect, arise from a calmer and inactive inner life. "Arise from": the phrase is vague enough to show that the relation of inner to outer is not fully understood. Or that it is not intellectually understood. Perhaps the alternation of inner and outer is best presented through the artistic imagination because it is a compound of the physical and the rational that evades the grasp of intellect. "There are tides in the body." There are tides in the mind too.

Bibliography

Literary Texts

Literary texts are usually referenced in the text only by page number—sometimes also by abbreviation.

Archer, J. *First Among Equals*. London: Harper Collins, 1984.

Bowen, E. *Afterthought*. London: Longman, 1962. Cited as "Aft."

———. *Collected Impressions*. London: Longman Green, 1950. Cited as "CI."

———. *The Heat of the Day*. London: Cape, 1954.

Forster, E. M. *Aspects of the Novel*. Harmondsworth: Penguin, 1958.

———. *A Passage to India*. Vol. 6 of the Abinger edition. London: Edward Arnold, 1978.

Golding, W. *Lord of the Flies*. London: Faber, 1958.

Gordon, L. *Virginia Woolf, a Writer's Life*. Oxford: Oxford University Press, 1986.

Green, H. *Loving*. London: Hogarth, 1945.

Greene, G. *The Heart of the Matter*. London: Heinemann, 1948.

———. *The Heart of the Matter*. Vol. 6 of the collected edition. London: Heinemann and Bodley Head, 1971. Cited as "CE."

———. *Ways of Escape*. London: Bodley Head, 1980. Cited as "WE."

Hartley, L. P. *The Go-Between*. London: Hamish Hamilton, 1953.

Lawrence, D. H. *Phoenix*. Edited by E. D. McDonald. London: Heinemann, 1936. Cited as "P."

———. *The Rainbow*. Edited by A. Fernihough. Harmondsworth: Penguin, 1995.

Mansfield, K. *Collected Stories*. London: Constable, 1945.

Rendell, R. *Simisola*. London: Arrow, 1995.

Trollope, A. *The Warden*. London: Everyman, 1969.

Trollope, J. *The Rector's Wife*. London: Black Swan, 1992.

Woolf, V. *The Common Reader*. London: Hogarth, 1925. Cited as "CR."

———. *Mrs. Dalloway*. Edited by E. Showalter. Harmondsworth: Penguin, 1992.

———. *Night and Day*. London: Hogarth, 1966. Cited as "ND."

Critical Works

Critical Works are cited throughout by year and page number, the author's name being evident from the text.

Allott, K., and M. Farris. *The Art of Graham Greene*. London: Russell and Russell, 1963.

Beer, J., ed. *A Passage to India, Essays in Interpretation*. London: Macmillan, 1985.

Beja, M. "The number of moments of vision. . . ." In *Clarissa Dalloway*, edited by H. Bloom, 36–40. New York and Philadelphia: Chelsea House, 1990.

Bennett, A., and N. Royle. *Elizabeth Bowen and the Dissolution of the Novel*. London: Macmillan, 1995.

Bennett, J. *Virginia Woolf, Her Art as a Novelist*. Cambridge: Cambridge University Press, 1964.

Bersani, L. "Lawrentian Stillness." In *Modern Critical Views, D. H. Lawrence*, edited by H. Bloom, 179–94. New York and Philadelphia: Chelsea House, 1986.

Bien, P. *L. P. Hartley*. London: Chatto & Windus, 1963.

Bloom, H., ed. *Clarissa Dalloway*. New York & Philadelphia: Chelsea House, 1990.

———, ed. *Modern Critical Views, Graham Greene*. New York & Philadelphia: Chelsea House, 1987.

Brown, E. K. *Rhythm in the Novel*. Lincoln: University of Nebraska Press, 1989.

Caserio, R. L. *Plot, Story and the Novel*. Princeton: Princeton University Press, 1979.

Church, M. *Structure and Theme*. Ohio State University Press, 1983.

Colmer, J. "Promise and Withdrawal in *A Passage to India*." In *E. M. Forster, A Human Exploration*, edited by G. K. Das and J. Beer, 117–28. London: Macmillan, 1979.

Delas, D., and M. L. Terray. *Rythme et Ecriture*. 2 vols. Paris: Cahiers de sémiotique textuelle, 1988–91.

Di Battista, M. *Virginia Woolf's Major Novels*. New Haven and London: Yale University Press, 1980.

Eagleton, T. "Reluctant Heroes: The Novels of Graham Greene." In *Modern Critical Views: Graham Greene,* edited by H. Bloom, 97–118. New York and Philadelphia: Chelsea House, 1987.

Eikhenbaum, B. M. "The Theory of the Formal Method." In *Readings in Russian Poetics: Formalist and Structuralist views,* edited by L. Matejka and K. Pomorska, 3–37. Ann Arbor: Michigan Slavic Publications, 1978.

Frank, J. "Spatial Form in Modern Literature." *Sewanee Review* 33 (1945): 231–52.

Fullbrook, K. *Katherine Mansfield*. Brighton: Harvester, 1986.

Genette, G. *Figures III*. Paris: Seuil, 1972.

———. *Narrative Discourse*. Ithaca: Cornell University Press, 1980.

Gibson, A. *Reading Narrative Discourse*. London: Macmillan, 1990.

Gindin, J. *William Golding*. London: Macmillan, 1988.

Hanson, C. *Virginia Woolf*. London: Macmillan, 1994.

Herbert, C. *Trollope and Comic Pleasure*. Chicago: University of Chicago Press, 1987.

Holmesland, O. *A Critical Introduction to Henry Green's Novels.* London: Macmillan, 1986.

Hormasji, N. *Katherine Mansfield, An Appraisal.* London: Collins, 1967.

Hough, G. *The Dark Sun.* London: Duckworth, 1968.

Jaques, E. *The Form of Time.* London: Heinemann, 1982.

Kenney, E. K. *Elizabeth Bowen.* Lewisburg: Bucknell University Press, 1975.

Kermode, F. *Lawrence.* London: Fontana Collins, 1973.

Kiely, R. "A Long Event of Perpetual Change." In *Clarissa Dalloway*, edited by H. Bloom, 137–46. New York and Philadephia: Chelsea House, 1990.

Lassner, P. *Elizabeth Bowen.* London: Macmillan, 1990.

Leavis, F. R. *"The Rainbow,"* In *Modern Critical Views. D. H. Lawrence,* edited by H. Bloom, 147–62. New York and Philadelphia: 1986.

Lee, H. *Elizabeth Bowen, An Estimation.* London: Vision and Barnes & Noble, 1981.

Levine, J. P. *Creation and Criticism. A Passage to India.* London: Chatto and Windus, 1971.

Lewis, R. W. B. "The 'Trilogy.'" In *Modern Critical Views: Graham Greene,* edited by H. Bloom, 9–32. New York and Philadelphia: Chelsea House, 1987.

McEwan, N. *The Survival of the Novel.* London: Macmillan, 1981.

Mengham, R. *The Idiom of the Time.* Cambridge: Cambridge University Press, 1982.

Meyerhoff, H. *Time in Literature.* Berkeley: University of California Press, 1965.

Moynahan, J. *D. H. Lawrence. The Deed of Life.* Princeton: Princeton University Press, 1963.

Mudford, P. *Graham Greene.* London: Northcote House, 1996.

Mudrick, M. "The Originality of The Rainbow." In *Twentieth Century Interpretations of The Rainbow,* edited by M. Kinkead-Weekes, 11–32. Englewood Cliffs: Prentice Hall, 1971.

Niven, A. *D. H. Lawrence. The Novels.* Cambridge: Cambridge University Press, 1978.

North, M. *Henry Green and the Writing of His Generation.* Charlottesville: University Press of Virginia, 1984.

Orange, M. "Language and Silence in *A Passage to India.*" In *E. M. Forster. A Human Exploration,* edited by G. K. Das and J. Beer, 142–60. London: Macmillan, 1979.

Orr, J. *The Making of the Twentieth Century Novel.* London: Macmillan, 1987.

Page, N. *E. M. Forster.* London: Macmillan, 1987.

———, ed. *William Golding. The Novels 1954–67. A Casebook.* London: Macmillan, 1985.

Patrides, C. A., ed. *Aspects of Time.* Manchester: Manchester University Press, 1976.

Pinkney, T. "Northernness and Modernism." In *D. H. Lawrence,* edited by P. Widdowson, 181–95. London: Longman (Longman's critical readers), 1992.

Rimmon-Kenan, S. *Narrative Fiction. Contemporary Poetics.* London: Methuen, 1983.

Sagar, K. *The Art of D. H. Lawrence.* Cambridge: Cambridge University Press, 1966.

Sinclair, J. "Lines about 'Lines.'" In *Current Trends in Stylistics,* edited by B. Kachru and H. F. W. Stahlke, 251–61. Edmonton: Linguistic Research, 1972.

Slade, T. *D. H. Lawrence.* London: Evans (Literature in Perspective), 1969.

Smitten, J. R., and A. Daghistany, eds. *Spatial Form in Narrative*, Ithaca: Cornell University Press, 1981.

Stevenson, R. *Modernist Fiction*. Brighton: Harvester Wheatsheaf, 1992.

Stewart, G. "Lawrence, 'Being' and the Allotropic Style." In *Modern Critical Views. D. H. Lawrence,* edited by H. Bloom, 163–78. New York and Philadelphia: 1986.

Stokes, E. *The Novels of Henry Green*. London: Hogarth, 1959.

Stone, W. *The Cave and the Mountain*. Stanford: Stanford University Press, and London: Oxford University Press, 1966.

Vivas, E. *D. H. Lawrence. The Failure and the Triumph of Art*. London: Allen and Unwin, 1961.

Vogler, T. A., ed. *Twentieth-Century Interpretations of "To the Lighthouse."* Englewood Cliffs, N.J.: Prentice Hall, 1970.

Wall, S. *Trollope and Character*. London: Faber, 1988.

Worthern, J. *D. H. Lawrence and the Idea of the Novel*. London: Macmillan, 1979.

Index